# TAMAR AT SEA

**a Memoir**

by Tamar Griggs

The stories in this book reflect the author's recollection of events. Some names, locations, and identifying characteristics have been changed to protect the privacy of those depicted. Dialogue has been recreated from memory and journal entries.



Developmental editing — Joelle Yudin
Copy editing — Robert Kinney
Proofreading — Jennie Cohen
Cover and illustrations — Anna Melious
Typesetting — Arjan Van Woensel and Marisa Garau
Technical, photo, and multifaceted office fairy services — Amy Melious

ISBN 978-1-7752111-2-9 (color edition, paperback)
ISBN 978-1-7752111-3-6 (black-and-white edition, paperback)
ISBN 978-1-7752111-4-3 (electronic)

Still Wild 4 Life Press

## Dedication

Hi Maya, Luna, and Maya Rose!
You will learn a lot about your mum and oma
when you read this book.

*Good judgment comes from experience,*
*and a lot of that comes from bad judgment.*
—Author Unknown

# Table of Contents

90° 85° 80° 75° 70° 65° 60° 55° 50° 45° 40° 35° 30° 25° 20° 15° 10° 5° 0° 5° 10°
60° 55° 50° 45° 40° 35° 30° 25° 20° 15° 10° 5° 0° 5°
North America
Atlantic Ocean
Europe
Africa
South America
Shannon
New York
Alicante
Santa Pola
Torrevieja
Ibiza
Gibraltar
Tangiers
Canary Islands
St. Thomas
Barbados
St. Lucia
Grenada
Only 2,700 miles to go!
N
W
E
S

# Introduction

When I look back on my life now, as an octogenarian with snow-white hair, to the young woman that I once was, I am delighted to witness how I plunged into the adventure of ocean sailing at a time when there was no GPS to guide us. There were no smartphones, internet, or computers, either, only celestial navigation, a few instruments, and our wits. How lucky I was to be free and able to embrace this escapade on the high seas.

My adventures at sea began in 1968, when I was twenty-six years old, and my good friend Arthur invited me on a short vacation sailing in the Mediterranean Sea. I leapt at the chance and had no idea those two weeks would expand into a year that would include being shipwrecked on the coast of Spain and crossing the Atlantic Ocean with two Englishmen I didn't know.

Years later, when my adult daughter asked me for a written story about my ocean exploits, I thought I'd write about the physical journey that occurred in the topside world—the great shipwreck in Franco's country, and blithely hitchhiking across the Atlantic. I thought the story would be short and sweet, as it happened over half a century ago; what could I remember of the details, which were buried in the archaeology of my past? As my writing progressed, however, layers of memory began to emerge, and the story developed an energy of its own, becoming richer and deeper in surprising ways.

As life moves on, our experiences become part of the fertile earth of our being, creating the complex garden of who we are in the present moment. It takes time and deep love to tend the hidden roots of that garden. When the memoir became difficult, I protested. I told myself I was too old to write a book. I didn't have the time. This project was just too darn hard! I wanted to quit. My challenge was to believe I had the time, even if this book never was finished.

I found it difficult to accept who I was when, starry-eyed, I fell in love with that old gaff-rigged ketch *Josefine* and ended up spending nearly half a year with her eclectic crew. I was one lost soul. I was confident in my physical body, showing a happy face to the world, but deep down I was terrified, hiding disturbing information about my family genetics, which I did not understand. Yet, while I wrote, I had to welcome the Tamar of long ago into my heart. Love contains us both. I wouldn't throw my young self into the trash like an unwanted scrap or pretend she never existed. She lived.

Perceptions of our lives shift as we grow older, affecting how we weave the stories we tell ourselves and others. We hide some facts and embellish others so our story is not too embarrassing, and we can be comfortable with how we want others to see us.

In these pages I've tried hard to create a full, honest image of who I was as a young woman with all her foibles and faults. Despite this being a challenging and difficult journey, writing this book has been a lot of fun, too.

I've called upon journals, calendars, and friends to help prod my recollections. Much of the dialogue and many of the details described were taken directly from my journal. Other scenes were conjured from where memory and imagination mingle. No matter how truthful I tried to be in telling my stories, I learned that a few friends remember our shared experience differently. Who knows which version is true? Truth is a shape-shifting actor in the movie of any life. *Tamar at Sea* rings true to me and reflects the essence of what I felt at the time.

I hope you enjoy the journey into the life of this free-spirited American girl, marching to her own drumbeat while sailing over the sea and into her inner world—where wonders and challenges that she could not have imagined awaited her just around the corner.

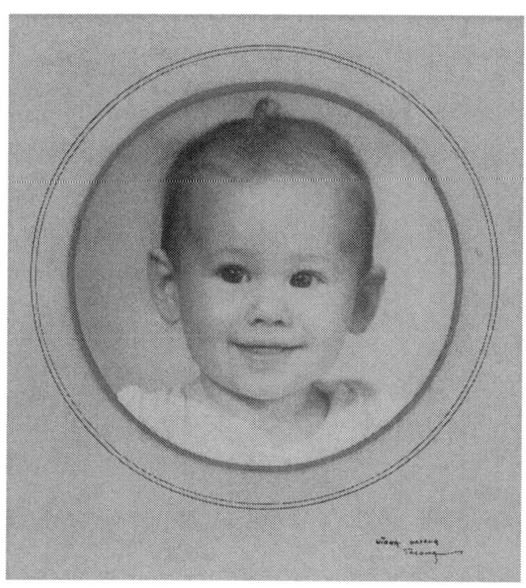

prelude
# Gig Harbor

Ever since I was a child I have been infatuated with the sea. For years, my family spent joyous summers in Gig Harbor, Washington, where we had a tiny cabin that we called the "shack." The harbor was protected by a long sandspit that was covered in tall, wild grass, with a red-and-white lighthouse at the entrance. While the sea in the harbor was relatively warm and calm, our cabin was outside of the harbor, where the swift currents were exciting, and the ocean was cold.

The shack was perched on wooden pilings right on the beach. The whole cabin would shake when loose logs banged into the pilings at high tide. It always sent a thrill up my spine.

My older sister, Naomi, and I slept in an enclosed porch. One wall was a dirt bank held in place by pilings spaced about a foot apart to keep the bank from cascading into the room. Creepy spiders lurked in the dirt. Naomi offered me the best bed, farthest from the dirt bank and close to a wall of windows that faced southeast onto the expanse of Puget Sound.

*Tamar, standing by sleeping porch at rising tide*

Lofty Mount Rainier raised its snow-capped top above Point Defiance, a densely forested peninsula.

Our cozy kitchen had a wood-burning stove. It served a double purpose as a cookstove and as heat for hot water to wash dishes and bathe us kids in a tin tub. It was great fun to collect kindling and bark on the beach. Naomi and I stacked it neatly under our beds, satisfied that we were helping Mother, who prepared simple, nourishing meals for us every day at the cabin.

During those endless summer days, when Daddy went to work by boat at the lumber mill that he founded on the tideflats of Commencement Bay, we had great freedom. We created our own entertainment and adventures.

We hunted for colorful agates, on our own, for miles down the beach. We played hide-and-go-seek in the tall grasses of the sandspit with a neighbor boy, and we found many ways to play with kelp. Naomi and I made kelp dolls that shriveled up into salt-covered old ladies as they dried. We braided their long strands of kelp hair and tied ribbons around them. Daddy taught us how to make kelp whistles. We jumped kelp rope on the cabin deck that Daddy built several years after we bought the shack.

*the shack with the deck Daddy built*

Growing up on the sea with the independence we had, we learned to solve problems as they occurred. Most of the dicey situations we found ourselves in were due to underestimating the power of the tides, and we had to use our wits and fortitude to get home safely.

We had a little square-bowed wooden dinghy we painted a soft orange and named *Salmon*. I loved that dinghy and spent many hours rowing her along the outside of the harbor, where the currents were swift, and inside the harbor, where the water was calmer.

One hot summer day, when I was seven-and-a-half years old, I fancied sailing *Salmon*. I rushed into the shack shouting, "Mother, I need a sheet and scissors and safety pins! And a pencil!"

"What for?"

"I'm making a sail for *Salmon*!" I could always count on Mother to humor my whims. Within moments she brought me just what I needed. With a hug, I was off.

A tall, smooth, straight stick that I had salvaged on the beach was to be the mast, and a smaller straight stick would hold the bottom of the sail in place. I'd seen many sailboats go by our shack and they all had sticks like these.

With the materials and tools laid out on the deck, I began marking lines on the sheet with a thick pencil. My sister, Naomi, appeared at my side and asked, "Can I help?"

Naomi and I played well together. We were a good mix of spontaneity and careful thinking. Inseparable as children, we never fought, thanks to her sweet temperament and her acceptance of me the moment I was born. "Sure! Hold the sticks so I can cut the sail."

A short while and many safety pins later, Naomi and I stood up and gazed at our masterpiece. The tide was good, and I was eager to sail *Salmon* right away. Excited to show Mother our homemade sail, I raced into the shack.

"Naomi and I finished, Mother, come see! Can I sail her now?" I grabbed her hand and pulled her out to the deck, my little three-year-old brother, Mark, trailing behind.

"Well done, you two! Go ahead, Tamar."

Barefoot, we dragged *Salmon* down the pebbly beach to the edge of the sea, delighting in the crunchy noise of the hull scraping the pebbles. Naomi and I then shoved the mast into a round hole in the dinghy's bow. I tied a rope to the end of the bottom stick, so I'd have control of the sail, letting it out wide over the ocean or keeping it tight against the side of the little boat, depending on the wind. Despite never having had a sailing lesson, I was eager to be on my way.

Salmon *with homemade sail*

Grabbing her sides, we heaved *Salmon* into the cold sea, and in I hopped, sitting down on the middle seat, where I could use the oars to back away from shore and turn *Salmon* around before heading off into the big unknown. Mother stood with my siblings on the beach and her Brownie camera in hand. Waving fond farewells, I caught the wind and sailed *Salmon* far out.

The sea was breathing gently; the sun was out. The tide was ebbing, but I knew it would soon become slack, then turn into a flood tide to help me home. I loved the freedom of being alone in our dinghy, the wind in the sail my sister and I had made, the scent of the salt air, and the sound of the waves lapping the hull. It was an exhilarating time in my life, and I was filled with confidence.

Hours later, I returned home in one piece, beaching the square bow onto the rocky shore. Out I scrambled, excited by the triumph of a successful expedition. Mother, Naomi, and Mark ran down to greet me and to help me pull the dinghy high up on the beach, where we tied it to a post. Sailing in the summers of 1949–1952 was my only sailing experience until I took to the high seas in 1968.

*Tamar with Sasafrass*

*Tamar, Naomi, and Mark exploring the beach*

chapter one

# Things Change

### *Boarding School*

My life was changed forever in the fall of 1957 on the day Dad sent me three thousand miles away from home to a boarding school in Massachusetts. As the plane rose higher and higher above the city and through the white clouds, I felt forlorn and empty. Leaving behind my familiar home, Siamese cat, my friends, and school, I felt totally unprepared for this chapter in my life.

Dad told me he wanted me to get a good education and learn how to think and dress like an easterner. Dad had graduated from Yale, so he knew what he was talking about.

Arguing with Dad was a losing battle. He ruled our roost, and neither Mother nor any of us kids had a say in our education. I loved Annie Wright Seminary, the private girls' school I had attended from kindergarten through grade nine in Tacoma. Every morning when I walked through the doors, I felt embraced by my teachers, friends, and the ritual of the Episcopalian chapel the entire school attended every morning of every day of the school year.

"Dad, I love my school! Please let me stay!"

"No, Tink. You're enrolled in Miss Hall's School." That was the end of the conversation. I stared at the father I loved and watched him walk down the long gallery and close the door to the master bedroom.

Mother took me aside. "I'm sorry, honey. I couldn't persuade your pa to let you stay home." She wrapped her arms around me and held me close. I hadn't a clue at the time that Dad had ulterior motives for sending me to a boarding school so far away from home.

Mrs. Charlotte McAllister drove her daughter, Robin, and me from New York City to Miss Hall's School in Pittsfield, Massachusetts. Dad had known Charlotte when she lived in Seattle and no doubt was thrilled that Robin was my age and going to the same boarding school. Robin seemed confident, bubbly, and full of big smiles. Unlike me, she was excited to be going away to school, only being nervous about the academics.

The school was set in the rolling hills of the Berkshire Mountains, which looked tame to my eyes, compared to the rugged Pacific Northwest. I already longed for Mount Rainier in the Cascade Range, majestic and snow-covered all year, and visible from Gig Harbor and Tacoma.

In the room where I would spend the school year with two girls I had yet to meet, I was relieved to discover there was a dormer window letting welcome daylight into our tiny world.

## *The Letters*

Shortly after I arrived at school, I received a letter in the dark cubbyhole of my mailbox, among all the other cubbyholes where the girls collected their mail. It was from my father. I was thrilled to hold something he had written and took it to my room to read in private. Sitting at my desk, I sliced the blue envelope open with the beautiful brass letter opener Dad had given me before I'd left for school, unfolded the letter, and read.

In type on the light-blue stationery, he told me that I had a bad seed in me, and that I was doomed to have a sick child. All that I saw was BAD SEED and DOOMED, which he had typed in capital letters and underlined twice in red.

I caught my breath, frozen to my chair. At this moment the foundation of my life cracked open; my happy childhood shattered like broken glass at my feet.

Tears pricked my eyes as I stared at the letter. I wanted to destroy it, but I didn't. Carefully I folded it and put it back into the blue envelope. Hoping that none of my roommates would pop into our room, I pulled my suitcase down from the top shelf in my closet, laid the alarming letter inside and locked the suitcase tight.

A week or so later, another blue envelope appeared in my cubbyhole. As I walked back to my room to read it, I wondered what he would tell me now. I had a glimmer of hope—that the previous letter had been a bad dream, and this letter would be filled with love and stories about my parents' English setters and our Siamese cat, which would bring me back to the comforting sense of home that I cherished.

In my room, I sat at my desk and contemplated the immensity of opening it. Dreading what was inside, I sliced the envelope open.

With urgency, Dad presented as absolute truth that there was another baffling illness that ran in our family. This illness prevented certain relatives from marrying or having children—a spinster gene, of sorts. To illustrate his point, he drew a family tree and put red dots next to the name of every relative and ancestor who never married or never had children. The tree was smothered in red dots. I held the letter and stared at it in disbelief.

Are you kidding? Are you telling me that I would become another red dot on our sick family tree? A spinster or a married woman with no kids? Why was he telling me these horrible stories?

My world as I knew it crashed. How could I possibly navigate life when any step I took would lead me into a bottomless abyss of doom and despair? I was damned if I had kids, and damned if I didn't.

I locked the second letter in my suitcase and told no one about them. When more letters came, I shut my heart tight as a moon snail's door, too afraid of what else I might learn, and stuffed them into my suitcase, unread. Dozens of letters would arrive over the next three years at school. I knew they were important, and I'd have to read them eventually, but not yet.

The letters were out of sight but not out of mind. The damage had been done. I was a wounded teenager even before I hatched into a fledgling young woman. I carried a burden of great fear that would influence my behavior and relationships for decades.

My greatest conflict was that I loved my father, and I believed him. He was a dignified and respected member of the Tacoma community, and he was the most handsome, delightful, educated, adventurous man I could have dreamt of having as a father. How could I question his reasoning?

A different person might have said, “Fuck you. You’re nuts. You need to see a shrink!” But not me. Without challenge, my dad could say whatever he wanted to the daughter he loved and who loved him in return. It was easy for him to pour his fears onto paper and post them with a seven-cent stamp. I was too ashamed of the messages in the letters to bring them into the light, and Dad never mentioned the letters, even when I was at home.

chapter two

# FLOUNDERING

## *Escapade on the Hudson*

In 1960 I enrolled at Barnard College in New York City. Irene and I were roommates our freshman year. We immediately became good friends over our shared love of the sea. Irene was born in Holland, grew up in Brazil, and moved to New Jersey with her family as a teenager. She had traveled across the ocean numerous times and was drawn to the romance of the sea.

I had grown up in the Pacific Northwest and had an abiding fascination and love of the ever-changing tides and salt waters of Puget Sound.

One fine spring afternoon, when earth was awakening from its winter sleep, we needed to escape the rigors of academic life in stultifying classrooms of bright, eager students, and we thought of an adventure on the Hudson River, which was at the doorstep of Barnard College and Columbia University.

Irene was a Dutch girl through and through, with long, thick blonde hair and a glorious smile. We both were young and felt like mermaids who could entice men into our net.

*Irene with howler monkey*

Sitting barefoot on the banks of the Hudson River, dressed in T-shirts and shorts, as spring was in the air, we were determined to hitch a ride in a passing speedboat. Freighters and passenger ships went by, wending their way to the sea. A few sailboats were out tacking back and forth on the wide river. It wasn't long before a curious fellow approached us in a speedboat.

"Irene, look! Here's one coming towards us!" We jumped up and waved our arms.

A man yelled, "You girls want a ride?"

"Yes!" Irene and I exclaimed simultaneously.

"Where're you off to?"

"Anywhere! We just want a boat ride!" Irene said.

"Hop aboard, then."

He nosed his boat into the rocks, and we climbed in without a thought to the risk we were taking. He sped us downriver, where we had dreams to continue on to the wide-open Atlantic Ocean, and no one would have known where we had gone. The lure of the ocean was deep in our bones, and the Hudson River, wending its way to the sea, was a link to our romantic dreams.

Several hours later, he dropped us off on the rocks where he'd found us. We were lucky that he was a decent fellow, and it was a lot of fun.

### *Halloween Party*

In the fall of 1962, I was a junior at Barnard College. The enigmatic Eric Britton, then in grad school for economics at Columbia University, notoriously chased after Barnard girls. He invited my best friend, Irene, to a Halloween costume party he was throwing. She asked me to join her.

Partying was not on my mind. My sister, Naomi, had died six weeks before. Irene knew I was struggling with heartache, and she tried to revive my spirits by encouraging me to have some fun at a party. I didn't want to go.

"Tamar come, please!"

A flicker of curiosity flashed through my mind. "What will you be?"

"A flamenco dancer—Carmen Amaya!"

"Oh Irene, you will be fantastic! I never could pull off something like that. I feel so sad."

"Tamar, what if you went as a fairy?"

Dressing as an elusive fairy appealed to me. I felt like an effervescent being with my feet barely touching the earth. Naomi's death had spun me into a different world, where the foundation of my life, shaken first by my father's letters, was once again shattered. I missed Naomi tremendously and often dreamt of becoming a fairy with wings so I could fly in the sky with her and play as we had when we were children. I agreed to go to the costume party with Irene.

The next day I created a simple costume, befitting my mood. I wore a white dress above my knees and wove ivy and flowers into my long hair. Irene was a splashy, eye-catching flamenco dancer, bedecked in a red dress that flared out in multiple layers below her knees, complete with castanets in her hands. Her thick blonde hair, flowing over her shoulders and past her waist, was the most astonishing feature on Irene and caught many people's eyes.

It was a gathering of flamboyantly costumed characters, with the sounds of clinking glasses, chatter that rose and fell like a garbled symphony, and music of the times, some of which I recognized, like Elvis's "Return to Sender," "Green Onions," and Little Eva's "The Loco-Motion" adding to the cacophony. I felt suffocated in all the smoke and out of place with people pretending to be who they weren't. I wondered how people could make so much noise. I wanted to disappear.

At that moment, a fellow approached dressed as a monk in an authentic brown robe with a rope cinched around his waist. He was slight of build, handsome, with thick, dark-brown hair, a neat beard and mustache, a turned-down Roman nose, and sparkly brown eyes. His monk's costume appealed to me. It was simple and spoke of a quiet nature, in stark contrast to the other characters in the crowd.

"Where do you come from?" he asked.

"I come from the fairyland of make-believe!" I said and lightly slipped away.

He followed.

"Who are you?" he asked when he caught up with me.

"I'm Tamar. I'm from Tacoma, and I'm a Barnard student. And you?"

"I'm Arthur and I'm a physicist. I study quantum physics."

"Oh. What's that?" I asked, truly stumped.

"It's the part of physics that studies how everything works. I study particles, which are very small objects, like atoms and electrons. Everything in the universe has a particle nature."

## *Arthur*

Arthur and I became good friends. I learned that besides being a serious scientist, he had a playful side that was intriguing and fun. He created a machine that was a tangle of wires and boxes, which painted abstract pictures, and drew a lot of gawkers in Greenwich Village.

I liked Arthur and enjoyed our conversations over coffee or dinners. We'd talk about everything under the sun: physics, inventing, art, the colorful students we knew, sailing, my courses at Barnard, and our families.

I wish that I had been available to have a relationship with him, as he seemed genuinely interested in me, and he was a stable, fascinating, and fun man, attractive and smart, too. But I was far from ready for a relationship, suffering from the confusion of my father's letters and the tragedy of my sister's death.

## *Don't Tell Anybody*

A mythical dragon slept inside my womb and did a very good job of keeping my secret fears concealed. On the surface I was carefree, vivacious, and healthy. Inside, I was suffering, broken, terrified, and insecure.

I had returned to Barnard not even two weeks after Naomi's death on September 13, 1962. Before I boarded the plane in Seattle, Dad said, "Don't tell anyone about Naomi."

At the time, I didn't question Dad's decree that I keep quiet. I could barely think. I didn't have the nerve or insight to challenge him about it. Was he hiding something? Was he ashamed of her death? Dad was a Griggs, and he came from an illustrious and well-known family in Tacoma. Was Dad's request for silence to avoid public scrutiny?

I did tell one soul. Against my father's wishes, I told Irene. I simply had to say something to my best friend, allowing her into my grief.

### *Floundering*

AT SCHOOL I COULDN'T ESCAPE my devastation over the loss of my sister. I decided to barely eat. That was my misguided way of empathizing with her death. I didn't want to die, but I loved my sister and reasoned this was a gentle way of being with her.

Even as an adolescent I knew that Naomi had been suffering from depression. When I was thirteen and she was fourteen, I witnessed her sitting on the floor of the bedroom we shared, banging her head against the wall, trying to knock the depression out of herself. She believed her depression was all in her head.

With an aching heart, I hugged her and told her all would be well. I thought her moodiness was a natural stage in growing up, which I just hadn't reached yet. Naomi didn't seem to have the close friendships that I had. She slowly became more and more withdrawn and told me she felt she didn't belong in our fun-filled family.

I had a blue-and-white Danish demitasse of hers that I brought to New York, and I'd pour Grape-Nuts cereal into it with a tiny bit of milk; that was my breakfast. It was less than a quarter cup of cereal, but I loved holding something in my hand that Naomi had enjoyed.

I doled out my lunch carefully over the noon hour from a little box of sun-dried raisins. I indulged in an apple or banana in the afternoon, and for supper I'd have a container of yogurt and a cup of soup. That was it; all carefully monitored. I lost so much weight I was eventually only ninety-three pounds.

Back then, therapy wasn't prevalent like it is today, and I was on my own confronting my loss. I am sure that I was anorexic, but nobody counseled me.

I was so lost and depressed that I was teetering on the edge of failing school. I had chosen to major in art history and had mistakenly thought that I would be able to dive into my studies and forget the tragedy back home. Before Christmas break, my faculty adviser, Mrs. Garcia Lorca, called me into her office. I knew that I was in trouble. She scanned my grades and my thin frame before suggesting that I take a leave of absence for a year and go home. She didn't ask me a single question. She clearly knew that something was causing me to flounder, and I was headed for failure if I didn't leave the rigors of academic life and get myself together.

I nodded, taking this in. I felt that I was in the presence of a remarkable woman who was perceptive and kind. I wanted desperately to confide in her that my sister had died, but Dad had forbidden me to speak of her death, so I left that immense event untold. Just before Christmas, I flew home.

## chapter three
# TACOMA

It was the perfect time for a break from academic life and to remain at home for the year. My parents met me at the airport, and we chatted away about my life in the city and their life on the creek. I was excited to be home again in the place I loved. On the surface, everything looked perfect.

My parents had transformed our massive cement-block house into a fairy-tale scene, with upside-down little fir trees bedecked in tiny white lights hanging from the gallery rafters. An elegant eighteen-foot noble fir Christmas tree, also laced in tiny white lights, with shining glass balls of purple, silver, blue, and green, stood in our open dining room by the large fireplace.

The house was lovely, yet there was a huge, unfathomable hole. This was our first Christmas without Naomi. Strangely, we never spoke of her death, yet I am sure we each held her in our hearts. We were a family of silences, orbiting each other in our private worlds of grief. I felt at once embraced by the house I knew so well and disturbed by the hush over her death.

*Naomi, 1960*

## *Heartbroken*

One cold winter morning I walked again over the arched bridge under which Chambers Creek rushes to Puget Sound. I knew it differently now as the bridge my sister failed to take when she came to say goodbye to me. I walked back to the house, where a huge fire was burning in the hearth, and all at once the night of Naomi's death became poignantly clear in my mind.

Although Naomi had struggled for years with depression, her death was a sudden, traumatizing shock. I was haunted by one of the last conversations we had only a few days before she died.

Naomi had been staying at our Gig Harbor cabin that summer and had been seeing a therapist in Seattle four days a week. My parents encouraged me to live with her during August, to give her company. I was happy to spend time at Gig Harbor. I loved the shack where so many of our happy childhood memories were made by the sea, and I loved and felt sad for my dear sister, who seemed so troubled.

One evening, we were sitting on the deck, with the high tide flooding underneath the cabin, when Naomi suddenly said, out of thin air, "Tamar, I don't want to die."

I was flabbergasted, wondering why she would say such a thing.

"Die? Naomi, you're not going to die!"

I didn't ask her questions. I didn't reach out to her in her anguish and sorrow. I simply didn't believe what she had said—that she thought she might die.

Shortly after that evening on the deck, I returned to my parents' house to pack for my junior year at Barnard. I left Naomi at the shack, begging her to come say goodbye to me before I had to leave in three days. I felt miserable leaving her, and guilty, too, and for a moment wondered if she'd be safe alone at the cabin.

I hugged her and drew back, looking into her blue eyes. "Will you be okay?"

"I'll be fine, Tamar. I'll try to see you before you go."

I left her, feeling heartbroken that she was so sad. Another part of me was excited to be packing up and returning to my studies in New York.

I drove over the arched Narrows Bridge spanning Puget Sound and down the winding dirt road to our family house on Chambers Creek. This was early September and there was a faint hint of cool mist in the air. The salmon-bearing creek bubbled merrily around the banks by our house, winding its way to the sea, and the Virginia creeper, climbing up our tall windows, was already crimson. Lola, our English setter, had a litter of puppies, and Mother kept them in a playpen in the gallery when they weren't outside. I loved sitting in the playpen with them as they scrambled over me with puppy-love abandon.

The night before I was to leave, Mother, Dad, my brother, Mark, and Uncle Bill, Mother's younger brother, who was visiting us from San Francisco, went out to dinner. I stayed home to finish packing and to play with the puppies.

The phone rang.

It rang and rang.

I didn't answer. I was having too much fun with the puppies.

When my family came home from dining out, we got into a crazy mood. I have no idea what possessed us, but Dad put dancing music on our record player. Inspired, I donned my slinky, long red dress, and Mother fetched her long black dress with a silver braided strap around her neck. We danced the foxtrot, samba, waltz, and tango on the polished, midnight-blue cement floors of the gallery barefoot with Uncle Bill and Dad. We all were good dancers, and we had the time of our lives.

Sometime during the evening Dad lit the five candles of our silver candelabra, and we carried it around recklessly, with wax dripping onto the heated floors, as we laughed and danced. I felt as if we were in a Fellini film, captive for a weekend party during which anything could happen.

Well past midnight, we trundled to bed. I was exhilarated, happy, and worn out from our crazy dancing, which had been pure magic and spontaneous fun. As I shut my eyes, glowing in joy, I briefly wondered about that phone call.

The next morning, Mother brewed a pot of coffee and set a box of cornflakes, bananas, and a pitcher of milk on the dining table. Dad had left for work. Mark and I wandered down the gallery towards the kitchen with its enticing scent of coffee.

Dad suddenly rushed into the house, weeping. He spoke to Mother and Uncle Bill. I stood near Mark, wondering what was going on.

Dad told us that he found Naomi dead in her car across the creek, close to the bridge. Dad said that she had fallen asleep with the windows rolled up and the engine running. There was a leak in the exhaust pipe; she died of carbon monoxide poisoning. He said it was an accident.

While Dad made all the arrangements, Uncle Bill was a solace to Mother. He lent a calm presence to the tragedy that shook our family to its foundations. Mark and I each absorbed the shocking news on our own.

My heart ached, thinking of my lonely sister contemplating whether to cross the bridge between her despair and our night of gaiety, or stay in the car with the heat on and the windows shut, falling asleep in utter desolation, not realizing that Death was knocking at her door.

I was haunted by what Naomi had told me at Gig Harbor. Had she come to say goodbye and witnessed our hilarity the night before, too desolate to join in? I wondered again about that call that I had neglected to answer. Had that been my beloved sister reaching out to me? I felt wretched and guilty that I hadn't answered the phone.

A few days later, we went to the funeral home to say goodbye to Naomi as she lay in her coffin. I was totally unprepared for what I witnessed. I stared at her still body, with her hands folded over her chest, her thick, dark-brown curly hair brushed neatly. She was wearing a slender off-white, short-sleeved scooped-neck dress that fell just below her knees. I didn't remember ever seeing her wear this dress. What I remember most was the bright red lipstick someone had painted onto her lips. I didn't remember ever seeing her wear lipstick. I wished I had never laid eyes on her lying so still in her coffin, with her blue eyes closed and those shocking red lips.

### *Too Many Secrets*

One evening when it was still winter, Mother and I made a big pot of split pea soup with a ham bone, onions, potatoes, and carrots. When Dad came home from work at the mill, the kitchen smelled inviting. The setters barked and raced to greet him with their feathered tails wagging like flags, and I joined them, hugging Dad a welcome home. I was happy to see him. He hung up his coat in the entryway, then stoked the fire in our open dining area, where my parents had moved the couches closer to the fireplace for winter warmth. Dad lifted the lid and poked his nose over the steaming pot, grinning. We all liked split pea soup.

He then fetched a can of beer and poured half a glass full of frothy beer and laced it with milk. This was Dad's signature drink—half beer and half milk. Mother, being a German frau, liked her beer straight. I hated beer. We settled on the couches close to the warmth of the fire, and chatted about our day, with the English setters curled up at our feet. Mother smoked a cigarette. Dad lit one but he let the ashes grow as he rarely inhaled. I think he simply liked holding a cigarette in his hand. I fetched him an ashtray and held it for him as he flicked the ashes into the tray.

"Dad, you've got to be careful with your cigarette," I said.

He looked at me and smiled. "Yes, Tink, I know."

Because my parents had lost a daughter, I didn't want them to worry about me, so I took on the role of being a strong and healthy young woman, showing a happy, confident face to my family and the world, while fiercely guarding my confusions. I believed that I was their only kid who could pretend to be sane! I wanted desperately to talk to my mother about Naomi but believed that it would be too painful for her.

We dined peacefully on soup, fresh bread, salami, cheese, and huge pretzels from the nearby German bakery. Then without saying a word,

Dad got up and walked down the long gallery into the master bedroom and shut the door. Mother and I looked at each other. "Just like your pa," she said quietly.

Dad often retreated to the bedroom when he wanted to think or write letters. I had a feeling of unease as Mother and I continued to sit at the table. I wondered if he was going to write my brother a letter. Mark had been with us over Christmas but had flown back to Groton School in Massachusetts. Would his missives to Mark be as devastating as the ones he wrote to me?

I had a strong suspicion that Mother didn't know about the letters, and I didn't want to trouble her with more trauma. As with Naomi's death, they were swept under the table as if they never had happened. Why didn't Dad discuss them? Was he creating a façade, even in his family, that all was great in the Griggs home?

My father had been worried about our family genetics when Naomi showed her first symptoms of being ill. He began to do massive research, as he suspected there was an inherited illness on his mother's side of the family tree.

Long before she died, when she was fourteen, Naomi had attempted suicide by slitting her wrists. Even though we were close, I had no idea. Her suicide attempt was one more secret that had been kept from me and my brother.

# chapter four
# NEW YORK

My year at home was coming to an end, and I looked forward to returning to Barnard in New York. I could have stayed at home, where life would have been easy, but I was twenty-one and longed for independence from my family. I wanted to carve out a life for myself, far away from home, and see if I could survive on my own without family connections. In New York City, I'd just be one of the millions taking the subways and walking the streets, going about their lives, and no one would have a clue about the illustrious and deeply warped family history that tagged along with me.

So, when the spring term began in February 1964, I took flight to the skies and once again landed in the jungle of New York, fully intending to resume my academic life at Barnard. Instead, I was met with a huge surprise. I learned that Barnard required me to reapply to the college, even though I had simply taken a leave of absence. The process seemed daunting, as I had been on the edge of failure when I left.

I phoned Irene, who was sailing into her last year at Barnard, and spent a weekend with her at her family house in New Jersey, where I had a good think. After considering the reality of my situation and the depth of my unresolved grief over my sister's death, I understood that I wasn't yet ready for the demands of academic studies. College could wait.

When I turned twenty-one, in December 1962, I had inherited a small trust fund from my uncle and great-aunt. If I was careful, I could live modestly and frugally without having to work. So, instead of returning to school, I found myself a beautiful one-room apartment at 7 East Tenth Street, close to Greenwich Village. I rented the second floor, which had exquisite teak carvings of elephants, birds and flowers surrounding the windows. These were crafted in India and shipped to New York in the early 1900s. Here, living in this sunny, serene apartment, I decided to explore anything that struck my fancy.

*7 East Tenth Street*

## *Therapy*

My sister's death compelled my search for a therapist in New York. I needed to open my suitcase with all the read and unread letters from my father. Dr. Franck was a lovely Freudian analyst, who didn't make me lie on a couch and say out loud everything that went through my mind. We both sat in comfortable chairs surrounded by his art, philosophy, and literature books. In this environment, I found myself able to open my heart and have real conversations over the letters.

During one of my first visits, he asked, "Are you happy?"

I thought a while.

"In comparison to Naomi, yes."

"But you—are you happy?"

"No!"

I explained my dad's ominous warnings about bad seeds and spinsterhood. I told him that I was scared, doomed to have a sick child, and all I wanted was to be a mother. My mother was gentle; I loved her dearly. I knew that my mother adored her mother—so if I had a child, it would be three generations of good mothers.

It took courage to face Dad's messages. I grew to understand that my father meant well. He wanted to warn me of the pitfalls in my ancestor tree so that I could avoid them. What he didn't realize was that he had checkmated me. Any step that I took that led off the knife's edge path of my life, which Dad warned I needed to follow, would plunge me into the fated abyss. What else could I do but freeze in my tracks?

Although a relief, reading the letters out loud and discussing them with Dr. Franck hadn't reached my deep grief, ingrained into every cell of my young body.

As if out of sheer survival instinct, I dove into the worlds of art and dance.

## *Pandora's Box*

I DEVELOPED A LIFELONG LOVE of dance in Nancy Jane Bare's creative classes in elementary school. Nancy had studied dance with Martha Graham in New York. She taught us barefoot, adapting Graham's technique to children. We performed fascinating pieces set to modern music and others based on Greek myths.

My favorite was *Pandora's Box*. Zeus was angry when Prometheus stole fire from the gods and gave it to humans. He wanted to punish Prometheus and devised a plan. He sent Pandora, a beautiful woman with gifts from the gods—wisdom, kindness, beauty, and curiosity—to Prometheus's brother, who fell head over heels in love with her and married her.

As a wedding present, Zeus gave Pandora a beautiful box and instructed her not to open it. Curiosity won, and she opened the forbidden box. All the evils and suffering of the world were unleashed upon humanity.

When she slammed the lid shut, there was still one being left inside, begging to be let out. With great fear, Pandora opened the box, and out came Hope.

In our school recital, Naomi danced Gluttony, wearing a papier-mâché mask she had created in art class. All the girls inside the box were masked as they danced the evils of the world. I was given the role of Pandora.

Little did I know that this fascinating story would become woven into my life as I journeyed forth, confronting the suitcase and the dark letters locked inside. Pandora became a metaphor for my life.

## *Dance*

I KNEW THAT MARTHA GRAHAM had a dance school in New York. I also knew that she had broken away from formal ballet to explore barefoot what it is to be human, expressing all our conflicting emotions. She choreographed many dances based on Greek tragedies.

I could relate to tragedy. So, it was with great expectation that I enrolled in her dance school. I yearned to come to a place where my body could express my deep sorrow, and I could heal.

The day of my first class arrived. Filled with anticipation and excitement, I entered the immense studio that had a wall of mirrors and a bank of tall, arched windows that reflected light off the lustrous dance floor. I sat in the front row facing the mirrors, as I was eager to see and understand the exercises. All the classes would be taught by Martha's company members. There was a hush in the room as the students focused on their own bodies, waiting for class to begin.

The teacher arrived, and with very little explanation, we began the warm-up exercises, sitting on the floor with the soles of our bare feet together and bouncing our heads down to our toes. Still on the floor, we were taught contractions and releases, which were the foundation of the Graham technique. The contractions came from the pelvis, and the releases began there, too. When you are in sorrow or deep trauma, your body naturally contracts. When you are joyful, your body releases, and you open to what is around you. Slowly but surely, I reached into the depths of my loss and began to access the pain from Naomi's death.

A few months after being steeped in the Graham technique, I discovered Merce Cunningham's studio, and eagerly signed up for classes. I found Cunningham's method playful, light, and fun. He had broken away from storytelling in dance and explored movement for movement's sake. There was a genuine warmth in Merce and a sense of humor and curiosity about all the ways we can move from point A to point B. During the warm-up exercises, which were always done standing up, I felt like a bird with wings to fly.

Dance soothed me in a way that talking never could. I felt strong and confident in my body, which changed my outlook on life as I walked the streets of New York. For me, the Graham and Cunningham techniques balanced the sorrow and joy in my life. Once I discovered Merce, I continued frequenting both studios. Dance became my lifeline.

## *Art*

The art and dance studios at Annie Wright Seminary, my school in Tacoma, were stable sanctuaries as we moved up the ladder towards high school. Mrs. Margot Seeley was another inspiring teacher. She taught art classes in a huge studio with high ceilings. Light flooded the room through banks of large windows. There were long tables covered in white paper, where we'd gather to create. The room smelled of paint, clay, glue, and turpentine. I eagerly went to her classes all through elementary school, never knowing what she'd planned for us.

Back in New York, I wanted to continue my art studies. I spent many hours at the New York Studio School of Drawing, Painting and Sculpture on West Eighth Street. The school had been founded by Mercedes Matter in 1964, and it was an exciting place to study. As we drew the nude models posing in elaborate settings, we studied how the light fell on the figures. I also spent hours at the Art Students League, where I studied etching. I loved the mystery of covering up zinc plates and dipping them into acid baths, creating images and textures, never knowing what the inked print would look like until I released it from the press.

*Clowns, etching created during my time in New York*

As much as I reveled in my immersion in the arts, the fact that I didn't have a job haunted me. My small trust fund set me apart from most others in a world where work is often wrapped up with purpose and meaning. My unusual circumstances felt like both a blessing and a curse, both a freedom and an emptiness, leaving me confused about finding my purpose in life.

## *The Loft*

By 1967 I had moved to a huge loft at 112 West Fourteenth Street, a few steps from Sixth Avenue. It was an open, spacious room on the third floor of a commercial building, and I was excited to create my own home that would reflect my spirit, and where I could do artwork and live in the same space.

My loft was in a mercantile district, where stores hung their discount clothing on racks on the sidewalk. I wasn't supposed to live in this building, but many artists lived in their New York lofts, and nothing was ever done about it.

On the floor above me was a thermometer factory that made a lot of noise from 9:00 a.m. to 3:00 p.m., and below me there was a gay nude theater called Dramatis Personae. The "madame" of this theater had taken a fancy to me, and looked out for me as I came and went from my loft. We often chatted in the evenings when she sat outside the door taking tickets. I loved her flamboyant appearance, which was my opposite: she was a voluptuous woman with masses of curly red-brown hair. She wore bright red lipstick and had long curved fingernails that she painted silver underneath and red on top.

The sixty-by-twenty-foot rectangular space looked onto bustling West Fourteenth Street. I set up my living area on the south side, where the sun streamed in through a large bank of barred windows. There, I placed my huge four-poster bed, and created a small kitchen furnished with a sturdy card table and two chairs. A claw-foot bathtub nestled up to a wall near the two-burner stove in the kitchenette.

Close to the north facing windows, I arranged my large wooden easel with a small table nearby for my oil paints, turpentine, brushes, and palette. I enjoyed laying out the Windsor & Newton oil paints in tubes—Cadmium Red, Indigo Blue, Burnt Sienna, Crimson, Titanium White and Ivory Black—just waiting to be mixed and worked into a blank canvas.

I brought a tall ficus tree with me from my apartment on 7 East Tenth Street, and I fervently hoped it would be happy and thrive in its new home.

My dining table, a bohemian improvisation, was an old door I had found in an alley, propped up by cement blocks. My guests and I would dine royally, sitting cross-legged on cushions on the floor.

Mother had given me a few oriental rugs, which added warmth to the rather industrial atmosphere. I couldn't wait to invite my friends into the realm I had so lovingly created.

This loft was my home and my sanctuary.

## *David Enters*

For reasons that were a mystery to me, I held a deep fascination for the ancient Roman myth of the abduction of the Sabine women. I was familiar with many different depictions of the story created by painters and sculptors throughout the centuries, and something in me resonated with the pain and anguish the women were experiencing at the hands of their captors.

Knowing that creative endeavors always offer a way to better understand ourselves, I felt compelled to explore the complex tragedy of power, sex, and violence through my artwork.

One afternoon, I invited a group of friends to my loft to stage a reenactment of the story so that I could photograph it and use those images as references for a painting. The bright afternoon light coming in through the loft windows would allow me to photograph at a high enough shutter speed to catch movement.

As the tale goes, Romulus was one of the boys raised by a wolf and he ruled a city that would become Rome. The men needed more women in their kingdom. After an unsuccessful appeal for wives from nearby towns, Romulus invited the residents of neighboring towns, including

Abduction of the Sabine Women *by Nicholas Poussin*

the Sabines, to a festival of games. At a signal from Romulus, the Roman soldiers grabbed the Sabine women and kidnapped them. The women were forced to accept the Roman men as their husbands.

We chose Eduardo, an art student, to be Romulus. Standing on a makeshift podium, he gave the rest of the fellows—his Roman soldiers—the signal to abduct the Sabine women: my friends Ruth, Bettie, Elizabeth, Elaine, and a few others. Chaos followed.

The dearest of my friends there was David, a quiet, creative, and gentle man. We'd met several years before through our parents. Although he'd been agreeable about coming to help me out, I was a little concerned that he'd be uncomfortable acting out the assault of women, as he had such a kind nature. When I glanced over to check on him, I noticed that he seemed fine. Then, I caught something else. His gaze was on my friend

Ruth, with stars in his eyes. I smiled.

That afternoon, I photographed like mad. In frame after frame, men were chasing and grabbing women, as they struggled to escape. I had more than enough material to work with for the painting I hoped to create.

## *Max*

IN THE SPRING OF 1968, Mother flew to New York to see me. We went to a performance of the Joffrey Ballet company, where we saw Maximiliano Zomosa dance Death in *The Green Table*, an antiwar dance choreographed by Kurt Jooss in 1932, when rumors of war were rumbling in Europe. Since Max had been to our house in Tacoma when my parents helped to sponsor the Joffrey Ballet for a summer residency at the University of Puget Sound, we were eager to see him perform. Death was on our minds, as Mother had lost her daughter, and I my only sister, way too soon.

That evening, as we sat in the dark theater, we were mesmerized by the power of Max's dance portraying Death. With relentless pounding feet and outstretched arms, Death was ready to claim everyone. In one tender scene a young maiden, grieving over the death of her love, longed for Death to take her away. He came to her and embraced her compassionately in his strong arms. I thought of Naomi longing for Death to end her own sorrows. Death had scooped her up in his fated arms, just like he had with the young maiden, and had brought her peace.

After Mother flew home, I invited Max to a party in my loft. I prepared a spread of Dutch cheeses, homemade bread, sweet butter, salami, and ham. Chianti festooned the low table, and candles were set in empty bottles. I wanted my loft to be romantic and beautiful for this occasion.

As the party time came near, I brushed my long, straight hair and put half of it back in a barrette. I put on a silver Indian necklace with three tiers and tiny leaves that danced as I moved. After lighting the candles, I started a record of Segovia playing classical guitar, one of my favorites. I felt an excited anticipation about what the night might bring.

I had draped soft, orange India-print curtains around the sides of the massive four-poster bed to give myself one private, cozy space in the open studio. As much as it dominated the room, in the low light, it looked quite pretty. For the party, I pulled one curtain aside so my friends could stash their belongings on the bed.

I loved that bed, which Eduardo had custom-made for me. The four posts, stained a dark brown, were four-by-four-inch wooden beams that rose eight feet above the floor. The crossbeams were mitered into the posts and set at different levels. The bed looked like a Mondrian painting.

I waited.

My thoughts were on Max. I was having intense fantasies of us becoming lovers, even soulmates.

Soon I heard footsteps and chatter coming up the stairs, and my friends piled into my loft, pouring themselves Chianti, nibbling on the goodies I had laid out, and talking about this and that.

Max became the center of attention that night. Eager to hear his stories, my friends gathered around him. We learned that he had been a medical student at the University of Chile when he saw a performance of *The Green Table* by the Chilean National Ballet. He told us he was so moved by the figure of Death, that he left university to become a dancer, simply wanting to dance that role.

David, who seemed entranced by Max, asked him how he could become a dancer, having trained later than most professional dancers. Max told us that he had been an athlete in university, so dance came easily to him.

It took three years for him to achieve his dream of dancing Death with the Chilean ballet company. Later, he danced the lead role of Death again, this time in New York City with the Joffrey Ballet.

I was in awe of this man. The evening carried on in a blur of laughter and longing. Max was the last to leave that night. With his trench coat on, he drew me into a deep, long hug that had me quivering with desire.

I wrapped my arms around his neck, and we stood together breathing in time to each other's heartbeat.

He then pulled away and said quietly, "Thank you for the party. I must go."

I watched him exit down the narrow stairs, then turned to face my loft with the debris of a party to clean up. I blew out the candles and replayed Segovia to soothe my spirits. I was stunned by Max's presence in my life and the emptiness I felt gazing at my bed.

## *Stormy Night*

A FEW WEEKS LATER MAX phoned. He asked if he could come see me. I thrilled at the sound of his voice and the thought of being alone with him.

I quickly lit candles and scattered them around my loft. Thunder boomed, and lightning flashed eerily over New York City. Rain pounded my back windows, which looked out on a desolate group of concrete commercial buildings. I left my hair loose over my shoulders and wore soft, royal-blue cotton pants that were patterned with roses, and a plain white top.

When I heard a knock at my door, my heart leapt. I opened it, and there stood Max—medium height, a beautiful figure with coal-black eyebrows and dark eyes, in a soft gray trench coat, drenched in rain.

"Jeez, you're wet! Come in!" He stomped his feet on the mat, kicked off his boots, and laid his coat on the door-table. Next, without warning, he turned and gave me a long, deep, intoxicating kiss. My mind exploded.

When we broke away, I poured myself into his eyes. My body was on fire. I buried my head in his shoulders, bringing him close. I was done for, totally spellbound. Tears welled up in me at the relief of feeling loved. I believed that we were connected on a deep level, in that death played a profound role in both our lives. It was reassuring, too, that he had been to my home and knew where I came from. In New York, no one knew much about me. In fact, no one, anywhere, really knew me.

He fetched a bottle of whiskey out of his raincoat pocket, offering me a sip.

"No thanks."

He took a long drink from the bottle. He then drank half the bottle while pacing up and down my loft, gazing at the storm that raged outside and, it seemed, within his heart as well. I sat on my bed and watched him. He seemed distracted, tormented, even.

After a while, he turned and spoke to me. He confessed that he was married to a Chilean woman and had two children with her, and that he was also married to a dancer who was pregnant with their child.

I was stunned.

"My God, Max. What are you going to do?"

"I don't know."

He tipped the whiskey bottle up and drank some more. Then he turned to face the windows again, deep in thought. His silhouette was illuminated when flashes of lightning blazed the sky. Despite his startling revelations, I was hopelessly drawn to this man and the power in him that I had never encountered in anyone else.

Silently, I stood up and approached him from behind, wrapping my arms around him. I felt his ribs rise and fall as he breathed, and I listened to his heartbeat, with my head laid against his back. Still deep in thought, he turned around, put his hands on my face, and pulled me into a kiss that tasted of whiskey. He scooped me up and laid me on the bed. I was totally, irrevocably done for.

When I woke the next morning, he was gone.

## chapter five
# The Invitation

### *Out of the Blue*

One day out of the blue, Arthur called me from Italy.

"Hi Tamar! I'm heading to Spain! How does a two-week sailing vacation in the Mediterranean sound to you?"

"Are you kidding? I'd love to come!"

"Great! Meet me in Ibiza in a few weeks. I'll be in touch soon with details."

I was keen to escape the city and have fun for a few weeks, and once again experience the joy and passion for sailing that had captured my childhood imagination—before the letters, before Naomi died, before my confusion.

By this time Arthur had married, but he and I were good friends. If he had no qualms inviting me, I had no qualms accepting.

### *Cliffs of Moher*

En route to Spain I visited Ireland. I wanted to explore the west coast, where I believed fairies and elves lived. I loved Irish fairy tales for their

worlds of magic and spirited beings flitting about the forests and open fields, invisible except in our imagination. These little folk were my fantasy escape world that I held dear to my heart. At that time in my life, I didn't have my feet planted firmly on earth, and although I was in my late twenties, elves and fairies still appealed to my imagination. I felt like an elusive fairy myself, effervescent as a bubble. *I sure could do with some magic right now*, I thought.

I landed in Shannon, rented a car, and drove to the Cliffs of Moher, where I stayed at an inn. I had fun in some smoky Irish pubs and walked miles and miles on the cliffs, which plunged straight into the Atlantic Ocean far below.

One afternoon I stood on the cliffs, breathing deeply the fresh, salty air of the Atlantic Ocean, with the gray waves crashing far below against the steep cliffs. Longing for my sister welled up inside me, and I called out to her from the depths of my being. She came to me. She was dressed in white, with gossamer fairy wings; her blue eyes shone, inviting me to join her in the sky and play.

"Naomi, why did you die? Why are you my angel sister now? I want you back!"

I felt her reply: "Tamar, I was too sad. I didn't belong in our family. You were having fun, and I couldn't join you. I was lonely and afraid."

"I'm sorry Naomi! I never wanted to get older than you. I miss you. Come back, please! Let me hug you here, now, on the Cliffs of Moher."

I reached out to her, but she vanished into the blue sky like an ethereal cloud disappearing in the wind. My sister was gone and would never get older than twenty-two. I had to let her go no matter how much I wanted her.

## *Ibiza*

ARTHUR MET ME IN THE tiny airport on Ibiza, looking dignified in his trim beard and white slacks, with polished shoes, a dark-brown leather belt, and a soft, blue long-sleeved shirt. I felt as if I'd come home even though I was far away from my physical home. He appreciated me, and in his company, I felt a comforting connection.

During our taxi ride to the harbor, I was enraptured by the bright white plaster houses nestled on steep cobblestone streets, the heat, and the dazzling crystal-blue sky. How can one be so swiftly transported from the dismal gray skies of New York, with its skyscrapers and sidewalks, to the windy cliffs of Ireland and on to this exotic place?

The sloop, *Tomboy Ann,* was tied to a wharf, waiting for us.

"She's beautiful, Arthur!"

Over dinner in a small restaurant, I said, "I can't believe I'm here! I needed a break from New York—you know how frantic the city gets. The Mediterranean Sea with you couldn't be better." We chatted away until it was time to settle into the sloop for the night, as we were leaving the next morning to explore the islands.

This was a bareboat charter, where Arthur was the skipper. For the next two weeks we sailed in the scintillating turquoise and cerulean blue of the Mediterranean, anchoring in isolated coves to explore the shores of the little islands that make up the Balearic group. We hiked for miles above white sandy beaches with the intoxicating scent of dry pine forests, juniper, thyme, and rosemary. We swam in crystal clear waters, drank wine, and feasted on board our sloop as the sun set and the sky became sparkled with stars. We fell asleep to the gentle rocking of the boat pulling on the anchor and the lapping of waves on the hull. The days blurred together like a beautiful dream.

### *A Huge Black Boat*

When the charter was over, things didn't go as planned. As we approached the harbor in Ibiza, our engine quit. Arthur was an excellent sailor, but his skills were put to the test. He had to get *Tomboy Ann* safely to the dock with only his wits and the wind. In his attempt to dock under sail without a motor, we got tangled up with a huge black double-masted sailboat moored to the marina dock, alongside many other sailboats.

I felt a frantic urgency in the air. That boat was massive, and we were in a charter boat that wasn't even ours. How would we get out of this mess without causing further damage to the sloop? I hadn't a clue how to help and stayed out of the way, apprehensively watching the scene unfold.

Arthur quickly let down the mainsail and threw the fenders over the side to protect both ships. I heard a dog bark and looked up. Staring down from the large vessel were a bearded fellow, a woman, and a young child. A black Lab, watching with its paws on the rail, barked excitedly at the strange scene below.

The man, backlit by the sun, yelled, "Throw me your line!" Arthur gathered the bow line into a circle and tossed it high up into the fellow's hands. He quickly secured the rope to a cleat on the boat and yelled for the stern line, which Arthur tossed high up. Once the lines were secure, the fellow let down a rope ladder and invited us to climb aboard his vessel. I inched my way up the steep sides of the boat and jumped over the bulwark—a three-foot-high wall that protects people from falling overboard—and onto the expansive wooden deck. I was embarrassed at the near disaster when docking, but excited to set foot on this huge sailboat with these mysterious characters.

On deck, I saw that the fellow who had called out to us was handsome: lean, tanned, muscular, early thirties maybe. He sported a neatly cropped beard and mustache along with wavy brown hair below his ears. He had gleaming white teeth and penetrating brown eyes that seemed to take in everything at a glance.

Arthur popped his bearded head over the bulwark and lithely jumped down onto the deck, shaking his head.

"I'm sorry. Our engine quit."

"No worries. I'm Olaf, the owner and captain of *Josefine*. This is Anja, my wife, and Bine, our four-year-old daughter."

He extended a strong hand to shake ours firmly. Anja smiled and nodded. Her blonde hair flowed like a waterfall over her shoulders. She was in full sail, stunningly pregnant, caressing her belly as if protecting the precious cargo growing inside. White-blonde Bine, clinging to her mother's legs, smiled and said a quiet, "Hi!"

Anja's Nordic features with high cheekbones and blue eyes, bangs and thick long blonde hair reminded me of my dear friend Irene. And her pregnant belly stirred my own deep longing to have a family.

"This here is Fang," Olaf said, rubbing the dog behind her ears. Fang had calmed down and sniffed us eagerly, wagging her tail in pleasure.

"Would you like to see the ketch?"

"You bet!" I blurted. I was already in love with her. Climbing the rope ladder and encountering her size, I was reminded of adventure tales I'd read as a teenager: *Robinson Crusoe* and *Two Years Before the Mast*. My favorite author was Joseph Conrad, who wrote many gripping sea stories, and this sailboat looked like it fit perfectly into his romantic, tense, and hair-raising fiction.

I was awed by the space, large enough, it seemed, to play tennis or at least throw a ball for Fang on the deck. We learned that she was sixty-six feet long and fifteen feet wide. She was a gaff-rigged ketch, built in Denmark in 1931 as a fishing boat. She had fished the North Sea for over thirty years, often staying out for two to three weeks at a time.

As we walked around on deck, with Anja, Bine, and Fang tagging along, we learned that Olaf had bought the ketch in 1965 to convert her into a sailing home. He had made money to purchase her in San Francisco, where he had also studied for his captain's license while his brothers in Denmark found *Josefine* and converted the fishing boat to a family home.

"Stefan, my youngest brother, is sailing with us as first mate. He has more sea experience than I because he fished the North Sea for years. But I'm the captain, so he must answer to me!" His whole bearded face split into a wide grin.

Olaf chatted away, obviously proud of his family's spacious sea home. He told us that they planned to sail around the world for a couple of years and raise their children at sea. Anja wanted to have their baby in the middle of the Atlantic Ocean, with Olaf delivering it!

"Follow me and I'll show you the rest of the ketch."

Clinging to the handrail, we climbed down ten steep wooden stairs to the belly of *Josefine*, where in the dim light we saw a vast space with a huge wooden dining table, surrounded by benches for communal meals, and lanterns overhead that swayed with the motion of the water. A yellow canary sang to us from within a hanging cage, its entire body trembling and throat moving fast as it made loud, rhythmic trills and chirps, happy for an audience. Anja, Bine, and Fang stayed on the deck above, and Fang stared down at us through the doorway, slowly wagging her tail.

Olaf continued to walk us through the large belowdecks area. The galley was tucked into a narrow room cut off from the open space. A corridor ran off the main communal area towards the bow and led to six small bunk rooms for guests or crew; there were three rooms on either side, each built in pine, with a door for privacy, a bunk bed, and a tiny open closet with a few shelves. Already, I could picture myself sleeping in one of these compact rooms. An additional room was devoted to the head, a boat's washroom with a sink and a toilet, where in those days you pumped your poop straight into the sea. Towards the stern were the captain's quarters, luxurious and ample, where the Danish family slept.

At the end of our tour, Olaf revealed more of their plans. They were taking paying guests along the way who would help with sailing, cooking, and the expenses of running the boat. They planned to pick up people and drop them off wherever they wanted. Two teenage brothers, originally from California and now living in Ibiza with their mother, were joining them for the trip across the Atlantic. Another American woman would be coming along. Gibraltar was their next stop.

My head was spinning. An adventure was presenting itself to me, something I never dreamt of doing before. *Josefine* was calling. These Danes seemed to embody the spirit of the hippie movement—cutting free from the standard work world and exploring ports of foreign countries into the bargain. They were chasing a wild dream, and I wanted to join them—for the safest part of their voyage at least—to Gibraltar.

Me, sail the Atlantic? No way! That notion frightened me. I was certain that at the first hint of disaster, I'd curl up in my bunk, be totally useless, and die in an unforgiving storm. But sailing as far as Gibraltar, in the Mediterranean Sea—that was a possibility.

Besides the romance of *Josefine*, I had been attracted by the familial spirit on board. There appeared to be strong ties within this Danish group. I was intrigued that Olaf's brothers all had a hand in making his dream come true, and I was drawn to the ambiance of a young mother with a child, a dog, and a canary on board. By the end of the tour, the idea of joining Olaf and Anja was burning in my mind.

As we were about to depart, two young men climbed on board, and Olaf introduced us. They were the American brothers Olaf had mentioned, who were joining the Danes on their ocean sailing adventure. Andy had masses of curly black hair, thick dark eyebrows, brown eyes, a hint of a mustache, and a stocky build. Steve was scrawny, with straight light-brown hair that fell over his eyes and a right hand that twisted towards his thumb. I liked them immediately.

After thanking Olaf and Anja for the tour and confirming that we could keep *Tomboy Ann* tied to *Josefine* until they departed for Gibraltar,

Arthur and I returned to our sloop and prepared to dine out. Arthur was preoccupied with getting word to the charter agent that there was a problem with the engine, but that had to wait until the next day, as we had spent so much time on *Josefine*.

## *Chance of a Lifetime*

OVER DINNER AND WINE IN a little marina restaurant, I mused about shifting my plans.

"Arthur, I was thinking... I want to join *Josefine* and sail to Gibraltar with them. I don't want to cross the Atlantic, but it would be fun to sail along the Spanish coast and fly to New York from Gibraltar. It might be a week or ten days. What do you think?"

Arthur took a sip of red wine, considering. He cared about my welfare, so I knew I could rely on the integrity of his opinion.

"Well, these Danes must be competent sailors if they sailed *Josefine* from Denmark to Ibiza. It's not too hard to sail in safe water like the Mediterranean Sea, and any reasonably competent sailor should be able to manage the trip to Gibraltar. You'll probably be okay."

I was thrilled he didn't think it an outlandish idea. After all, we had planned to return to New York together. Even if he had misgivings, Arthur knew me well enough not to protest my wild dreams. Still, I was thankful for his encouragement.

The next morning, I mustered up courage to ask Olaf if I could sail to Gibraltar with them. Here was the chance of a lifetime. My excitement bubbled over into our negotiations at the communal dining table in the dimly lit cavern of the ketch. During our conversation, I learned that Andy and Steve's mother had paid two thousand dollars for their educational trip across the Atlantic. Olaf agreed to take me to Gibraltar for $125. No chores were laid out for me, except to help Anja in the galley.

A bearded fellow in ragged cutoff blue jean shorts, barefoot and bare-chested, approached the table, smoking a cigarette. I learned that he was Stefan, Olaf's younger brother, who was sailing as first mate on *Josefine*.

Like the teenage American brothers who seemed so different in appearance and behavior, as if they could have had different fathers, Stefan was Olaf's opposite: fair-skinned, blond hair and beard, blue eyes, and a little shy, perhaps because he wasn't fluent in English; whereas Olaf, who spoke perfect English, was darkened by the sun, and talkative.

As I left the boat I couldn't believe my luck, headed on an adventure sailing along the Spanish coast in an old gaff-rigged ketch.

The next few days were a scramble. *Josefine* was leaving port imminently, and Arthur had to negotiate the repair of the engine on *Tomboy Ann*. He rented a small room in a pensione, where I joined him until it was time for me to board the ketch.

All I brought with me was an orange backpack stuffed to the brim with my Pentax SLR camera, a few rolls of film, my alto recorder, my 1968 Metropolitan Museum calendar, and scant summer belongings: panties, T-shirts, shorts, a cotton dress with yellow flowers sprinkled over it, a pair of bell-bottom jeans, a light sweater, rain jacket, sandals, sneakers, and toiletries. I didn't even have a bra or book to read, and regretfully I didn't buy a journal. I needed to purchase a sleeping bag and pillow, as well as cable my parents that I was delaying my return to New York City and sailing to Gibraltar.

## *A Diverse Crew*

It was time to begin my life on *Josefine*. Either the universe had provided me with this opportunity, or the devil had some part in negotiating it. No matter, I was oblivious to consequences or prudent thinking.

In the early morning light, Arthur and I hugged on the dock and stood still a moment, gazing at each other. There were so many unspoken words between us. I waved to him from the deck of the boat with an ache in my heart. I felt sad parting ways with him but was elated about the journey ahead.

"Stay safe!" he cautioned. He appeared concerned and a bit forlorn.

"I will! I'll see you in a week or two!"

I climbed the rope ladder to the deck above, with my backpack jammed full and my sleeping bag and pillow strapped onto the top. I waved to Arthur before disappearing into the living quarters of the ketch.

Anja showed me to my tiny room in the bow. There were no porthole windows to open for fresh air or to glimpse the sea and sky, but I didn't mind, as I planned to spend most of my days on deck, watching the ocean and sails.

Already I loved this tiny room lined in fresh pine with the bunk bed and wee open closet, where I stored my things. Eager to meet the other American woman who would be traveling with us, I soon had the pleasure. As I was unrolling my sleeping bag, a young woman appeared in the doorway. She seemed to be in her early twenties, buxom and blonde, and a sight to behold in tight white shorts and braless in a low-cut T-shirt that exposed her deep cleavage and revealed her pert nipples.

"Hi! I'm Suzy Creamcheese! I'm sailing to Gibraltar with the Danes."

"I'm Tamar and I'm sailing to Gibraltar, too. What a boat this is! Don't you just love her?"

"Totally!" She grinned. "Gotta split!" And she vanished down the hall in bare feet.

Did she say that her name was Suzy Creamcheese? I didn't believe that was her real name, but I had no idea she was using a name coined and made famous by Frank Zappa on his 1966 debut album. There never was a Suzy Creamcheese; she was just a figment of Frank Zappa's imagination. When he toured Europe in 1967, so many people were asking, "Where is Suzy Creamcheese?" that he hired a girl to play her. Suzy Creamcheese was part real and part myth, and we had one on board.

We were a diverse crew sailing on this captivating old ketch. I imagined Chaucer writing about our pilgrimage, as in the *Canterbury Tales*, and the dreams we all carried in our hearts. I wished I were as perceptive as Chaucer or Josef Conrad, so I could write a gripping story about the characters together in a boat for a week—their foibles, intrigues, and conflicts. Instead, I was trapped on a merry-go-round of my own inner dialogue.

By midmorning, we were ready to depart. Food had been stowed for eight people, as well as for a dog and a bird. It was a beautiful, bright blue summer morning, with white gulls soaring above. The halyards clanked against the masts of sailboats anchored in the harbor, sounding like tinkling bells.

We all stood on deck, except for Stefan, who stayed on the dock, waiting for Olaf to start the engine in the wheelhouse. When he heard the *putt-putt* of the motor, Stefan unwound the bow line from the cleat on the dock, wound it into a neat circle in his hands, and heaved it up to the deck, where Andy deftly caught it. Andy then coiled it into a neat sailor's circle on the deck. Stefan tossed Steve the stern line, and Andy raced to help his brother make another tidy sailor's circle of the rope. Stefan climbed up the ladder and we motored out of the harbor.

## chapter six

# A Ship of Sorrows

***The true adventurer goes forth***
***aimless and uncalculating***
***to meet and greet unknown fate.***

—O. Henry, *The Four Million*

We were an international menagerie, bound together by the good ketch *Josefine*. She could very well have been flying the pirates' skull and crossbones flag—an idea that thrilled me because it seemed so absurd and yet so real.

When we were clear of the harbor and other boats, Olaf put the engine in neutral and prepared to hoist the sails. There was considerable excitement on deck as this was the moment that marked the beginning of our journey under full sail. I stood by and watched, entranced. Never had I been on such a glorious old boat, and I couldn't wait to witness all her sails taut in the wind.

The men untied the mainsail, which was folded onto the boom, ready to raise the heavy canvas. "Andy, take hold of the rope and pull!

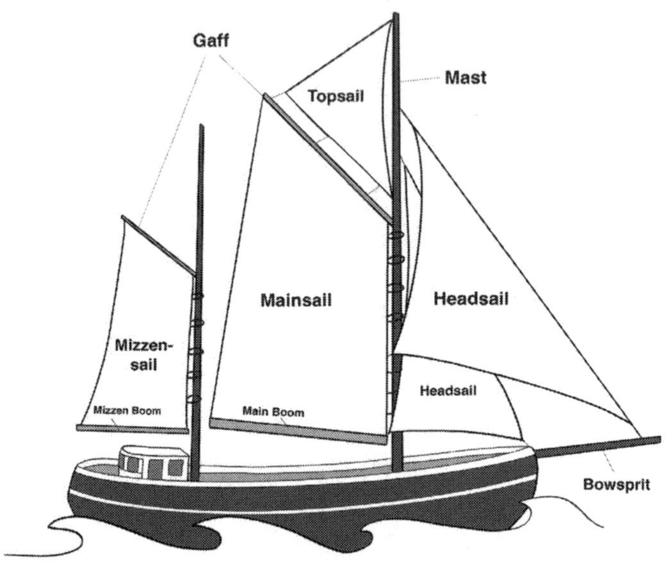


*Gaff-rigged ketch*

You, too, Steve!" Olaf commanded.

Together with Olaf they pulled down on the halyard with all their weight, rhythmically bending almost into a squat, as the top of the sail, which was attached to the mast by large wooden hoops, rose higher and higher. Stefan attended the gaff pole, raising it in tandem with the leading edge of the mainsail. The repetitive movement was hypnotizing as the sun beat down on their half-naked bodies, their muscles rippling, their hair soaked with sweat.

Andy got into the rhythm easily, while Steve struggled a bit because of his twisted hand. Without a moment's hesitation, Suzy jumped into action, joining Steve on his rope. I stayed out of the way in the bow, with Anja and Bine, watching in fascination.

Witnessing all that exertion up close, I understood how compelling it would be to sing sea shanties while raising the heavy sails of an old boat. Shanties were work songs sung on the high seas to help large groups of men keep a steady, even pace while raising the sails. They often had naughty lyrics about drinking, chasing ladies in different ports, punishing sailors, and how miserable their life was with cruel captains or cooks. I thought of one I knew and imagined all of us singing the jolly tune in time with hoisting the sails. I wished we had all broken into song at the top of our lungs, and that I had been bold enough to initiate it.

*What shall we do with a drunken sailor,*
*What shall we do with a drunken sailor,*
*What shall we do with a drunken sailor,*
*Earl-eye in the morning?*

*Way-hay, up she rises,*
*Way-hay, up she rises,*
*Way-hay, up she rises,*
*Earl-eye in the morning*

After the mainsail and mizzen sail had been raised, there were the two triangular headsails to raise at the bow of the boat. To crown *Josefine's* glory, the Danes raised the small, triangular topsail.

At last, we were officially under sail. Olaf cut the engine, and we were at once in a quiet world of warm wind and sea. *Josefine* was glorious with her masses of white sails etched against a clear blue summer sky and her hull cutting through the deep blue waves of an inland ocean. It was July 29, and we were headed towards the Spanish coast under perfect conditions.

### *Topless*

Shortly after we were underway, Suzy stripped as if in celebration, revealing her full, pale boobs in all their glory. She stretched luxuriantly and walked barefoot towards Stefan. I could tell she was hot for him—and how could he resist? Seemingly without words, they disappeared into the dim belly of the boat.

Olaf shook his head and returned to the wheelhouse.

Anja looked on, saying nothing.

Andy and Steve stared after them, their lips curling into private smiles, as if appreciating the quick glimpse of naked flesh. "Far out!" I heard Andy whisper to Steve under his breath.

## *Happy Beginnings*

WE WERE RAVENOUS, AS IT was well past noon. While Bine stayed on deck to play with Fang, and the boys got pleasantly stoned, Anja and I went down to the galley to prepare an easy lunch of pickled herring with capers, liver pâté, salami, bread freshly baked in Ibiza, sweet butter, a block of cheddar cheese, a jug of water, and beer, which we spread out on the communal table for all to eat at their leisure. We also boiled a pot of coffee.

"There's a bell on deck at the top of the stairs that you can ring to announce lunch is ready," Anja said. I dashed up the companionway to clang the bell.

Anja made a plate for Olaf and brought it to him in the wheelhouse. Stefan and Suzy were nowhere in sight. The boys grabbed some food and went up to eat on deck. I took my plate and ate on deck, too, sitting against the bulwark of the bow, enjoying the motion of the waves, and feeling quietly ecstatic that we were on our way. A few white gulls reeled in the blue sky, crying sharply, bringing me back to my idyllic childhood in Gig Harbor. For me, seagull cries will forever be the haunting call of the sea, and I was overcome with gratitude for this surprising moment in my life. Fang lay down beside me, flapping her tail on the wooden deck while I rubbed her silken ears.

A few feet away, the boys lit a joint and smoked contentedly, passing it between them.

"This is cool," I heard Andy say to his brother. Being stoned seemed to be their way of enjoying the moment. It was evident that their bond was strong, and I appreciated how protective Andy was of Steve. They were young, on a grand adventure, and I could imagine how excited they must have felt. Occasionally they'd gaze at the sails, stunningly white against the deep ultramarine blue sky. The wind puffed out the sails and ruffled the boys' hair and my own. It was magnificent to feel both the heat of the sun and the gentle breeze on my face.

The boys brought their plates back to the galley, and—bless them—washed and dried their dishes. Once Anja and I put away the food and finished tidying up the galley, we spent a leisurely afternoon left to our own devices. I passed the time on deck in the fresh Mediterranean air, thoroughly enjoying the moment. The hours flew by in bliss: blue sky, blue sea, and a strong yet gentle wind that moved us so swiftly that a white frothy trail of foam spread out behind. The boat rolled up and down in the waves.

Once the sun began to sink to her bed, the time came to prepare the evening meal. Anja and I again descended into the dimly lit interior of the boat. Almost as soon as we got to the galley, we both braided our hair, as it was stifling hot inside. There was barely room for her to turn around with her big belly, and she sighed, standing still, contemplative.

"Let's keep it simple tonight and have spaghetti and a salad. We have fresh bread from Ibiza, as well as butter and cheese." Anja took a gentle lead, and I did as she asked, happily.

"Boy, it's hot down here," I said. "The others are lucky to be outside." Anja nodded in agreement, and her hands instinctively went to her belly.

As we worked in silence side by side, I tried to grasp the reality of her situation and contemplate the immensity of her decision to take off across oceans with a young child and a baby soon to be born on the high seas. She was merely a year older than I, yet already had a family. I envied her, and wondered if my dream would ever become a reality.

I already knew that these folks had been living in San Francisco when their dream took root to buy a sailboat and sail around the world as a family. I wondered if the couple spent time in the Haight-Ashbury section of San Francisco. It was a mecca for hippies throughout that era, where young people rebelled against the capitalist culture of America, musicians formed bands that became famous, and street theater troupes performed parodies on the American Dream.

### *The Dinner*

OLAF PUT *JOSEFINE* ON AUTOPILOT, and we gathered around the communal table for our first dinner together. As everyone scrambled to find their place, Anja put the big pot of spaghetti on the table, and I brought out the piping hot tomato sauce. We laid the sliced bread on a large platter, surrounded by Dutch and Danish cheeses. Olaf sat at the head of the table, king of *Josefine*, and Anja, his lovely queen, sat opposite, on the far end. Their subjects squeezed around them.

Stefan and Suzy sat beside each other on the bench against the wall. Suzy, flushed with happiness, was once again wearing a shirt. Stefan was obviously pleased. They nuzzled each other when they thought no one was looking. Steve sat between Suzy and Olaf. Bine was nestled between her mother and me on the opposite bench. Andy was on my other side, completing the circle back to Olaf. We were all excited and in good spirits.

The overhead lanterns were lit, swaying to the motion of the waves, casting shadows on our vastly different faces in the subdued light. This scene, on the old creaking boat, gave me the sense that I had entered into an exquisite Rembrandt painting.

*Who are these characters,* I wondered. In the dim light of the ketch, I was overcome by how handsome the Danes appeared, shrouded in shadow. Anja was demure and beautiful in the somber light.

A weird image came to my mind—of Jesus sitting at a table surrounded by his disciples and followers. Would Olaf be Christ? Would Stefan be a faithful disciple? Would Anja be the Virgin Mary, and Suzy our Mary Magdalene? Would Andy and Steve be followers eager to learn what their elders had to teach?

I'd fit in as Tamar. My life had already revealed a curious parallel to the Tamar in the Bible. In fact, I was named after her.

As the story goes, Tamar was King David's only daughter. He loved her immeasurably, and she was happy. Sadly, though, her fate led her to be dishonored, no man would marry her, and she was doomed to lead a childless life. Her father failed to protect her.

Anja dished out the spaghetti, Stefan scooped up the sauce with a ladle, and we passed the plates around until everyone had one. Wine was poured freely. Once our glasses were filled, Olaf tapped a knife on his wineglass. All eyes went to him.

"Anja and I want to welcome you into our home. We've spent years making our dream a reality, with the help of my brothers in Denmark."

He told us that they planned to create a seagoing community to explore the potentialities of life, seeking freedom, adventure, and good vibes as they sailed around the world raising their children. I felt lucky that I had landed on a boat with people who expressed such familial and loving ideas. We lifted our glasses and drank, and I felt the warmth reach my belly and my brain.

Towards the end of the meal, Olaf brought out a pipe of hashish. He inhaled deeply. As he exhaled, the pungent smoke swirled over his head. He passed the pipe to Andy, who took it, inhaled, and passed to me. I shook my head. I had never smoked hash and had only smoked pot once, years before, with my mother and brother in Tacoma.

After Naomi's death, my brother began smoking marijuana regularly, and experimenting with hallucinogens. Mother wanted to understand Mark better.

One afternoon during the year I was on leave from Barnard, when Dad was at work, Mother, Mark, and I were hanging out in our dining area by the fire, when my brother rolled a joint.

"Mom, try it! Tamar, c'mon."

Mother took the joint. She had smoked cigarettes since the 1930s, so inhaling pot was easy for her. I hated smoking, but like Mother, I wanted to find out what was happening to Mark when he got stoned. Before long, each of us entered an altered state of consciousness. We connected in a surprisingly happy way that day, and it was groovy. I could understand how Mark might enjoy being stoned. However, after that experience, I realized I didn't want to live my life in an altered state! I wanted to be present to each moment, even the hard ones, and pot transported me to a different place.

"Tamar, try it! Go ahead."

I felt a shift in the room. Olaf's eyes seemed to challenge me. I wanted to belong to the group, to be accepted, but felt anxious. I knew hashish was stronger than pot, and I feared having a "bad trip," especially in the company of strangers.

I objected. Still, I took the pipe and inhaled, feeling the bitter sting in my throat and lungs. I coughed profusely as I exhaled.

A faint smile exposed Olaf's white teeth, gleaming through his full beard. He seemed amused at this naïve American woman. The pipe went around again and again. The smoke filled the room and enveloped the table with a heavy woody scent. We got stoned. Really stoned.

My hearing was magnified a thousand times. My attention was drawn to the musical sounds and rhythms of the knives, spoons, and forks clinking on the plates as we ate. Words lost all meaning. I was truly frightened, convinced that I was losing my mind.

Olaf remained oddly focused on me. I got the feeling he was playing a cat and mouse mind game with me, taking pleasure in my inability to hold a conversation, while he was being perfectly rational. This is when Olaf's character changed in my eyes. Where he had once appeared charming and affable, he now appeared menacing. Was this simply a bad trip?

Late that night we went to bed.

Olaf and Stefan took turns on the night watch in the wheelhouse to make sure the boat stayed on course. They were the only two on the boat capable of managing *Josefine*, and they both were stoned out of their minds. I simply went to my little bunk bed and fell into oblivion.

## *A Single Click*

The next morning, I felt groggy and lethargic, and I had a raging headache. It was late, already midmorning. I yawned and stood unsteadily on my feet. I hated myself for getting stoned. I couldn't recall if I had ever caved into peer pressure.

Slowly, I got myself dressed, brushed my hair, and went barefoot to the galley to get a cup of coffee. On the counter, I found a large pot of oatmeal for everyone to dig into. Anja must have made it. I had no appetite for food.

I climbed the companionway with my cup of coffee to the bright light of the midmorning sun beating on the fir deck. We were close to the Spanish coast and heading west towards Gibraltar. I made my way to the wheelhouse, where I found Stefan manning the huge wooden wheel.

The wheelhouse was a comfortable cabin built close to the stern of the boat. The boom of the mizzenmast floated above the roof of the cabin—just barely. The cabin had dark wood paneling, a canvas door in the back, many windows looking over the sea, and a huge old-fashioned wooden wheel with multiple handles to grasp firmly. I was glad Olaf wasn't there. I wasn't ready to see him after that unsettling night. I felt at ease with Stefan, however. This morning he was meditative, and I wondered if he felt as rotten as I did.

Eventually, I broke the silence and announced I wanted to take a photo of *Josefine* under full sail. I was enthralled with the romance of sailing in this tall ship, and I was dying to catch an image of her in all

Josefine *under full sail, hours before her shipwreck*

her glory. Stefan kindly offered to take me out in the wooden clinker dinghy during Olaf's shift. It was a beautiful fourteen-foot lifeboat built of overlapping planks with wooden seats, two oars, brass oarlocks, and a small motor.

I waited on deck as Stefan and Andy lowered the lifeboat onto the sea. Stefan climbed down the ladder and into the dinghy, started the motor, and yelled, "Tamar, come down!"

With my camera around my neck, I climbed down the rope ladder into the boat and sat on the middle seat. A rush of adrenaline went through me as he revved the engine and we raced ahead of *Josefine*. The waves were surprisingly big for the Mediterranean Sea, causing the ketch to barrel down on us swiftly. When Stefan judged we were far enough ahead, he put the engine into neutral. I didn't have a moment to spare. I leapt up, spread my bare feet wide apart, focused the lens, and snapped one photo. There wasn't time to get another.

"Sit down!" Stefan hollered, sounding worried I might fall out. I sat with a thump, clutching the sides of the dinghy with white knuckles as Stefan raced back to the ketch.

All the others, except for Olaf, were crowded along the rail watching the action. After I was safely on deck, Stefan turned off the dinghy's engine and climbed up the ladder holding the small boat's stern and bow lines.

"Hey, Andy! Give me a hand!"

The two of them hauled the lifeboat up the deep sides of the ketch and returned it to its rightful place on deck.

I realized what a risky thing we had done, yet I felt empowered by the adventure.

## *The Boys*

AFTER ANOTHER DELICIOUS BUFFET-STYLE LUNCH, we had a relaxing day at sea. The brothers and I chatted a bit on deck. I learned that their mother had been a schoolteacher in Palo Alto, California, and had decided to move to Ibiza, where life was more laid-back. She had enrolled them in public school on the island, but when the Danes appeared in the harbor with that old, black gaff-rigged ketch and she discovered they were sailing across the Atlantic, she thought it would be a grand experience for her boys to participate in an ocean voyage and learn about sailing. Andy was eighteen and had graduated from high school; Steve, seventeen, was in his last year. Both boys enthusiastically embraced the adventure.

Steve explained he was born with a "club hand." It could have been fixed at birth, but his mom was afraid of surgery, as it could cause nerve damage. So, she left it. He was teased a lot at school.

"I'm so sorry, Steve. That must be hard for you."

The three of us were quiet. Then Andy lit up a joint, inhaled deeply, blew the smoke out, and passed it to Steve. As they escaped into their own worlds of enjoyment, I was left to my thoughts.

My gaze turned to the sea, sky, and sails. Leaning against the bulwark with my elbows on the rail, I soaked up the sailing experience. I didn't need a novel to fill in the time. These intriguing individuals, captive on *Josefine*, provided enough of a story.

### *A Walking Contradiction*

THE HEAT AND THE HYPNOTIC motion of the sea lured me to sit on deck with my back to the bulwark, my legs stretched out in front of me. Fang joined me, wagging her tail in pleasure as I stroked her. I reflected on the bizarre night we had, stoned out of our minds.

My effort to belong to the group, by accepting the pipe, had backfired. Instead, I came away with a vivid awareness of how different our values were.

In many ways, I felt I was an anomaly, a walking contradiction: part hippie and part capitalist. I was a mix of where I came from and a product of my generation. I wrapped the cloak of a flower child around my shoulders while disguising a deep-rooted connection to the American Dream. How could I revolt against capitalism when my life benefitted from the hard work of my ancestors?

Another thought frustrated my brain. I couldn't understand why I was so meek in the face of powerful men. I was a tangle of messy feelings.

## *Disaster*

In the late afternoon, sailing along close to shore, a mauve spit of land, like a mirage, appeared in the distance, far enough away that it presented no immediate danger. However, we would have to turn away from shore now to avoid it.

From the wheelhouse, Olaf yelled to Stefan to prepare for a tack to port, away from the beach. Anja, Bine, and I quickly moved far away from the boom. If it knocked you in the head, it could kill you. Stefan, with the help of Andy, Steve, and Suzy, jumped into action. As Olaf turned the wheel, the boom swung around, making a loud noise. The boat veered to port, but not enough, as the sails drooped.

With urgency, Stefan yelled to Olaf, "Turn on the engine!"

Olaf ignored his brother's command. "Tacking now!" Olaf yelled back. Goose bumps appeared on my arms, and I gripped my camera tightly as tension mounted on the ketch.

Stefan had no option except to adjust the sails. I had been so wound up in the drama between the brothers that I hadn't fully realized where *Josefine* was. Suddenly, the entire boat shuddered violently and made a terrifying noise. *Josefine* had run aground.

I froze. I'm sure that my heart stopped beating for a moment. Panic broke out on deck. All the men, plus Suzy, rushed to lower the sails, and they came tumbling down, causing Fang to bark and race around the ketch. The heavy sails now lay in confused heaps around the booms. Bine cried as she clung to her mother, who watched in horror. Her dreams had shattered in a sudden twist of fate, and I ached with her.

Our leisurely afternoon sailing blithely along the coast of Spain had turned into a nightmare in an instant. I hadn't a clue how to help. At the same time, the scene was too urgent to do nothing. Instinctively, I tucked myself behind my camera and recorded the drama.

*Josefine* was lodged on sand in shallow water, facing the beach. Awestruck tourists and Spaniards gathered nearby, gazing at our misfortune.

Stefan was furious. His face was red and filled with rage as he shook his head at the wreck. He went towards Olaf. "What the fuck were you doing?" he said, glaring at his brother.

Once again Olaf ignored him. "Go below to see what happened!"

Stefan stormed off to investigate the damage, yet the tension between Olaf and Stefan felt like a bomb ready to explode.

"She's taking on water!" Stefan yelled as he climbed back on deck. We learned that the huge five-hundred-pound rudder had ripped off on impact, causing the shattering noise and a massive hole in the stern. The ocean was pouring into the living quarters. If it rose another two feet, it would be above Bine's head. *Josefine* was no longer livable.

Olaf ordered Anja, Bine, and me to collect our things and get off the ketch. He told the boys to help us and to return to the ketch.

The panic in his voice snapped me out of my trance. There was no time to be afraid or to wonder about our future. Pumped with adrenaline, Anja and I dashed down to the living quarters to fetch our belongings. I could not believe what I saw: the ocean was everywhere—in the common area, over the benches surrounding the communal table, and in the galley. I stepped off the lowest companionway stair, holding on to the rail, and then slowly waded through water above my knees, holding my arms high up, clinging to my camera. Tentatively, my bare feet felt the wooden floor under the seawater.

When I peeked into my pine room, I stood frozen for a moment. The water had crept close to my bottom bunk, but if I hurried as the ocean still poured into the ketch, I could salvage my belongings in time. Quickly, I stuffed my clothes and camera into the backpack, rolled up my sleeping bag and pillow, and fastened them securely to the top of my pack. Taking one last look at the tiny pine room I had so happily settled

*Chaos on board*

*Andy and Fang*

into only the day before, I said a fond farewell in my heart and turned to escape up the companionway to the deck, where the havoc continued.

Olaf and Stefan were frantic. Bine was crying, "Fang! What's going to happen to Fang? Mommy, I can't leave her! I won't go!" Anja embraced the devastated child, and quietly said, "We must get off the boat. Someone will bring Fang down."

One by one, Anja, Bine, and I climbed down the rope ladder and waded through knee-high water to shore, Andy and Steve giving us a hand. Safely on the beach, we stood in a line, staring at the wreck that was once our hope-filled boat. Twilight was falling and a cool breeze wafted around our stunned bodies.

Andy brought the black Lab down the rope ladder. He let go of the dog and she swam to the beach, where she shook her fur and raced to Bine.

Meanwhile, officers from Generalissimo Franco's Guardia Civil, in gray uniforms with machine guns slung over their shoulders, were pacing the cement wall above the beach. An ominous cloud engulfed me. The dictatorial atmosphere of Franco's regime was not a joke, and I knew that he was clamping down on drugs and rebellious university students. The possession of drugs was a criminal offense punishable by imprisonment. The Danes must have been aware of the political situation, which no doubt added to the stress of the moment. We were, after all, dope-smoking hippies with long hair, shipwrecked in Franco's country.

## *A Strange Joy*

Anxious and unsure what to do, Anja and I stood around until a tall, handsome, blond man approached and introduced himself. He was Swedish, and he told us that the beach we had grounded on was in Alicante. Possibly because of noticing how pregnant Anja was, he generously offered us free lodging at his vacation house for however long it took to remove the boat from the beach. He explained that he and his wife were leaving for Sweden the next day, and they could stay in a hotel for the night. The universe certainly showered us with an unexpected blessing. I marveled at the gift this stranger gave us.

"Thank you! Let me tell my husband." Anja walked down the sandy beach to the shipwreck and spoke quietly to Olaf. He came back and shook hands with the Swede, thanking him. "Anja and our child would have been in a bad way. Stefan and I must keep watch over the boat." Then he turned to Anja and said, "I'll see you in the morning. Have a good night."

We followed the Swede, Fang trotting along beside Bine, tail high, no doubt happy to be on land and with the child. The canary would remain in her cage, hanging from the ceiling of *Josefine* throughout the ordeal.

Our benefactor's vacation house was a beautiful two-bedroom bungalow with an open dining, living room, and kitchen. Anja claimed one bedroom with a double bed, and I the other, which had two twin beds. It was perfect, adding a strange joy to a worrisome time.

### *Back on the Beach*

WHILE WE HAD A HOT shower and a good night's sleep in a dry house, we knew the men hadn't fared so well. The next morning, we were eager to hear their stories.

Anja had thoughtfully grabbed some food off *Josefine* before abandoning the ketch, and after a quick cup of coffee, some bread with butter, and cheese, we walked back to the beach where, once again, we were witness to the sad fate of *Josefine*, stuck in the sand, listing to starboard. The sea was breaking into whitecaps at her stern and sending up frothy foam.

Olaf and Stefan walked up to us, and we learned that they had taken turns sleeping on the slanting deck of the boat and camping on the beach. There needed to be at least one of them on *Josefine*, at all times, or the Spaniards could take possession of her. Overnight, the Danish brothers had cut their hair and trimmed their beards, no doubt recognizing how important it was to give the appearance of being normal, law-abiding people in Franco's country. They had tossed all the hash and marijuana

*Stuck!*

on board into the sea.

Andy and Steve didn't seem to be as concerned and took it all in stride. They had camped on the beach in their sleeping bags and continued to smoke their own marijuana, ignoring the Guardia Civil pacing the cement wall close by, and naïvely endangering us all through their affiliation with *Josefine*. They also refused to obey Olaf's command to cut their hair. Though their hair was not much past their ears, it was long for the times, and in places like Franco's country, that could be considered a dangerous statement of rebellion.

These boys were young and naïve; they no doubt felt that their hair was a personal matter, and that Olaf had no right to boss them about their appearance.

Suzy was the only American who understood the gravity of our situation and had the sense to split. At some point, either right after the crash or in the darkness of the night, she made a dash onto land, and we never saw her again. No one revealed details about her disappearance.

It never occurred to me to bolt for freedom. When *Josefine*'s rudder ripped off and she filled with the sea, I was in such shock that I was swept away by the urgency of our shared situation and my love for that ketch. Anja and I were nearly the same age, and I wondered how she felt watching her dreams shatter, with a child to take care of and a baby on the way.

Clustered on the beach the morning after our shipwreck, Olaf, Anja, Stefan, and I gazed at the sorrowful boat stuck in the sand. Andy and Steve were farther down the beach, where they had camped out during the night. I could imagine the despair in the Danes' hearts as they grappled with how challenging it would be to get the big ketch off the beach. There was tension in the air, and they spoke at some length in Danish.

Suddenly, Olaf announced in English, "We need money to repair her," looking straight at me. It was clear that he was challenging me to fork over money.

I felt insecure and caught off guard. Was it up to me to bail them out of this mess? I hesitated, not wanting to be seen as the rich American. And just like the night before, I caved. "Perhaps I can ask Arthur. He's still in Ibiza and may be able to loan you money. How much do you need?"

"Two thousand dollars."

That was a huge sum, but I didn't dare question it. I wanted to help so we could be on our way but hadn't a clue how much damage there was, how long it would take to get *Josefine* out of the shallow water or how much it would cost for her rudder and hole to be repaired. I gulped and nodded. I didn't want to argue with Olaf and show him how fragile and timid I felt.

"I'll see what I can do."

## *Arthur's Loan*

I wondered what I was getting into as I walked into town to find a phone. I had a feeling that Arthur would lend Olaf the money. I didn't want to ask my parents, mainly because I hadn't relied on them financially for years, and I didn't want to worry them. I knew that my mother would be dismayed, and my father would tell me to abandon *Josefine*, which I did not want to do.

I found an American Express office and dialed the number of the pensione in Ibiza where Arthur was staying while he arranged the return of *Tomboy Ann*. Luckily, he was there.

"Arthur, it's Tamar! I'm in Spain..."

"Tamar! Why are you calling? Are you all right? You just left a day ago." I could hear the worry in his voice.

"I'm fine, but *Josefine* isn't."

"Oh God. What happened?"

I gave him the rundown.

"Is everyone okay?"

"Yes, we're fine, just a bit freaked out. We're safe, with a place to stay for the time being. But *Josefine* needs to get off the beach and be repaired. Olaf said they need two thousand dollars to fix the rudder, and I know it's a lot, but would you be willing to loan it to them?"

"Well, yes, I could, I guess, but are you sure you don't want to come back to Ibiza?"

"I want to see this through."

"I wish you'd come back, but okay... Do you have the wiring instructions? I'll send the money."

"Thank you, Arthur. This is wonderful!"

"Don't worry about it, Tamar. Just be careful and keep in touch. Do you want me to call your parents and tell them what's going on?"

"No, thanks. I'll send them a cable."

Deeply appreciating his support without judgment, I returned to the beach and told Olaf and Anja that Arthur would wire the money. Anja gushed with sincere gratitude. I had never seen her so animated.

As promised, with nothing more than a gentleman's agreement between them, Arthur wired the money to Olaf in Alicante. After that, Olaf never mentioned the money to me again. I wondered if I had done the right thing.

While Olaf went to town to collect the money, I chatted with Andy and Steve. They looked rather rough around the edges, with unkempt hair and wearing only their tight bathing suits. It seemed like a long time since we had abandoned *Josefine*, and I felt a kind of protective affection for these boys. The three of us were in limbo, with no certainty of the future. The boys could return to their mother in Ibiza and I, to New York, yet I had a suspicion we'd stay with *Josefine*.

For a moment we stood and stared at the sorrowful boat perched directly on the sandy beach.

## *Seeking Solutions*

Time passed. Everyday Olaf and Stefan discussed with the Spaniards how to get the boat back into deep water so she could be towed to a repair facility. Unfortunately, the tides in the Mediterranean Sea are minimal, rising and falling only a few centimeters a day, as opposed to the eight or ten vertical feet in the Pacific Northwest. So, we couldn't depend on tides to help dislodge the boat, which kept digging deeper and deeper into the sand and her watery grave.

As the weeks went by, we fell into a kind of routine. Anja, Bine, and I would walk from the house to the beach and spend most of the day there. I would photograph the scenes around me as Bine played in the sand, making castles and pools, and learning a bit of Spanish as she chatted with the locals. She was happy and carefree.

Anja sometimes donned a bikini, with her beautiful swollen belly visible and long hair falling over her shoulders, keeping one watchful eye on Bine and the other on her husband, who was completely engrossed in his epic task. If she was feeling worried, she never expressed any fear, doubt, or dismay to me. Andy and Steve joined us on the beach during the day to observe the near-constant negotiations going on in earnest near the boat. Andy was attentive to what was going on, while Steve often played in the sand with Bine. Despite all efforts made, *Josefine* remained stubbornly stuck.

Olaf seemed to have met with everyone to try and find a solution. Some of the local men who came to speak with the Danes looked like mafiosi, with their dark, impenetrable sunglasses and heavyset bodies, cigarettes, or cigars in their thick lips. If our situation wasn't so urgent, some of the scenes I witnessed would have been hilarious.

One day, the Danes lured tourists and locals on the beach to grab hold of a long, sturdy rope Olaf and Stefan had attached to *Josefine*'s starboard side and pull with all their might to try to move the boat farther over onto its starboard side. At the same time, another group of gawkers, knee high in the ocean, lined up, side by side, and pushed hard from the boat's port side. *Josefine* still did not budge.

On another day, Olaf, wearing only his tight black-and-white-striped bathing suit and holding Bine in his arms, met with a priest, whose white collar poked out from the black cassock that ended at his polished black

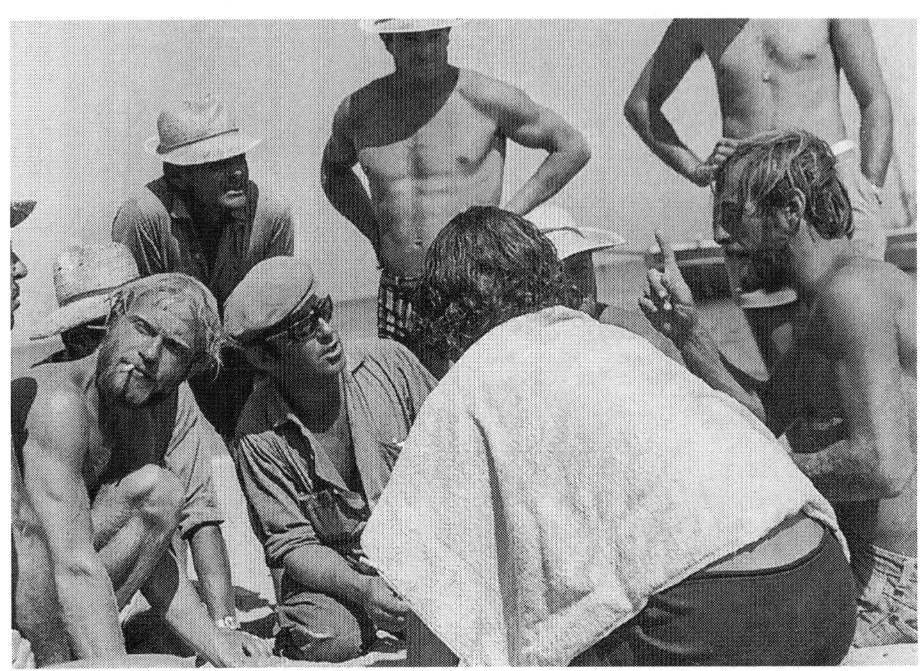

leather shoes. The priest reached out to Bine with his right hand, while holding a cigarette in his left. Both Olaf's and the priest's attention were focused on Bine, who looked shyly curious at the strange apparition in front of her.

Word had no doubt spread in Alicante about our unfortunate shipwreck; people, including the priest, were insatiably curious and flocked to the beach to witness the disaster.

## *Naomi's Birthday*

AUGUST 9 WAS MY SISTER'S birthday. We had been on the beach for little more than a week. She would have been twenty-eight. Naomi! How my heart yearned for her.

As I watched Bine rolling in the sand, playing, laughing, and paying no attention to the tensions and negotiations around her, my thoughts once again drifted back to the idyllic summer days that Naomi and I spent as children at Gig Harbor.

A vast and mysterious divide now separated my sister and me. She felt so close yet impossibly far away. I wished with all my heart that we could have journeyed through our lives together. Listening to the muffled chatter among the people on the beach, with Bine's sweet voice sprinkled in like chimes, I dug my hands into the hot sand, lifted them up, and watched the grains pour down between my fingers.

## *Anja and Bine Depart*

ANJA'S PREGNANCY WAS NEARING FULL term. Olaf had arranged for her to deliver her baby in a convent in Gibraltar. We were to meet them there once *Josefine* was repaired. I was sad to see Anja and Bine go. Now it would be just me and the four men.

I continued to stay in the Swede's house with Fang, relieved to be a safe distance from Olaf and his intensity. Andy and Steve camped on the beach, having no interest in joining me at the comfortable vacation house. They unabashedly smoked dope in broad daylight. It

was a wonder that those boys weren't arrested—and us along with them.

News of our shipwreck had reached the United States. Intended as a heartbreaking appeal for donations, Olaf had written an article about it for the *San Francisco Chronicle*. "It was the sort of message you might expect to find floating in a bottle in the sea, although it came to the *Chronicle* by regular mail," the reporter wrote. If Olaf received any responses, he didn't tell us.

## *Driftwood Shelter*

I could have flown back to my life in New York at any time. Ready to bail from the tense and discouraging scene, I did book a flight at one point. But then Stefan happened.

The September days were getting cooler, and the weather more temperamental. One day, Andy, Steve, Stefan, and I built a makeshift shelter on the beach out of found driftwood and blankets. It was great fun and a big relief to be occupied with something constructive after the chaos of weeks slipping by, with no resolution in sight. This shelter was intended for the teenage brothers, but they gladly let Stefan and me stay out in it some nights.

I liked Stefan. He seemed sad, lonely, and kind. We fell into an unlikely romance due to circumstances and nothing more. We scarcely spoke, but we enjoyed the warmth of each other's bodies, wrapping our arms and our solitary souls around one another on the beach, with the sound of waves lapping nearby and the waxing moon sailing overhead.

## *The Oil Drum Scheme*

One Spaniard, who smoked thick cigars and wore spooky dark glasses, suggested we roll a bunch of empty oil drums down the beach and attach them to the ketch. The oil drums would have to be tied tightly enough on both sides of the boat and partly submerged in the sea, so that when they were all secured, they'd have the force to lift the heavy boat out of the sand.

QUESADA HERMANOS
TORREVIEJA

The next few days were spent collecting thirty oil drums in Alicante. The local Spaniards were a huge help in this endeavor. Those were exciting days, filled with hope and anticipation.

A day that we thought we'd never see came on September 16. Miraculously, the oil drum scheme worked, and *Josefine* was released from her watery prison. The ketch was lifted by the oil drums just enough for two fishing boats, tied to the stern of the ketch, to dislodge *Josefine* from the sand.

Everyone on the beach stared dumbfounded as the big ketch trembled and moved for the first time in seven weeks. A tugboat was waiting farther out to tow her to Santa Pola, a nearby harbor with a dry dock facility, where her damage could be assessed, and she could be repaired. The oil drums kept her afloat.

*Josefine* was on her way, and so were we, eager to join Olaf and Stefan at the dry dock facility. I tidied up the Swede's house and left a note of gratitude. In high spirits, Andy, Steve, and I took Fang, and hired a taxi to Santa Pola, a short drive west along the coast, moving us a little closer to Gibraltar.

## *Dry Dock*

ONCE AGAIN, WE TOOK SHELTER on *Josefine*, this time at the dry dock facility where she awaited repairs. She had been towed onto a large, submerged dock which had heavy-duty posts on either side, called cribs, to keep the ketch safe. There were two rails, like railroad tracks going up the beach. The dock and boat were pulled up the tracks, about twenty feet away from the sea, where *Josefine* could be far enough above the beach for repairs to be done underneath her hull.

It felt like a huge step forward to be back on board, even though many questions remained about the boat's condition. I had imagined that we'd only need to physically repair the damage to the hull. When we climbed down into the interior of the ketch however, I was blown away by the foul smell and the massive amount of work in store for us to clean up the mess. After being partially submerged for seven weeks, *Josefine* reeked of rotting seaweed and dying creatures. Despite the dismal scene at hand, I felt oddly and boldly committed to the ketch.

Like little mice, we scurried to check out our sleeping quarters. My former sanctuary had become a dank dungeon, especially since there weren't any portholes to air it out. Even though the seawater had drained out as *Josefine* was pulled up the beach, the bottom bunk beds in our tiny pine rooms were drenched. We were blessed that the sea hadn't reached the top bunks.

Steve and Andy took separate rooms, and Stefan had his private room, too. We all lived in the upper third of our rooms. Almost everything on the boat was drenched. Fortunately, the gimbaled stove had escaped the salty sea, and we were able to clean the fridge. We could not, however, use the toilet, as it wasn't possible to flush the contents onto the beach, so while the boat was up on the ways, we used a toilet provided in a nearby building.

My unease around Olaf had not lessened since that first night on board and after he had put me on the spot regarding money for repairs. In Alicante, it had been easy to avoid him. Here in dry dock, we'd be living in close quarters again, and that concerned me. As I walked through the stinking belly of the boat, I wondered, *Am I crazy to stay here? Probably.* But I saw a chance to contribute, hands-on, to the restoration of that beautiful vessel. I made up my mind—I would see this through. After stashing my belongings, I went on deck to hear Olaf's plans.

He explained to us that we Americans would clean the interior of the boat, while he and Stefan would do the repairs. It was something all three of us could do, and there was no question that *Josefine* had to be scrubbed.

### *Stefan Close, Max Far*

That first night on *Josefine* I thought about Stefan and our nights on the beach. I wondered if we'd be together on the ketch and if he was thinking about me, too. There was no passion drawing us together, like there had been with Max in New York. Still, I craved the comfort of snuggling with a man. I waited, hoping he would come, but he never did. Neither did I seek him out. Hard work over the days and weeks that followed left us all too exhausted at night to remember our desires. Besides, my heart belonged to Max.

We spent the next seven and a half weeks in dry dock, scrubbing *Josefine*'s insides and fixing her leaks and rudder. There was a sense of camaraderie among Andy, Steve, and me; even though it was a stinky job, we had a common goal to tidy up our home and to be on our way. The seawater had risen four feet in the ketch, so we spent a good part of each day on our hands and knees, furiously scouring the inside walls with stiff brushes and buckets of sudsy cold water. I twisted my hair into a braid to keep it out of my face, as it was sweaty work. Andy and Steve wore cotton bandanas around their heads to keep the sweat and their growing hair out of their eyes.

## *The Price of a Lemon*

ONCE WE RETURNED TO THE boat, and with Anja still away, I took over the "woman's work" of making all the meals. Our standard breakfast of oatmeal, which we ate every morning, was nourishing but disheartening, so I thought it would be nice to have more special meals in the evening. A few days after we were safely in dry dock, I approached Olaf to see if he'd like me to go to the market to shop for provisions. We sorely needed to stock up on fresh produce, meat, and fish. He agreed and disappeared into the captain's room to fetch me some Spanish money.

How glorious I felt, walking the mile to the market along the hot, dusty path by the sea, carrying a wicker basket over my shoulder, free to stretch my legs and be alone at last.

When I reached the bustling market, I heard laughter and conversation, all in Spanish. Skinned rabbits and plucked chickens covered in flies hung from wooden poles in the market booths, where bronzed Spanish women sold their produce. There was a variety of offerings from the sea—mackerel, herring, crabs, and prawns—as well as eggs and plenty of fresh vegetables and fruits. I spoke little Spanish but had studied French and Italian in school, so I could get by, mixing three languages into any one sentence.

"Quanta costa le lapin?" This made-up mix of Italian and French is how I asked, "How much does the rabbit cost?"

"Yo prendre *that* lapin, por favore! Grazia!" was my way of saying "I'll take that rabbit, please! Thank you!" My attempts to communicate brought giggles from the market women.

Back on board, I tucked our provisions into the galley. I planned a rabbit stew and was excited because I had never eaten rabbit before.

Olaf suddenly appeared in the galley doorway. "How much was that lemon?"

"What? I don't know!"

"How much was the rabbit?"

"Honestly, I don't know. But I can add up how much I spent in total."

He shot me a disgusted glare. "Wake up and pay attention. We must be frugal and know where every dime is going."

Salty tears pricked my eyes. All I could say was, "Okay. I'm sorry."

I was humiliated. We were all working hard, and I was doing my best to be helpful. I understood the need to be thrifty, but the way Olaf spoke to me was cruel. I could take criticism spoken with kindness, but Olaf's words weren't kind.

### Miss Witherspoon

Miss Witherspoon, a skinny, bitter, unctuous teacher of religious education, was head of the boarding students' residential life at Miss Hall's School.

One day she summoned me into her office and lit into

me like a viper. I had forgotten to go to an appointment the school had arranged to have my feet measured for shoes for a formal dance with a nearby boys' school. With a flu epidemic in Pittsfield, the students couldn't shop in town, so the shoe man came to us. While I was supposed to be in the gym with my fellow students, I had been out by the pond, listening to a chorus of spring frogs and lifting my face to the rain, tasting a bit of the Pacific Northwest, which I missed so dearly, on my tongue.

"How dare you forget the appointment! The school arranged it especially for you girls. What do you have to say for yourself?" She rubbed her hands together, and her head bobbed on her skinny neck.

"I'm sorry! I'm really sorry!" I covered my tear-stained face with my hands and sobbed.

"If you think your tears will soften my heart and make me forgive you, you are wrong. You are selfish and inconsiderate and think only of yourself." I continued to cry, not sure what to say or how to reply. I knew nothing could appease her.

"Get out of my office. You are on probation for two months." After being dismissed from Miss Witherspoon's presence, I went to study hall and buried my face in my books, with tears streaming down onto the pages. I hated this woman for being mean and unforgiving. I was so ashamed that I kept this confrontation a secret from my girlfriends; I truly believed I was a selfish, thoughtless girl.

The relentless, dark predictions from my father exploded like a volcano inside me, because this horrible woman was also a spinster. In my mind, I was looking into the mirror at the woman I could become—a bitter old maid—just like Miss Witherspoon.

## *Meaningless*

Slaving away with our scrub brushes for an entire morning, Andy said, "That's it. Let's take a break!" We emerged out of the dim cavern belowdecks into the bright sun. Reveling in the fresh air, we were enjoying a good, lighthearted chat on deck, when Olaf approached.

"Get back to work. There's a lot to be done."

"We're just getting some air, Olaf!" I said.

He turned his full attention onto me. "You're spoiled and can do whatever you want. But your life is meaningless. You wander about with no purpose in pursuit of irrelevant things. Now get back to work."

"What an asshole," Andy said under his breath. I didn't say anything. I simply withdrew into silence and simmered in anger, like a volcano, raging at the ungrateful treatment our captain showed me and his paying crew.

We returned to our task, where I threw every ounce of my aggravation into my work. Sweat poured down my face, mixing with hot tears, which I hid from the boys. I hated the feeling I had when my mind rushed in to agree with Olaf. My life *was* meaningless. I *was* spoiled and *could* do whatever I wanted. I was twenty-six and hadn't yet found a guiding vision for my life; I was, indeed, wandering.

Like a storm, painful thoughts whirled in my mind, opening memory after memory: my father's letters, Naomi's death, Max. This scrambled universe inside me was invisible to everyone in my life. No one knew who I really was, not Olaf, not anyone.

Still on my knees, on the wet floor of the ketch, I straightened my back to stretch. I realized that Olaf was curt with the others, but I felt an extra animosity pointed at me, and since I never said anything, he kept going. I didn't have the self-confidence to respond. Perhaps that made him feel even more comfortable criticizing me, as I was an easy target—just like I was with Miss Witherspoon.

### Boundary Issues

In Dad's letters, my father worried that I was too loyal to my girlfriends. He believed that loyalty was a masculine tendency; therefore, my loyalty to my girlfriends would lead me down the long, treacherous road to spinsterhood.

To be a desirable woman, and to snag a husband, he instructed me to flirt with men and make them feel good, even if they were married or had girlfriends. Neither had I been taught to defend myself from verbal abuse. I had to flirt and be nice—no matter what.

## *Assassination Dream*

Olaf's comments and treatment of me had affected me so thoroughly that first week in Santa Pola that he was infiltrating my dreams. Only four days after we arrived at the dry dock, I dreamt I assassinated our captain.

Olaf stood on a stage wearing sandals, loose white pants, and an unbuttoned white cotton shirt. He was in perfect physical shape—slender and tan; his brown eyes were alert, his beard and mustache were neatly trimmed, and his wavy, dark-brown hair fell to his shoulders. He looked like Christ and moved with elegance and confidence.

He came towards me slowly, welcoming me to a private session. I pretended to be humbled in front of this handsome guru and reverently bowed and kissed his feet. With a serene motion, he bade me to stand up and follow him to his high-backed wooden chair in the center of a platform, where he invited me to sit on a cushion at his feet. There was a long silence during which his eyes bore a hole into the darkest depths of my soul, and when he finally spoke, his words turned me to dust.

Stealthily, silently, a figure dressed in a hooded cloak colored mauve and charcoal, with flared sleeves, appeared in the doorway behind the guru's back carrying a shiny sword. Suddenly, the ghostly apparition raised the weapon high over his head and plunged it straight into Olaf's back. Olaf keeled over in a pool of blood.

It was Andy who gave the fatal blow. We had staged this gruesome murder before I pretended to be Olaf's obedient pupil. Triumphant, we hugged each other and twirled around, celebrating our freedom from the tyranny of this self-declared Almighty, who was captain of our boat. We stared a moment at the mess.

I woke up shaking at the vivid images my mind had conjured. In life, I was a mouse in the presence of Olaf. Deep down in my subconscious, however, I had the guts to stage a gruesome murder. I sensed there was fight in me that hadn't surfaced yet.

## *Why Say Thanks*

Life with Olaf continued to degrade. One morning over breakfast during our second week in Santa Pola, Andy poured me a cup of coffee and I said, "Thank you," appreciating his gesture. Olaf cocked his head, considering the situation. A faint smile appeared on his bearded face. We all were at attention because we never knew what he would say, and there was tension in the air.

"Why did you say that?" Olaf asked me.

"What do you mean?"

"Forget verbal politeness. Words are meaningless games we play with each other. Why say 'please' and 'thank you'? We should just give and take without playing the social games we've invented."

Once again, I didn't say anything, but in my head, ironically, what I shouted was anything but polite. *What the FUCK is up with this guy?* His words were a far cry from the words he spoke during our first communal dinner together at sea, about camaraderie and establishing a harmonious community while exploring life's potentials.

For once Andy said nothing.

Olaf stood up and walked away from the table with his coffee cup in his hand, leaving us to muddle over his caustic words and to clear and wash his empty bowl. Stefan joined his brother in silence, offering nothing to soften Olaf's words.

Finally, Andy announced, "What an egomaniacal shithead!" We had to laugh.

"I don't care what he says! Even though he's our captain, I'm not going to abandon goodwill on this boat. *Thank you*, Andy, for pouring me the coffee!" At that, we laughed again, in a spirit of mutiny against our eccentric captain. The three of us cleared the table and tidied up the galley, feeling the warmth from our shared experience and our resolve to disobey our captain.

As merciless as Olaf was, he was also bright and well-read. That seemed to be another way he liked to disarm people. He quoted Hegel, Kierkegaard, and Hesse regularly. His reading focused on philosophy and argument. Olaf enjoyed intellectual thought and contradiction.

In college I had read a few novels by Hesse—*Siddhartha*, *Demian*, and *Steppenwolf*—and enjoyed them, but I never would have felt comfortable discussing them with anyone, and especially not Olaf. I clearly wasn't a match for him. I remember the feelings I experience from reading books, but not specific details or philosophical points to guide me into lively discussions.

I couldn't tell if he enjoyed the disparity or if it irritated him.

### *Anja, Bine, and Baby*

Anja and Bine joined us with their new baby after we'd been in dry dock for ten days. Olaf had found a safe place near *Josefine* for his wife and children to stay more comfortably than on the boat, which still smelled of dying sea creatures. It would have been nearly impossible to manage a young child and a baby on the ketch, climbing up the steep rope ladder, and having no working toilet. Olaf met his family at the train station and brought them to their cottage, where they settled in before they came to *Josefine*.

When Andy, Steve, and I saw the little family clustered on the beach, we raced to greet them, eager to meet the baby. Fang stayed on deck, standing on her hind legs with her paws resting on the bulwark rail, watching the scene below.

Anja looked tired yet clearly healthy and happy, proudly showing us their baby boy, whom she cradled in her arms. My heart melted to see the baby and Bine once again. I had sorely missed that lovely, innocent child while we struggled on with *Josefine*. She was a bright spark of love and joy in this adventure.

"Can I take Bine up to see the boat?" I asked Anja. "I'd love to show her what we've been doing, and Fang will be happy to see her!"

Anja nodded an okay, and Bine eagerly scrambled up the rope ladder ahead of me and jumped onto the deck, where she was knocked over by Fang. I felt tears well up watching the two friends reunite after such a long time.

We descended into the dimly lit interior.

"Ugh, it *stinks*!" she shouted, standing still, and plugging her nose.

"Yeah, it's pretty gross."

Then she brightened, hearing the canary sing loudly in its cage.

"The canary's happy to see you! She's been very quiet. I think she's been sad without you here."

Bine went over to the hanging cage, greeting her other friend. The presence of Anja and her children softened our remaining days in dry dock. Bine spent a lot of time around her damaged home and played with Fang on the beach.

When Olaf and Stefan ate dinner with Anja in the rental cottage, it left us Americans to our own devices, when we were able to relax and let down our guards.

Stefan had become a shadow on the ketch during our days in dry dock. He didn't reveal what he thought about the whole thing or us, the crew working away in the background. Throughout everything that had happened, the strong bond between the brothers was evident. Stefan kept quiet when Olaf lashed out at any of us.

### *Jay Enters*

WANTING A CAPABLE MAN TO help sail from Gibraltar to the Canary Islands and on to the West Indies, Olaf placed an ad in a Gibraltar paper. A gentleman named Jay replied and came to Santa Pola to see the ketch and meet all of us. After Jay climbed into the boat, the Danes invited him to the communal table. Andy, Steve, and I were allowed to witness the discussion.

Jay was clean-shaven and slender, with short gray hair and blue eyes with smile lines. Pleasant and straightforward, he was retired from the American military and wanted to learn how to sail a tall ship. After sizing up this fellow, Olaf said, "I need to discuss this with Stefan."

The Danish men went up to the deck, where they had a private conversation.

The boys and I chatted with Jay. He seemed kind, levelheaded, and I thought he could be a welcome addition to the crew. I really hoped that he'd join us and bring a sense of greater civility on board the boat.

When the Danes returned, Olaf bluntly announced their decision.

"We don't think you fit the bill. We want someone with experience, with more muscle power than you. Someone who can handle the heavy sails, who can take night watches. Sailing is dangerous. We almost got run down, and we wouldn't trust you with night watches. But if you pay more, we could take you across the Atlantic Ocean and perhaps hire someone with more experience with the extra money."

Jay hesitated. "Well, okay. Fine. I'm game."

He gave Olaf a deposit and planned to join us in Gibraltar. Olaf would be in touch with him once we were on our way.

### *Bine's Fifth Birthday*

Bine turned five shortly before *Josefine* was ready to continue her voyage to Gibraltar. I felt honored to be invited to the intimate family ritual and loved knowing that Bine, especially, wanted me there. Anja had made a beautiful spread of Danish delicacies, including a white-frosted cake sprinkled with chocolate bits. Bine hugged her papa, her Uncle Stefan, and me, before dashing off to give her baby brother a kiss. They sang "Happy Birthday" to her in Danish. Bine made a wish and blew out all five candles, clapping her hands in delight.

On this day, I witnessed the Danish family in a very different light, apart from the struggles that existed among us on *Josefine*. In this moment, I felt a sense of belonging.

To our delight, the day drew near when we would test the restored seaworthiness of the ketch. Olaf had arranged for his family to return to the convent in Gibraltar until we arrived there. I walked over to the rental cottage to say goodbye to Anja and Bine.

Looking into Anja's blue eyes, almost hidden by her straight bangs, I said, "Stay safe. You've got a precious bundle and a delightful child."

"You take care, too. Thank you for all the help you've given. It's been a hard time for everyone."

"You can say that again! With any luck, we'll be seeing you soon!" I said.

I hugged each of them and returned to the boat.

## *Back on the Water*

THREE MONTHS AFTER THE SHIPWRECK, on November 2, Olaf declared that *Josefine* was ready to continue the voyage to Gibraltar. Our next destination was Torrevieja, about thirteen miles by sea from Santa Pola, and an easy test run to make sure the ketch was sound.

By late morning we were all aboard, tense, and apprehensive. I held my breath as the winch slowly deposited the ketch, sliding on rails, backwards into the sea with a splash, setting us free. Olaf started the engine, and we motored out, waving to the folks at the marina. We were elated to be on our way.

Once safely out of the harbor and well away from the perilous shore, Olaf put the engine in neutral to raise the sails. It was a magnificent sight to watch the men hoist the sails once again, and then set the jaunty gaffs on top, so the mainsail and mizzen sail looked appealing with their lopsided appearance.

A hefty wind propelled us along under an ominous gray sky with huge, puffy, dark clouds. We were racing west, the waves were large and curling into whitecaps behind us, and the ocean swooshed past *Josefine*'s wooden hull as she sliced the waves.

I claimed the bow, which had been my favorite place in a boat ever since I was a child and Daddy took us camping and boating in the San Juan Islands.

Sailing on this creaky and magnificent old ketch gave me the sense that I was going back to the time of rough old sea captains plying the oceans on pirate, whaling, exploration, or mercantile voyages. Painted black, *Josefine* looked rather devilish.

Arriving in Torrevieja that evening, we encountered a storm brewing, but we made it safely into the harbor before the winds picked up and howled into the night. We were tired and happy at the success of *Josefine*'s first day back at sea.

The following morning, Olaf announced that we'd be staying in

Torrevieja for two weeks. News of the long delay took me by surprise. I wondered if Olaf and Stefan had noticed something ominous in *Josefine's* performance the day before. I had thought they were eager to get to Gibraltar and be on their way to the Canary Islands. All morning I mulled over the delay. I decided it was an opportunity to step away from *Josefine* and try to get a refreshed perspective on my options: return to my life in New York or continue to the Canary Islands.

## *Madrid*

After checking with Olaf, I chose to head to Madrid. It was the chance of a lifetime to visit the Prado art museum and stand before works by some of the great masters I revered and had studied in school: Titian, El Greco, Rubens, Bosch, and Goya.

Lingering in the Prado Museum, I was struck by how much love and skill the artists had poured into their work. It was incredibly inspiring. I wondered what I could create when I returned to New York that would shine with equal passion.

As my thoughts returned to New York, a wave of longing for Max overwhelmed me. I missed him intensely.

After the Prado closed, I walked for a long time in the old center of Madrid. Tapas bars on what seemed like every corner overflowed with cheerful groups of friends laughing, snacking, and drinking wine. Watching ordinary life unfold, I felt an urgency to book a flight to New York and rush to find Max. I knew that would be insanity, further complicating his life and my own. But my heart was dominated by my fantasy of being with him. The power and mystery of Max drew me to him like a magnet.

## *Dilemma*

I also pondered what I would do if I *didn't* return to New York. Perhaps I could stay with *Josefine* until we reached the Canary Islands. The idea of sailing on the sprightly tall ship down the coast of Africa appealed to me. I craved a full, uninterrupted experience of ocean sailing after being stuck for so long on the beach and in dry dock. But could I stand to spend more time with Olaf, and would he even agree to take me farther? The lure of the sea beckoned, although a shadow of fear lurked over this option.

*Josefine* was still in port when I returned to Torrevieja; I'd half expected Olaf to leave without me. I was refreshed from my sojourn to Madrid, yet I decided to postpone asking him about sailing to the Canary Islands until we reached Gibraltar. This would give me a bit more time to consider my approach and decide if a longer sail was indeed what I wanted to do.

## *Off to Gibraltar*

We finally departed for Gibraltar after another couple of days in Torrevieja. The first evening at sea, I went up to the wheelhouse and sat with Stefan while he was on watch. *Josefine*'s many sails glowed white against the starry sky. Everyone was asleep except for me and Stefan, who stood at the wheel. The red and green lights designating port and starboard were shining at the bow, alerting ships of our direction.

Someone below turned on the kitchen light, spreading a warm illuminated patch from the companionway into the dark night. Fang was curled up at my feet. She was such a sweet, affectionate dog, holding none of the tension we humans created on board. I sat quietly, enjoying the peaceful feeling. We had only been at sea for one day, but it was enough to rekindle my passion and fondness for *Josefine*.

That night I became sure that I wanted to sail to the Canary Islands and farther, across the Atlantic. I couldn't fathom any other way to go home to New York, except by sail.

To ease concerns that tried to nudge their way into my bliss, I reasoned that sailing down the African coast to the Canary Islands was safe enough to do with the Danes, as we'd be close enough to shore that if anything went wrong, we could probably be rescued. Did I forget so quickly the disaster we met close to the Spanish shore? Safe? Are you kidding?

One never knows what might happen at sea. Egos can get in the way. One hasty, foolish mistake or twist of fate can plunge an entire vessel, with its passengers and crew, into the depths of the sea. Was the ocean a temptress, luring men and women to challenge her? No matter. I felt the call of the ocean, and I would go.

## *A Request*

ONCE WE DOCKED IN GIBRALTAR, neither Olaf nor Stefan mentioned that this was where we had planned to part ways. It was time to clarify my plans and see if I could continue with the boat to the Canary Islands. Over breakfast, with everyone gathered around the communal dining table, I mustered up the courage and presented my request.

Olaf was quiet and looked at me while he considered his response. Everyone was silent, listening. The spoons had stopped dipping into the oatmeal. Since he hadn't said anything, I nervously filled in the emptiness and offered to pay for the extra passage.

Andy showed a hint of a smile. Stefan was attentive.

"Let me think about it."

I let out my breath not realizing I had been holding it. My desire to reach the Canary Islands propelled me like a straight arrow, and I was willing to risk whatever might arise between Olaf and me to get there.

In the late afternoon, Olaf announced that I could stay on board for another $150. Andy and Steve burst into big smiles.

If I had been reasonable, I would have flown to New York, got my head and heart straight, and forgotten Max. But I was not reasonable.

## *You're Nuts*

THE NEXT DAY I SENT a cable to Arthur and my parents from the American consulate to inform them of my change of plans; we'd be stopping in Tangiers before heading to the Canary Islands. I'm sure my cables, which I sent sporadically over the months I was away, had been received in surprise and apprehension. I could hear Arthur say, "You're nuts!" while shaking his head in dismay.

I could hear my mother sigh, "Oh Tamar, why? Why put yourself through this when it has already been so difficult?"

I could hear my dad say, "Honestly, Tink, your loyalty to these hippies distresses me. They obviously don't know how to sail. Come home before more disaster hits!"

### Fishing with Daddy

Dark clouds crowded the sky above Westport, Washington, as we loaded into *My Sonnet*, our beautiful, open Chris Craft boat. Naomi and I were heading out into the Pacific Ocean with Daddy to a catch a big salmon for Uncle Bill, whose birthday was the next day. A few men on the dock warned us not to go out. "It's no good to fish out there. It's rough. I wouldn't take them girls out if I was you!" Daddy wasn't worried, and I was super excited. We hopped into the boat, and Daddy started the engine, ignoring the advice from the fisherfolk mumbling on the dock.

No sooner had we rounded the jetty than we encountered huge waves rushing at us, curling over in fierce whitecaps, and tossing our little boat wildly, threatening to tip us over.

"Daddy, go back!" He ignored me and went farther out, to meet the next one.

"Daddy, no!"

Naomi and I began to cry.

Daddy swallowed hard.

The Coast Guard was out, rescuing boats that had tipped over. Finally, Daddy turned around and we made it back to the harbor, where we tied *My Sonnet* to the dock, crowded with fishermen and people who had gathered to see what was happening. On the wharf we had to climb over large black plastic bags that held the corpses of fishermen who had drowned. I held on to Naomi's hand tightly.

We followed Daddy to the end of the wharf, where he turned to us and announced, "You girls stay here on the beach. I'm going to see how *My Sonnet* handles the waves."

"Daddy, no! Don't leave us!"

"I won't be gone long."

We watched Daddy return to *My Sonnet*, start the motor, and leave the safety of the harbor.

"Naomi, what's going to happen to Daddy?"

"I don't know," she said, wrapping her arms around me.

"I'm scared! Don't leave me!"

"I won't."

We sat down on a log and held each other close for some warmth and waited, shivering.

"What will we do if Daddy doesn't come back?" I said.

"Let's not think of that."

After what seemed like an eternity, I spied Daddy. "He's here!" We raced to the dock and hugged him tight, sobbing in relief. He was soaked from the huge ocean waves that had crashed over his boat. He was shaking, too.

"N and Tink, I love you!" He hugged us both. "Let's get warmed up and dry."

Was sailing down the African coast in *Josefine* any more reckless than so many of the things my father had done with us kids? At least I was only putting myself at risk. A dream had taken hold of my heart, which was stronger than any of the imagined cautionary words that might have caused me to doubt my decision.

### *Gibraltar*

OLAF AND HIS FAMILY SPENT a week off the boat while we were tied to the marina dock in Gibraltar. Stefan remained on board to oversee the ketch and her crew, which now had one new member: Jay had joined us. He had a good sense of humor, lightening up the atmosphere on the ketch.

Early one morning Jay, Andy, Steve, and I took a taxi up to the Rock of Gibraltar, which rises far above the ocean, guarding the entrance to the Mediterranean Sea. Over the centuries there was much conflict between the Christian people of Spain and the Muslim people of North Africa, who live a mere eight miles away from each other across the Strait of Gibraltar. The rock was previously heavily fortified with guns, which now were silent. The view was stupendous.

Golden-orange monkeys with no tails ran around the fortifications, entertaining the tourists. The Gibraltar monkeys are the only wild monkey population in all of Europe. They are inquisitive creatures, a protected species, and we were warned to give them plenty of space.

On this day, a few monkeys were sitting on the fortified wall in the heat of the sun, grooming each other and staring at us with their large golden eyes. I was fascinated but stayed about ten feet away. I didn't want one jumping onto me and picking through my hair.

### *St. Michael's Cave*

ST. MICHAEL'S CAVE IN THE rock of Gibraltar is a series of caves with impressive limestone stalagmites and stalactites, formed drip by drip over thousands of years. We entered the cool environment—a welcome relief after the blazing sun—and stared in wonder at the eerie underground world.

"Far out!" Andy said, admiring the vision of kaleidoscopic changing lights.

We learned that live concerts were held in the Cathedral Cave—a natural auditorium with superb acoustics that could seat four hundred people. How thrilling, that we were in time to attend a concert of Stravinsky's *The Rite of Spring*, one of his most famous compositions. Having grown up with classical music and the "modern" music of Debussy and Stravinsky, I was delighted to hear this piece in the mysterious environment where the limestone formations heightened the effect of the music.

I was at once totally present to this moment in Spain and drawn six thousand miles away to my family's home on Chambers Creek the day the Joffrey Ballet company came to our house for a party in 1967. Dad loved to entertain, and he was especially proud of our Frank Lloyd Wright house that was designed for our family in 1946 and built in 1954.

*Luis Fuente and his wife on our bridge*

### Joffrey Party at Home

It was a beautiful summer day. The salmon-bearing creek merrily wound around banks of salal, fern, and ocean spray, flowing down to Puget Sound. The arched wooden bridge over the creek was lined with pots of pink geraniums, blue lobelia, and creeping charlie that Mother had planted.

As the guests arrived, Dad played Debussy's *Prelude to the Afternoon of a Fawn* and, later, Stravinsky's *The Rite of Spring* on the record player. The dancers spread out, admiring our house, and enjoying the spacious terrace, where we served drinks, salmon, and yummy broiled crab and cheese hors d'oeuvres. It was a fabulous party, and I mingled with the dancers.

Max stood out from the other male dancers. I was drawn to his dark hair and eyes, strong face, and extraordinary body. Only he and one other dancer, a woman, changed into bathing suits and played in the shallow creek. Max picked the woman up and carried her across the creek in his arms. It was no small feat to carry a lassie across the bubbling creek in bare feet, with the slippery, slimy-smooth rocks covered in algae and tiny black snails on the bottom.

I gazed longingly at the two dancers. I wondered if I'd ever be held by a man like that.

In St. Michael's Cave, I felt nostalgic for that magical afternoon in the Pacific Northwest when I saw Max for the first time.

My reverie ended with the onset of deafening applause. As we shuffled out into the sunshine, we blinked at the blinding light and, once again, delighted in the curious monkeys.

## *Sailing the Strait*

Olaf returned with Anja, Bine, and their baby to reprovision *Josefine* and continue our adventure to Africa. It was a huge relief to have female companionship on the ketch again. Even though Anja continued to be distant, involved with her children, I was in a more familiar world with their presence.

In the predawn morning of December 2, the men hoisted the sails, and we were on our way sailing towards the Rock of Gibraltar. I was once again overcome by the sense of adventure, the huge unknown, and the vision I had of sailing down the coast of Africa on shining blue seas, where everything would go gloriously well.

We had just turned south towards Tangiers when we faced a huge confusion of ocean waves, topped by whitecaps, from the Atlantic Ocean. The sea was dark gray, and the sky was shrouded in ominous clouds.

It can be tricky to navigate a boat through the Strait of Gibraltar, an open channel that is only a few miles wide. In the strait, warm, dense water from the Mediterranean Sea flows deep down in a steady westward current, while the cold, less dense water from the Atlantic Ocean moves closer to the surface in a steady eastward flow. Because the Atlantic Ocean is so much larger than the Mediterranean and has bigger tides, most of the movement is eastward. Vessels headed for the open ocean to the west must time their departure precisely, or they can encounter challenges bucking the strong tides.

The seas we met that day were surprising and turbulent. We could have timed our passage better, but we made our way without incident.

## *Tangiers*

We entered the port of Tangiers, on the north coast of Morocco, in the evening of December 2. It was too late to clear customs, so we remained on the boat and were entertained by the haunting sounds of Arabian music, so strange to my Western ears.

After we cleared customs the next morning, I was excited and ready to explore this mysterious new world. The boys disappeared down a narrow cobblestoned street. Olaf went off with Stefan, while Anja stayed on *Josefine* with the baby, Bine, and Fang.

Jay and I hung out in the streets, listening to the lively, exotic sounds of Arabian music played on instruments I'd never seen before: the oud, a fretless lute; the quantum, a flat wooden board with many strings stretched over it, like a zither; as well as cymbals, drums, and wooden flutes.

The bustle of the Arabian locals going about their lives in the city was intoxicating. The men wore long wool or cotton robes with hoods. Women wore silk scarves over their heads and curious barefoot children flocked around us.

## *My Twenty-Seventh Birthday*

IT WAS MY TWENTY-SEVENTH BIRTHDAY, December 4. We had agreed to return to the boat in the late afternoon for a little celebration. Anja baked me a cake, and we all sat around the table in *Josefine*'s interior while I cut pieces and passed them around. They sang "Happy Birthday" in the rollicking Danish version, and then in English.

Anja offered to prepare dinner on her own that night, leaving me free to escape to the bow of the ketch and contemplate the challenges and joys of my life. At twenty-seven, I was well past the age by which my father had warned me I had to find a mate. Ten years before, when I was seventeen and in my senior year at boarding school, he sent me a letter in which he outlined the ideal time frame for marriage and how I had to be "ruthless" in finding a mate.

*Dearest Tink,*

*I have spoken to you at considerable length about the time cycle in a girl's life. The next six years of your life are far and away the most important because during this period you will choose a life partner.*

*I have told you and Naomi again and again that you must be absolutely ruthless and relentless in finding the best solution to this problem. Nothing is important enough to interfere with this ultimate goal.*

*Much Love, Honey-Pie*

*Dad*

I knew Dad cared about my welfare, but he showed it by interfering in every aspect of my life. He believed he held the key to my happiness. He couldn't see the paralyzing effects his messages would have on me. He was an intelligent, creative, complex, and troubled man. How could he have been so blind to the contradictions in his counsel?

Based on my father's beliefs, I was now a miserable old maid.

Despite everything, old maid or not, here on this boat, on this night, I was glad to be alive. In the harbor under a full moon, I sent my parents abundant love and gratitude across the intervening miles for giving me the best gift of all, the awesome gift of life.

We spent six days in Tangiers. Everyone went their separate ways by day, exploring. In the market I bought two Arabian wool robes, one black and the other striped gray, brown, and white, that reached to my feet, with huge hoods and long sleeves that flared out. I planned to give the striped one to my mother, whose taste in clothing had become rather comfortable, free-spirited, and hippie-like—the opposite of the tailored, conservative style that Dad had preferred when they were newly married and attending social events in Tacoma. Back then, in the late 1930s and 1940s, Mother's radiant beauty was magnified by the elegant, simple black suits and dresses that Dad would buy her. Now, I knew she would love the Moroccan robe I chose for her.

### *Rough Waters*

We encountered wild seas as soon as we left Tangiers on December 9, and turned south along the African coast. The wind was directly against us; the waves rose like confused mountains, sullen gray, racing towards us and curling into frothy white foam as they broke. An occasional immense wave splashed over our deck, dousing all of us brave souls who were outside. We held on to walls or walked with our feet wide apart, lunging from side to side as the boat rolled mercilessly in the rough waters.

Andy was sick. "Fuck *Josefine*," he muttered, retching over the side of the ketch, clutching his stomach.

I was exhilarated by the force of the sea and glad that I wasn't seasick, although I did feel woozy. It was better outside in the open air than in the closed-in living quarters below. So, I stood at the bow, holding on to the bulwark for dear life as *Josefine* bucked the waves, climbing up the steep peaks and plunging down the other side. For the most part I remained on deck but occasionally retreated downstairs to visit Anja and the children. The little canary swung in her cage, gripping her perch.

We barely ate that day.

### *More Trouble*

The seas subsided during the night, but by morning, we were in trouble. We had sprung a leak, and we began pumping water out by hand, nonstop. The distance from Gibraltar to the Canary Islands is immense, over one thousand miles as the crow flies. Stefan, Andy, Jay, and I would be forced to pump in stints of two hours each, twenty-four hours a day for five days, until we reached the Canary Islands.

Sitting on a stool on deck, we pulled a lever back and forth with both hands, much like rowing a boat. It was grueling work, the hardest physical task I had ever done. If I hadn't developed the strength and flexibility that I had from dance training, I don't think I could have endured it. Giving in to the rhythm of the movement, I entered a meditative state that helped me forget my exhaustion.

Of course, this new crisis and the strenuous labor didn't ease the atmosphere on *Josefine*. Over the next days, tensions between the Danes and the Americans mounted steadily to the point of tears. The fact that Olaf didn't pump with us caused resentment, while at the same time, he became stricter about how much water we Americans drank.

The morning after the leak was discovered, and we had pumped all night, Olaf set a jug of water out on the communal table. "This is for you Americans. I'll refill it every morning."

"Are you kidding? That's not nearly enough for all of us," Andy said.

"It's plenty. Don't be such a spoiled American."

Andy's eyes narrowed as his resentment exploded. "You Danes get to use as much water as you want for those damn diapers and even for drinking! The water should be rationed equally. We're working hard to keep this boat from sinking! It's not fair!"

Olaf glared at Andy. "Christ, too, was hated in his lifetime."

"Fuck off, Olaf!" Andy turned and walked away.

Once again, I found myself aghast at Olaf's behavior. I had never encountered such an outrageous ego in my life and sensed danger in the presence of his unpredictability. Our captain acted like a pyromaniac, lighting emotional fires everywhere and adding fuel to them with Machiavellian abandon.

Stefan and Anja were deaf to our complaints. It seemed like everything became us versus the Danes because all decisions were made behind closed doors, and no information was shared with us. Although it was only five days to Gran Canaria, the trip felt a lot longer. Olaf's cruelty and abuse chipped away at the glory of the ketch.

Jay was a diligent helper, working alongside Andy, Stefan, and me, and he was a pleasant diversion. Even as a paying passenger, he enjoyed the hard work of caulking, scraping, varnishing, and even pumping. I don't remember Jay ever having cross words with Olaf. If he wasn't in agreement, he kept it to himself.

### *Gran Canaria*

*Josefine* limped into Las Palmas, the capital of Gran Canaria, on December 14 at 6:30 a.m. We were finally in the legendary hopping-off point for ocean crossing. The famous trade winds blow steadily from the west coast of Africa to the West Indies, and for centuries these winds have aided captains in sailing voyages across the Atlantic Ocean to the Americas.

This should have been a happy time of celebration—but we were shell-shocked after the arduous trip down the African coast. Everyone was uptight and exhausted. Relationships on board were so taut that something was going to explode.

We were all on deck as the men secured *Josefine* to the dock. After Olaf radioed customs of our arrival, he said, "You should all get cleaned up and look presentable. Get your passports. We must be on our best behavior."

Anja made a huge pot of oatmeal and coffee, and we gathered around the communal table to wait for the customs official. Stefan, dressed in a clean white shirt and neat blue shorts (not the frayed jean shorts he usually wore), stayed on deck to watch for the official to arrive. I had put on my yellow cotton dress and had braided my hair into one long braid over my shoulder. We all had our passports ready.

Olaf approached the boys and ordered them to cut their hair. Andy, who always took the lead with his brother, bristled. "No way! You can't tell us what to do!"

The boys hadn't cut their hair for the past five months, ever since

they first boarded *Josefine*. Andy's hint of a mustache had blossomed into a full statement above his lips, and his beard had sprouted. His dark hair was a wild mass of thick curls to his shoulders. Steve's straight light-brown hair was loose, constantly falling over his eyes. He'd shake his head or move his hair aside to catch a glimpse of what was going on.

At that moment, Stefan poked his head down the companionway and announced that the official was climbing aboard. There was nothing Olaf could do to continue his fight with the boys. He was boiling mad and gritted his white teeth, staring the boys down. Andy glared back at him, defiant.

Olaf had to appear calm during the interrogation. He did most of the talking, and by hook or by crook, he managed to steer the official down the path of accepting us without a search. We were free to explore Las Palmas, and for the time being, Olaf abandoned his confrontation with the brothers.

Andy, Steve, Jay, and I walked into the old town, which was about two miles from the port. This part of the city was a cluster of crumbly little buildings, dusty narrow streets paved with cobblestones, and Spanish architecture. I felt lighthearted escaping Olaf's anger towards the boys but uneasy, too, realizing that the confrontation was not over.

We stopped in the market square, where men sat on benches smoking cigarettes and tossing breadcrumbs to pigeons that flocked and cooed nearby. As there appeared to be no policemen around, Andy lit up a joint, inhaling deeply and blowing out the aromatic smoke as he passed it to his brother. I was apprehensive and worried about the brothers. Smoking pot was illegal in Spain and in the Canary Islands, which were still under Franco's rule, and punishable by imprisonment. It was unsettling how naïve these boys were, and I wondered if Jay or I should talk to them.

I was also preoccupied about what I would do next. After everything that had happened on board *Josefine*, I knew I had to make a change. I imagined approaching different ships in port. Surely, one of the boats continuing to the West Indies would have room for me!

The following morning, tensions escalated. While we were on deck, Olaf flew into a brutal rage because Andy and Steve wouldn't shape up and cut their hair.

"Cut your hair or get the fuck off this boat!"

I grew up in a family of silences and had never witnessed anything so raw and unpredictable as this. I froze, my eyes open wide.

The brothers took in Olaf's ultimatum silently, looking straight into their captain's deranged eyes and, without a word, turned to collect their belongings. I was sorry to see it come to this but not surprised. When they returned to the deck, we hugged and said our farewells. We had shared a lot in the past five months. The brothers climbed down the ladder to the dock and quickly disappeared.

Jay shook his head at this irrevocable rift. We both liked those stubborn, sweet boys.

### *Conflict at the Consulate*

I was between two worlds, the known, with its heartaches and challenges, and the unknown, a blank canvas. I needed to shake the cobwebs out of my brain and decide what to do. I walked into the old town alone. Despite the troubles aboard *Josefine*, she'd been my home for nearly half a year. The idea of finding another boat both scared and excited me.

I was thrilled when I spotted Andy and Steve in the market square. They had spent the night God knows where, and I was eager to hear their news.

"Andy! Steve!" I shouted as I waved and raced up to them. "Hey! Where have you been?"

They looked rather shaggy and tired, carrying all their belongings in large backpacks. "We slept in a shipwreck on the beach. It was damp, but we felt safer on the beach than being on *Josefine*." I nodded, understanding completely what they meant.

At that moment, Olaf appeared in the square. I was surprised to see him. He scanned the market and caught sight of us.

The boys visibly tensed, and so did I. We never knew what would come out of our captain's mouth.

"Hey, Andy and Steve. I've got good news for you!" Olaf announced without waiting for a greeting. He was smiling broadly through his dark beard and acting like nothing was wrong. "You can return to *Josefine* if you agree to cut your hair. I'll happily take you to the West Indies if you repent and tidy up. Let's go to the American consulate to sort this out."

Olaf's language was curious. "Repent?" Why did they have to seek his godly forgiveness? What was all the fuss about? We had cleared customs, and no one would see them for forty days once they were at sea! I wondered why he wanted to do this at the American consulate.

Glaring into Olaf's eyes, I said, "Olaf, you need to change, too." This was the first and only time I ever confronted him.

I was outraged. "Andy, this is madness!"

Olaf said, "I'm generous. I'm not as hard as you think. There's a soft spot in my heart." No part of me believed that. I felt a foreboding dark cloud descend on the brilliant day. Still, we all trudged to the American consulate. I was nervous about going, but I didn't want to leave the boys alone in this situation.

In front of the consulate officer, Olaf laid out the situation. Those penetrating eyes, his neatly trimmed beard, his loose white slacks and long-sleeved white cotton shirt, his confident posture, and his fluent English gave the impression of a perfectly reasonable man. He told the officer that he had an agreement with their mother to take them across the Atlantic Ocean to Barbados and required that they cut their hair, but they refused. Rather than obeying, they abandoned the boat. "So, Andy and Steve, will you cut your hair and join us once again on *Josefine*?"

There was a thick pause. Looking at his brother and then defiantly at Olaf, Andy calmly said, "No." Andy and Steve said a quick goodbye to me and walked out of the consulate. Olaf shook his head with an odd, faint smile. I walked away from Olaf without saying a word. I needed to be alone.

Finding a café, I sat down to have a good think. I believed that Olaf knew Andy would never bend to his offer, so he had secured an official witness to the drama and checkmated the boys. As it was their decision to leave *Josefine*, the responsibility would be Andy's if he forfeited the two thousand dollars his mother had paid for their educational voyage across the Atlantic. Olaf had played this well. Witnessing this scene put the final nail in the coffin. I had to leave *Josefine*.

## *Goodbye to* Josefine

After the brothers left the boat for good, there was a glum feeling on board. Olaf ruled with a condescending tone. There was no joy and I felt miserable. The only person on board whose company I felt comfortable in was Jay.

The next days swirled around in a blur. I was determined to leave *Josefine* but was nervous, too. Then on the morning of December 22, I packed my belongings, took one long, last look at the pine room in the bow of the boat that had been my home for nearly half a year, and went to find Olaf and Anja. They were on deck, along with Bine and Stefan.

"I've come to say goodbye. I'm going to look for another boat to cross the Atlantic." After a moment of awkward silence, Olaf simply said, "Fine." I felt sad and wished things had turned out differently. I knelt and hugged Bine. "You're in for a grand adventure. It's been fun knowing you. Take good care of Fang."

I climbed down the rope ladder with my backpack slung on my shoulders. Once I reached the dock, I stood for a moment, gazing up at the glorious boat. Jay, watching from above, waved and hollered,

"Perhaps we'll meet in Barbados!"

Desperate to throw off the heavy atmosphere, I rented a car and explored the island. For a week, I drove up steep, narrow roads and into misty mountains, passing lush valleys and quaint villages, feeling more carefree by the hour.

## On the Hunt

Upon my return to Las Palmas, I checked into a cheap boarding house in the old town and began in earnest my search for a voyage across the Atlantic. *Josefine* was not in port. I was relieved, as their physical presence would have haunted me.

The wide expanse of the shimmering ocean called to me. I was determined to cross the Atlantic by sail. The unknown no longer appeared threatening to me; rather it seemed sparkling and brilliantly blue. Now, how I could I snag a ride?

The boats were gathered on a huge dock with many fingers, and it was easy to wander around and introduce myself. When you're hanging out in ports among sailing folks, you're bound to see some splendid boats and meet a few characters. Sailors are generally friendly and enjoy telling yarns about their adventures on the high seas. You chat about where you've been and where you're going. Sometimes you're invited on board for drinks and, if you're lucky, for a meal.

So, here I was, a long-haired hippie, all alone, pacing the docks barefoot. Having no sailing experience to bring to the equation, I could only entice people to take me on board by offering to cook and clean.

## A Trio of Boats

There were three sailboats preparing to cross the Atlantic that attracted me. One was *Tamure* (pronounced *tam*-ur-ray), a sloop manned by three fellows from New Zealand—David, Jerry, and Mac—and an Irishman named Tim. The New Zealanders, all fit as a fiddle and fair-skinned, with light, short hair, and clean-shaven faces, had been sailing around the world for two and a half years and were eager to get home. They'd picked up Tim in Ireland. He was engaged to a gal back home but wanted an adventure before tying the knot.

I was immediately attracted to Tim after spending just a short while visiting with these fellows. Tim had handsome dark features, played fiddle, and sang Irish ballads from the deck of *Tamure*. It could have been fun to join these men, but seeing how many people were already on board, I didn't even ask.

Another sailboat preparing to cross the Atlantic was *Zia*. She was a large luxury yacht, about the size of *Josefine*, but she wasn't gaff-rigged like *Josefine*; *Zia*'s sails were triangular, making her an ordinary but still lovely ketch.

One day I asked the Colonel, who seemed to be the owner of the yacht, if he'd like help preparing for their transatlantic voyage. I hoped to win an invitation to join them by being industrious and helpful.

"By all means. Come on up." He extended his hand as I stepped on board. Two women, maybe in their thirties, stood on the deck in slinky dresses, with plenty of bangle bracelets, watching me.

"This is Michiko and Anita. Tamar wants to see *Zia* and help us get on our way."

Compared to the crew of *Josefine*, the *Zia* folks seemed very fancy. The Colonel showed me the formal salon, where everything was neat, tidy, and palatial.

One wall of dark wooden panels was filled with sparkling bottles of spirits: wine, whiskey, gin, vodka, and rum. From the top shelf hung crystal glasses on hooks, like a fancy bar in New York City. A stereo set was playing *Carmina Burana* by Carl Orff, a choral piece that took as its text several lusty songs from a collection by Benedictine monks from the thirteenth century. I had heard the recording many times in my parents' house. To top off the salon, there were fresh carnations and gladiolas in crystal vases on a large table covered by a black-and-white-checked tablecloth. I briefly wondered what would happen to all this finery in a rolling sea.

I was gaga. Stars in my eyes, I suddenly asked, "Do you have a vacuum cleaner?"

I proceeded to dive into a three-hour cleaning binge, thinking I'd prove myself invaluable. Imagine my chagrin when they didn't invite me to join their transatlantic party.

Then there was a beautiful sloop named *Alban*. I had heard that two English fellows were on board who were busy preparing to sail to Barbados in the West Indies. When I approached the sailboat, a tall blond man with a fair complexion was on deck, checking the mainsail.

"Hi! I'm Tamar!"

"I'm Patrick. It's nice to meet you!"

"I was recently on the Danish ketch, *Josefine*—I'm sure you saw her when she was in port."

"Yes, we heard something of your misfortunes. We broke our boom while sailing from England in rough weather and limped into port, too. It's taking us longer than expected to mend the boom. But soon we hope to barrel down to the West Indies." He smacked his thin lips and crinkled his sea-blue eyes in a delightful chuckle.

With my most beguiling smile, I asked, "How would you like a cook? I'm looking for a ride to the West Indies."

"I'll have to ask the boss. Why don't you come back in an hour? We're leaving tomorrow afternoon."

Sitting on the edge of the dock with gulls soaring overhead and my bare feet dangling in the warm sea, I contemplated the immensity of my decision should they agree to take me on board. I hadn't even met the owner of *Alban* yet. I'd be sailing across the open ocean with complete strangers. Oddly, that didn't worry me. Patrick seemed perfectly normal and too congenial to be a threat. Of course, the Danes had appeared "normal" at first, too.

I felt I was rolling the dice, and the stakes were high. I was willing to take the gamble on this being a harmonious and an enjoyable experience sailing the high seas with the two lads. What concerned me most was a nagging fear of not making it to Barbados. Nature is, after all, a powerful and unpredictable force. If I joined the *Alban* crew, would I ever see my parents again? What in heaven's name was I doing? Yet, the lure of adventure filled my heart and won. If Patrick and his boss said yes, I would take the leap.

## Alban *Says Yes*

AFTER SOAKING UP THE WARMTH of the sun and ruminating over the unknowns that lay ahead, I returned to *Alban*. Both Englishmen were outside, sitting in the cockpit.

"Hi guys. I'm back!"

A dark, lean fellow smiled at the obvious. "You're welcome to come with us," he said.

"Thank you! That's fantastic!"

Mike Lynch was the owner of *Alban*, and Patrick Blackwell was the skipper he had hired to take them across the Atlantic. Mike told me to gather my belongings and spend the night on board. I couldn't believe my luck. Here we were, about to sail 2,700 nautical miles together to Barbados, almost no questions asked! We'd be in Barbados in about three or four weeks.

Patrick, Mike, and I paused our chat for a few moments to watch as four truckloads of food were delivered to *Zia* for its projected two-week journey across the ocean.

"That's Daddy's pleasure yacht!" Patrick said. "All they'll do is drink and party. But the Colonel is a grand ol' chap. We're going to keep in radio contact with them and the lads from *Tamure* while we're at sea."

I skipped down the wharf and into town, feeling lighter and happier than I had for months. Dancing and spinning around, the wind caught my hair as I sang the kids' song, "If you're happy and you know it, clap your hands." I clapped my hands: *Clap! Clap!* I didn't care what anyone thought of this crazy expression of joy.

## *Letter Home*

I checked out of the old town inn and walked to the post office to get the mailing address for Barbados. Then I found a little café, where I ordered coffee and a slice of almond cake to celebrate my new adventure. With a sigh of pleasure and relief that I was finally on my way again, I sat down to write to my parents.

As I took a sip of coffee and a bite of the sweet cake, I put pen to paper. Hopping on board *Alban* and striking out across the vast ocean was a bold move. Our umbilical cord to land would be cut, and there'd be no way to connect to our loved ones or call for help, should anything go wrong. I felt as if I'd be dropping off the face of the earth for the trip's duration.

I worried that this might be the last letter I ever wrote to my parents. What if we got lost and drifted aimlessly on the ocean, running out of food and water? Would we draw straws to eat each other? I'd read enough sea stories to know this desperate choice was possible.

Despite these morbid reflections racing through my mind, I chose to write a cheerful letter to my parents. As their only surviving daughter, I truly hoped to come out of this alive. After I posted my letter, I sent them a cable as well. I also cabled Arthur. I was sure he'd appreciate knowing my plans.

*Dearest Mother and Dad,*

*I'm off to sail the Atlantic with two Englishmen on* Alban. *Mike Lynch owns the boat and Patrick Blackwell is the skipper. I'm excited about sailing the high seas in this graceful sloop, and a little nervous, too.*

*We'll be at sea for twenty-five to thirty days at the whim of the sea gods.*

*We plan to keep in radio contact with two other ships that are crossing the Atlantic but leaving a few days behind us*—Tamure, *with three New Zealand fellows and an Irishman named Tim, and* Zia, *a luxury yacht with a formal, dressed up crew. I like the down to earth feeling from Mike and Patrick. The energy on* Alban *is way happier than on* Josefine.

*You can write to me in care of General Delivery, Bridgetown, Barbados, West Indies. I'll call you as soon as we reach Barbados.*

*Wish me good luck! Give my love to Mark.*

*With lots of love,*

*Tamar*

I was sure my news would come as a surprise to my parents, to say the least. I hoped they wouldn't be too worried, and I hoped instead they'd appreciate my gumption. Of all the people I knew, they should understand. Each of them had been an adventurous risk-taker.

Dad was a rare breed. During World War II, he joined the Tenth Mountain Division, comprising army ski troops, one of the most highly trained divisions in the war, enduring grueling training in the Rocky Mountains. Fortunately, Dad became so ill at Camp Hale in Colorado that he was reassigned to San Francisco to manage shipping up and down the Pacific Coast instead of going to war in Italy. The Tenth Mountain Division entered the war in the winter of 1945 and staged one of the most daring series of nighttime attacks in US military history. Many fine young men were killed in the Apennine Mountains.

It was only because Dad had become ill that he escaped playing Russian roulette with his life.

Mother had spunk, too. In her younger years she leapt into the unknown with both feet. When she was twenty-two, she took the train to Washington State after answering an ad for a masseuse job in Lakewood, a sparsely populated suburb of Tacoma. She had been schooled in Swedish massage and had worked in a beauty salon at Marshall Field's department store in Chicago.

Lured to the Pacific Northwest by the promise of lakes and forests after her parents had died, she left her sister and brother in Chicago to strike out on her own. Mother traveled with all that she owned in one suitcase, including her doll from Germany. Soon after she arrived, she caught Dad's eye after he rescued her, when her solo sailing kayak tipped over in American Lake.

## *More Farewells*

After cabling Arthur and my folks, I happened to bump into Andy again in the market square. What splendid timing! I learned that the brothers had been sleeping in the shipwreck on the beach, then in a haunted house, and even in a cave up in the mountains.

Andy also told me that he had fallen in love with an English girl named Dusty, who lived on the island. They planned to elope to Ibiza once Dusty finished high school. She was only sixteen and had six more months of school, so Andy planned to stick around Las Palmas waiting for her. He was seeing her after school and wanted to know if I'd like to meet her.

"Sure! I'd love to."

I couldn't wait to see the girl who had stolen his heart. Andy and

I sat down on a stone bench, enjoying a good chat while observing the comings and goings of the local people. Shortly after three, Dusty appeared with a school satchel slung over her shoulder.

She was beautiful: slender, tanned from the sun, with masses of light-brown curly hair, blue eyes, freckles, and a tipped-up nose. She wore sandals and a thin, short-sleeved cotton dress of faded apricot that fell above her knees. I liked her immediately. I could see how they would make a sweet couple.

After a fun visit, we said our goodbyes, and I begged them to visit me someday at my parents' island property in Canada. I knew they'd love it there.

"Andy, you can let your hair grow to your knees if you want!" With that, he smiled. "I'll miss you. Please keep in touch!" I said.

When I got back to the marina, I found Steve waiting there to say goodbye. I was very touched. My heart ached, not knowing if I'd ever see him or Andy again or learn how their lives would unfold. I hoped I would.

## *Welcome Aboard*

FOLLOWING MY CHANCE ENCOUNTER WITH Andy and Steve in the old town of Gran Canaria, I returned to *Alban*, where Mike and Patrick welcomed me into the little sloop that was to be our home for the next month. Feeling exhilaration and anticipation, I climbed up a ladder hanging over the side of the boat, carrying my backpack and tightly rolled up sleeping bag, with my Pentax camera hanging around my neck. I stepped over the thin wire cable that ran along the entire edge of the boat to keep people from falling overboard.

"Welcome aboard," Patrick said, his sea-blue eyes flashing. Mike, with his dark-brown eyes, offered a friendly smile.

*Alban* was a wooden sloop, built in 1939 in England, forty-two feet long and nine feet wide, with a sixty-foot mast. She was very narrow, and this gave her elegance and charm. Boats with beautiful lines and designs have always made my heart flutter, and *Alban* was one of them.

"Let's give you a tour." Patrick held out his hand as I stepped down into the cockpit, a recessed well in the stern, where the steering wheel and compass were located. Built-in benches formed a U-shape around the cockpit.

With Patrick in the lead and Mike behind me, I climbed down five steep wooden stairs that led from the cockpit to the cabin, and stood transfixed, gazing at the tidy and compact living quarters. I could see that we would all be sleeping in the open cabin.

"This is the quarter bunk where you will sleep. Why don't you park your things here?" It was a relief to be free from my backpack. As I wiggled out of the straps, Patrick grabbed the aluminum frames. I set it on the bed to be sorted out later.

I loved my quarter bed instantly. My feet would be tucked under the port side of the cockpit above, and my head would be out in the open, so I'd have a clear view of the companionway leading up to the open air. I felt that Mike and Patrick had given me the best bed on the sloop.

Under my bunk was a storage cabinet, and above were small shelves where I could stash my belongings. These shelves had raised edges about two inches high, to prevent items from falling off in rough seas.

Forward of my quarter bunk was the galley, where I would prepare meals. It was teensy-tiny and L-shaped, with a gimballed stove on the port side, and a little sink facing the bow. The mini fridge was under the sink. There was a round porthole above the stove, so I could look out to the sea when trying to stay stable in rolling waves, cooking over a hot stove. This porthole could be opened to let steam out when the galley got too warm. We'd be traveling west and south towards the equator, and the days would become hotter and hotter even though we were sailing in January.

Patrick pointed to a table along the starboard wall, across from my bed. "This is my navigation table," he said. It was here that he kept his charts, almanac, chronometer, marine radio, ruler, pencils and, of course, his sextant. This was old-fashioned sailing, dependent on the sun, moon, stars, and planets to navigate us across the ocean. I hoped with all my heart that Patrick knew what he was doing.

"And this is where Mike and I will sleep." He motioned to two benches nestled up against the sloop's walls, with foam cushions covered in green canvas, like my bed.

"I'm on the port side in front of the galley, and Mike is on the starboard side, in front of my navigation table." If we were all sitting up in our beds, we could see each other clearly. Obviously, there was very little privacy, but this didn't concern me in the least. *Alban*'s compact cabin simply seemed cozy and friendly to me.

Above the benches were a few shelves crammed with books that would keep us entertained throughout our journey. These Englishmen obviously enjoyed reading. "Feel free to borrow any books from our wee *Alban* library," Patrick said. I couldn't wait to see what the lads had on board. The books one keeps tell a lot about a person. I'd grown up with tons of books in our house and loved reading.

The lads' beds were on either side of a table, which took up the center of the sloop's interior. There was barely a foot of space to walk between the table and the benches. The table could be folded down on one side, to make more space to walk in the cabin when we weren't eating.

Patrick said they liked to keep their beds tidy during the day so they could sit around the table for meals, but mostly they dined in the cockpit. This made sense to me. I vowed to keep my bed neat so as not to disappoint the lads, and of course, I liked the idea of eating out while enjoying the warm air, sunsets, and sea breeze.

Patrick thought I'd like to peek at our provisions, since I was the cook. He pointed out fresh food that hung from nets and canned food stored under their beds. My heart sank as I imagined the horror of having to prepare every meal for nearly a month for two hungry men. When I'd offered to cook, they had failed to ask me if I *could* cook.

The head, or bathroom, was directly forward of Patrick's bed, closer to the bow. Enclosed for privacy by a narrow door, it had a teensy sink and toilet where you pumped salt water in and pumped it out. Even though one could barely turn around, it was the only space on the sloop where one could be alone.

Across from the head on starboard was a storage locker for emergency equipment: life jackets, lifelines, flares, an extra radio, an inflatable boat, oars, food, water, and flashlights—a reassuring sight.

"There you have it! That's *Alban*! Why don't you make yourself comfortable? Mike will cook dinner tonight, and we'll dine in the cockpit."

"Sounds good to me! I can't wait to set sail with you guys."

I stashed my newly acquired journal and toiletries on the shelves above and laid out my sleeping bag and pillow on the narrow berth. The storage locker under the bed was full of supplies but had just enough space for my knapsack, camera, clothes, Arabian robes, and a towel. Then I took a deep breath and relaxed; I had found my home for the next month.

As the sun vanished, a breath of cool evening wind swept over the bay, and the sky turned an indigo blue. Sitting in the cockpit we could hear the chatter of yachting people from other boats, and fiddle music from *Tamure* drifting over the sea. Mike brought out a plate of appetizers: sliced cheddar cheese, fresh bread, and olives, along with a bottle of aquavit.

I was fond of aquavit because it reminded me of Mother. We would enjoy nips of it after dipping into the icy ocean in a rocky cove in British Columbia. That night in Las Palmas, the aquavit warmed my stomach and my brain, just as it did when the cold Canadian waters had shocked my body.

As the stars popped out, sprinkling the sky with glittering lights, Mike brought out our supper: fresh chicken breasts cooked in garlic, onions, and curry powder, with white rice and glazed carrots and a bottle of white wine. We ate in satisfaction, becoming mellow with our wine. All three of us seemed to be at ease and excited about the impending journey.

The night wafted away in perfect harmony. Then we made our way to bed to get a good sleep while tied safely to the wharf in the harbor. The next night, we'd be cast out on the open ocean. Not totally sure what I had gotten myself into, I kept my worries to myself.

chapter seven

# Across the Atlantic

***You cannot change the wind,***
***but you can adjust the sails.***
—Unknown

## *High Spirits*

A*LBAN* SET SAIL ON A WARM, sunny January afternoon. As our sloop motored out of the harbor of Las Palmas, my companions and I were in high spirits. The air was balmy; the sea was a silken blue; and each of us, no doubt, entertained our own dreams of what lay ahead. Despite an underlying shadow of fear, I was emboldened by optimism and visions of a grand and fun adventure.

It was January 11, my brother's birthday! I wondered how he was, and if he had come to some peace over Naomi's death. I shouted, "Happy birthday!" over the vast ocean, and hoped that he'd pick up the vibes.

Shortly after leaving Gran Canaria, Patrick called Mike to help raise the sails. The lads pulled on the rope in unison, raising the mainsail higher and higher as it swayed against the cobalt sky. Next, they set the

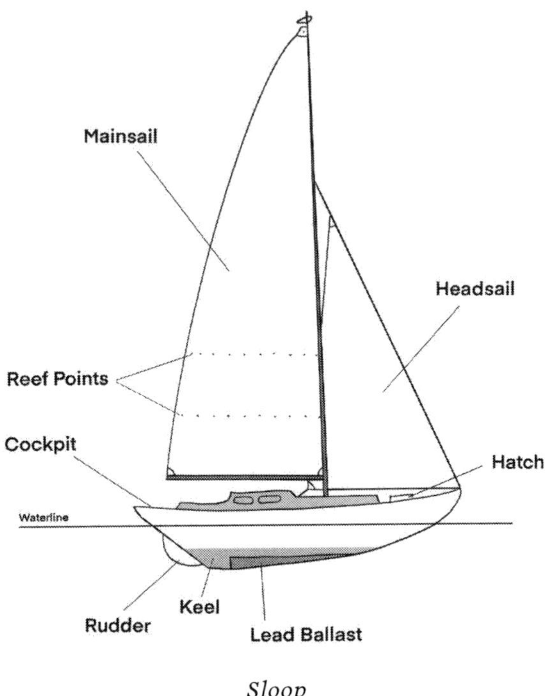


*Sloop*

two headsails, which spread out like wings on either side of the sloop and picked up the wind following from behind. *Alban*'s mast was incredibly tall, much taller than the mainmast of *Josefine*. I was in for a completely different sailing experience. Not only were my companions different, but the boats were, too, and this thought pleased me. There was no turning back. I was terrified and excited, with a dash of hope sprinkled in for good measure.

Patrick cut the engine after the sails were set. Now there was silence—serene, glorious silence, with just the warm wind in our sails. I claimed my favorite place on a boat—the bow. It was pure magic to feel *Alban* slice through the huge, even waves. Lying on my belly and drowsy from the warm sun and Dramamine I had taken to calm my stomach, I gazed into the deep ultramarine sea, hoping to catch sight of dolphins. The swells were large and even, like the breath of a sleeping dragon.

This moment was perfection, and I didn't want it ever to end. I felt at one with the gentle swells of the sea, the blue sky above, the white sails picking up the warm wind, and our fair sloop, *Alban*. I was overcome with gratitude that these fellows had invited me along, and that I had the courage or craziness to take this leap into the unknown.

Patrick called us to the cockpit. Reluctant to leave my treasured spot, I joined the men in the stern of *Alban*. Patrick explained our watch schedule, informing us that we'd be doing four-hour watches throughout the night and day, which would give each of us an eight-hour break.

"I'll take the eight to midnight watch. Tamar will do the midnight to 4:00 a.m. watch, and Mike will take the 4:00 to 8:00 a.m. watch. During the day, we'll cover the same times. The schedule will give Tamar time to cook supper," Patrick said with a chuckle.

For my benefit, he laid out our responsibilities on watch duty. "On watch, you'll need to keep an eye on the compass and steer the boat. I'll let you know what direction to sail using the compass. On some nights we may let our automatic pilot, which we call Harry, steer the boat, but we'll have to be on duty and watch the compass. Harry sometimes goes astray!"

It came as a surprise that I'd be taking part in night watches. I liked the idea of standing under a sky filled with stars, steering the sloop, and watching out for us all. Patrick had no idea who I was nor what my skills were, and yet he had entrusted me with a serious responsibility.

"This is exciting! Thanks, Patrick!"

"No problem, luv. We'll get more sleep with you aboard."

### *Panic*

The sun was sinking low on the western horizon, bringing a welcome breeze over *Alban*, and Gran Canaria was becoming a faint mirage behind us. When it was time to prepare our dinner, I felt a mild panic. What would these fellows think once they learned what a lousy cook I was? I figured they wouldn't toss me overboard, but I hated to disappoint them, as they had been kind enough to let me come along. These poor lads were in for a surprise.

There seemed to be lots of food, but what did I know about rationing food to last a month at sea? Or perhaps even longer if a storm knocked us off course, or Patrick didn't know what he was doing, and we became lost at sea. I carried on pretending that life was groovy in front of the men, yet I was scared out of my wits that something could go awry.

I gazed at *Alban*'s pantry, which was stacked with jars of dried herbs. Baskets of fresh fruit and vegetables hung in nets from the galley wall. There was nothing to do except to plunge in. The fresh produce needed to be eaten first, so I went to work chopping up veggies for a salad and making a dressing of olive oil and vinegar sprinkled with dried herbs. Rummaging in a locker, I found a bag of macaroni and a large can of Irish stew. That would do. I collected a bucket of seawater, as I knew that we had to conserve our precious fresh water, and I poured the sea into a big pot. When this was boiling, I tossed in some macaroni. Then I opened the can of Irish stew and spooned it into another pot, adding a chopped carrot, an onion, and two tomatoes. To top off the meal, I grated a bowl of cheddar cheese to sprinkle on the pasta.

I felt guilty being so stingy with our meal. One can of Irish stew for two hungry men and me? I had no idea if being cautious was a wise decision; it seemed to be the only way to operate to make our provisions last.

It was hot in the galley, and I envied the fellows on deck. I wanted to be outside enjoying the sunset with the lads, but I was stuck in the stultifying heat of the cabin and feeling very sorry for myself. Yet I couldn't complain because this cooking for my ride was the deal, and it was my big idea.

When all was ready, I passed our dinner up to the cockpit, where we enjoyed the simple meal with red wine. I was relieved that the lads didn't complain about the meager offering. It was a glorious evening. The air was warm, the sea was blue. *Alban* rose up and down the huge, gentle swells.

## *My Companions*

While we sat in the cockpit, soaking up the reality of our adventure, I wondered, *who* are *these fellows?* I begged them to tell me a bit about their lives.

I learned that Mike was thirty-two, and he had been a "big shot" at an advertising firm in London. He'd made lots of money. As time passed, he felt trapped in his city job. Remembering a picture of a sailboat in his dad's study when he was a child, the idea of an adventure on the high seas filled his imagination. Divorced, with no children, he could do what he pleased.

He bought *Alban* and planned to sail her to the West Indies, where he wanted to charter her. The only hitch was that he knew nothing about sailing. When he placed an ad in a newspaper, he found Patrick, whom he hired to skipper *Alban* across the sea.

Patrick was thirty-seven. He had auditioned for many Shakespearean plays but had only received bit parts. He lived alone in a small apartment in London and visited his aging mum in Devon as often as he could. When his dreams of acting came to naught, he turned his attention to celestial navigation and skippering sailing ships in the Mediterranean Sea.

I was fascinated by their different stories. Our skipper had a passion for Shakespeare! This sounded intriguing. And I found his devotion to his mother sweet, especially because I loved my own mother so dearly. I had more in common with Patrick's world of literature and stars than with Mike's business and advertising life.

Venus appeared bright in the changing indigo sky. A warm breeze filled the sails and gently moved us south-southwest. The two headsails spread out on either side of the sloop, white against the twilight sky. We were poised in the center of an ever-moving circle that darkened as night swallowed the day.

"Any seconds?" Patrick asked.

"Sorry, no! But you can have cookies and tea!"

"Mmmm. Tea. Now that's the spirit."

I washed the dishes and boiled a pot of water for tea. Everything had to be kept in order on a small sailboat, and I would continue to be careful about the water I was using. Mike went below to write in his journal over his cup of tea. Patrick did a sighting with the sextant on Venus and remained on deck for night watch. I wrote a bit in my brand-new journal while tucked into my cozy sleeping bag, then closed my eyes, content with our first day at sea.

## *Night Watch*

I was in a vivid dream when Patrick tapped me on my shoulder.

"Wake up. It's twelve o'clock."

*Merde!* Night watch.

I yawned, stretched my arms and legs, and shook the carnivalesque dream out of my hair. Slipping on my black hooded Arabian robe, as there was a bit of a chill, I climbed up the steep companionway to the cockpit. Patrick followed, to make sure I understood his instructions. He reminded me to keep an eye on the compass and steer 220 degrees south-southwest.

"Watch the sails—they should stay tight—and look out for ships. We're not in a shipping lane, but you never know. If anything happens, don't hesitate to wake me."

I grasped the seriousness of my job and knew I must remain standing at the wheel for four hours, attentive to every nuance of the sea, watching for lights from other ships, and mindful of the sails and compass direction. It was a glorious night, and I was looking forward to these few hours alone on deck.

"Any questions?

"I think I've got it! Sweet dreams!"

"Good luck, luv," he called as he disappeared into the cabin to catch his forty winks.

Oddly, I felt confident taking on this job, and I was happy to be an active part of the crew. I knew I could handle *Alban*. On this first night watch, I realized what an elegant lady she was. She felt like a living being, with her own personality, our fourth companion as we traversed the ocean. She was graceful and serene and sliced through the waves with confidence. She was a queen.

Alone at last, sailing swiftly south-southwest! We glided over a shiny black sea sprinkled in starlight. The white mainsail stood out against the sky, and the two headsails caught the following breeze. I stood at the helm, my hands peeking out through the flared sleeves of my Arabian robe, gripping the wheel, my bare feet placed far apart for balance, and I danced to the rhythm of *Alban* rolling in the heaving ocean waves. It was exhilarating to surrender my body to the motion of the sea and the sloop. Every ounce of my being was alive, both physically and mentally. For four hours, by myself, with the cool breeze blowing through my hair, I steered our sloop under billions of glittering stars.

This was a peaceful time, with everyone asleep, when I could enjoy the magic of the night sky that rose like a vaulted cathedral over our tiny boat, and mull over the dream that had been disrupted by Patrick's tap on my shoulder.

Dream

My mother and I were sailing quite fast in a small boat on the turquoise waters of an exotic tropical ocean. Suddenly, our vessel encountered ground and transformed into a carriage with four wheels. We rolled along a country road until we came to the top of a hill, and the road dropped swiftly to the sea below. Mother was driving, trying to keep the thin right wheels of the carriage from going over the edge of the crumbly road, which dropped for miles over a mossy, sea-blue valley. The carriage swayed.

"Mother, don't do that!" I yelled, aghast. She didn't listen and drove on, tempting fate, too near the precipice. After one more bend in the road, we lost our balance and fell over the edge, but the carriage didn't crash. It bounced serenely like a balloon down into the valley. At the bottom, the road ended in a gate topped with barbed wire, with a sign that said, "Keep Out!" We ignored the warning. The gate opened, bringing us to a road that led to the ocean. When we reached the end of the road, we slipped back into the sea and once again became a tiny boat.

In the dream I was tired, so I lay down in the boat until my sister tapped me lightly on my shoulder. "Would you like some chocolate? It's very good." It was at this moment that Patrick woke me for night watch.

My dream that night was a curious one. It had all the elements of disaster and doom, yet it was not menacing. It was as if we were in a fairy tale, where rusty gates opened, boats changed to carriages and vice versa, and the effects of recklessness were gently avoided. The dream was a surreal, smooth journey through a magical land of impossibilities.

Was it a dream to trust in the universe, that everything would be all right? Did I have a protective angel or fairy close by, sprinkling magical stardust along my path so locked gates would open and all the energies in the universe would combine to provide me with what I needed? I wanted to believe this was true.

The hours passed. I soaked up the black, starry sky and watched a pinprick of light appear on the eastern horizon and burst suddenly into bright orange behind the swiftly moving sloop. The horn of the crescent moon was rising over the ocean. When her entire crescent was visible, she looked about ten feet long, with her rounded belly down towards the sea. Slowly she changed to pale gold as she rose higher. She was so slender that she did not wash away the brilliance of the night sky. We were far away from civilization with no haze of city lights dimming the spectacular display of stars and planets.

At 4:00 a.m. I slipped downstairs to tap Mike on his shoulder. "Wake up. Night watch!"

"Huh?" He grumbled and rolled over, unwilling to climb out of his cozy sleeping bag and take command of the watch.

"It's time to get up. It's beautiful outside!"

"Oh fiddlesticks. I haven't slept a wink." He covered his head with a blanket.

"Mike, it's your turn for watch." I returned to the cockpit, where I waited for him to wake up. In a few minutes he stumbled out.

"I can't wait for this bloody trip to be over, so I can get a good night's sleep."

I went below to catch my wink of sleep, curled up in my cozy quarter berth before the day began in earnest. With our watch schedule I sure wasn't going to get a full eight or even six hours of sleep. Climbing into my sleeping bag shortly after 4:00 a.m., I'd sleep no more than four hours because the men would be hungry, and I'd have to prepare breakfast.

When I woke a little after eight, Mike was sitting at the table, writing in his journal, and Pat was busy taking sights. After rubbing the sleep out of my eyes, I changed into my shorts and T-shirt in the open cabin without feeling the least bit shy, brushed my hair and teeth, and poked my head into the cockpit.

"Good morning, Pat!"

"Morning, luv. Sleep well?"

"Great, and you?"

"I don't really sleep well until we hit land. How about making a bit o' breakfast?"

"Would you like scrambled eggs and bacon?" I wanted to make

something nice for the lads I'd nearly starved the night before.

"Sure! And a pot of coffee, please!"

"You bet."

Soon the cabin filled with the enticing smells of coffee and crisp bacon. We still had fresh bread from Las Palmas, so I sliced up a few pieces and served it with salted butter and raspberry jam. I gave Patrick his substantial breakfast in the cockpit.

"Thank you, luv!"

Breakfasts were easier to make than dinners, and I felt a blush of satisfaction that Patrick appreciated my efforts. Mike nodded a thank-you when I brought him his breakfast and paused his writing to dive into his platter. I often caught myself wondering what Mike was thinking about in his long silences sitting with his journal.

I fetched my plate and joined Pat in the open air. It was a supremely beautiful morning. The sky was a pale yellow and turquoise towards the horizon, deepening into a cerulean blue, and high up in the dome the sky turned a clear ultramarine blue. The sun was a misty yellow-white disk in the ever-deepening blue. The sea was a maze of mountains and valleys following us. I wrote in my journal:

*This is the life. Perfect! Just the three of us in our little sloop, sailing along on the wide ocean and in the vast universe.*

### *Swimming Naked*

Later that morning, there was barely any wind, and the sails flapped listlessly. Sitting in the bow with my journal, I began to feel woozy and hot. The blue ocean below beckoned.

I asked Patrick, "May I go for a swim?"

"Sure, we're going nowhere."

"You won't sail away without me?"

"I promise."

I dashed into the cabin, where I quickly stripped and found my towel. I emerged on deck stark naked and couldn't wait to slip into the warm water. I climbed down the ladder and into the sea. Swimming and splashing near the boat, I laughed with pure joy as the ocean caressed my body. When I climbed up the ladder, my skin and hair glistened with salty seawater. In this moment I felt utterly happy.

Wrapped up in my towel, I went into the cabin to change into a T-shirt and shorts.

When I was back on deck, Patrick announced he'd turn on the engine after lunch, as we were going nowhere under sail. He said that we had thirty-six hours of fuel, and we could use some now.

Before starting the engine and after Patrick took the noon sighting, we clustered around the navigation table and called *Zia* on the radio, looking forward to connecting with our friends. She had left the day after us and could have slipped by us with her many sails. We could hear them, but they couldn't hear us. We were quite disappointed.

When Patrick started the engine, it wasn't as noisy as I feared. *Putt-putt-putt.* It sounded like a tugboat engine, which had always been a romantic sound of the sea for me. In Puget Sound, I saw many tugboats plying the waters, towing logs, sawdust, or homes behind. I loved their sturdy appearance and the sound of their engines.

Yet here, out in the wide sea, I far preferred the natural sounds of the ocean swishing past our wooden hull. Fortunately, we didn't have to motor for long. The wind picked up and we were soon sailing at an exhilarating pace.

I wondered how far ahead *Josefine* was, and if the crew was still pumping. I opened my journal to write some thoughts.

*Our little sloop is like a toy in the vast ocean with an incredibly tall mast. You can walk across her in two giant steps. It seems almost ludicrous after being on* Josefine. *I'm nostalgic for the ketch, even though there was rarely a good scene on board. Olaf and Stefan were constantly on fire with tension.* Josefine *is beautiful but she is a ship of sorrows. That little canary sang away when we were all talking, arguing, or fighting, and was silent when we were silent.*

*The work on that ship and the effort to repair her was arduous. I can see her now floating on the black sea, moonlit sails, shadows of clouds, ropes banging in the bow, and a belly full of angry rumblings. Why do I miss her? I'll always miss her.*

## *A Terrible Cook*

As the sun slipped fire red into the sea, leaving a glow of amber along the horizon, Patrick said, "Hey, luv, how about some dinner?"

I cheerfully agreed, hiding the same performance anxiety that I'd had the first night. I found a can of chicken curry and a can of peas. *There! I'll make a big pot of rice to fill out the meal.* In a short while, dinner was ready. I felt a tremendous sigh of relief that I'd pulled off one more meal, and without any dire consequences.

Our meal's entertainment that evening was a brilliant sunset with myriads of clouds lingering in the sky. After supper, while we were enjoying the warm evening in the cockpit, Patrick sang a familiar sea shanty in his beautiful baritone voice.

*I've been a wild rover for many's the year*
*And I've spent all me money on whiskey and beer*
*But now I'm returning with gold in great store*
*And I never will play the wild rover no more*
*And it's no, nay, never*
*No, nay, never, no more*
*Will I play the wild rover*
*No never, no more*

Mike smiled and tapped his fingers on his legs, enjoying the rollicking tune yet reluctant to sing along. I joined the chorus in my soprano voice, and Pat and I sang to the stars above.

## *Second Night Watch*

I danced again, loose at the wheel, on my second night watch. The sloop glided effortlessly over the silken sea, casting a trail of brilliant bioluminescence behind. The moon got brighter as it swept over the dome.

Standing for four straight hours on a swaying sloop, keeping watch on the compass, sails, and marine traffic, all the while steering the boat, was challenging. I was sorely tempted to tiptoe downstairs and doze a bit, but what would I say to Pat if he caught me sneaking a snooze? Instead, I made a quick cup of tea, nibbled a few pieces of dark chocolate, and settled into my watch, wrapped in my Arabian robe.

That night, my mind drifted to my parents. They were so far away, on the west coast of North America. I had sent them letters and cables, but we had only spoken a few times over the past six months. I wondered if they were worried about me. I imagined them sitting by the huge fire in our home on Chambers Creek, the setters curled up at their feet, looking out at the rain pounding the windows. Those windows rose an impressive twenty feet tall and were laced in Virginia creeper vines that Mother had planted years before, providing a lovely natural curtain for our home.

My parents were likely smoking cigarettes, drinking coffee, and wondering, *Where is Tamar? Will we ever see her again?* I knew that if anything happened to me, their lives would be shrouded with double desolation. I imagined that Mother was worried sick. But Dad probably cheered me on, never having thought his daughter would embark on such a wild venture.

I loved my mother with all my heart. I loved my father, too, but my love for him was complex. I felt that he had given me life and taken it away.

At last, 4:00 a.m. arrived, and I was free to wake Mike. Bending over his snoring form, I thought, *What a strange fish!* However, I felt a little sorry for him, as 4:00 a.m. was a wretched time for anyone to wake up. He rolled over muttering, "Shit!"

A little while later, the scent of coffee woke me. Mike had made a pot after his watch and was writing in his journal, while Patrick was on duty outside. I yawned, stretched, and climbed out of my cozy sleeping bag to pour a cup of coffee and greet another day. I wrote the following in my journal.

*It's a supremely beautiful morning. The sky is pale blue, turquoise, cerulean blue, with gray-white fluffy clouds, and the sea is a limpid ultramarine blue. There's a misty yellow-white circle around the sun. The sea rolls in huge mountains and valleys following our ship. Pat says we traveled 131 miles in the past twenty-four hours.*

*I'm now sitting in the warmth of the morning sun. There's a long freighter to our starboard, which is odd because we aren't in a shipping lane. Pat tells me that international sea law created shipping lanes in all the oceans of the world, where cargo ships can pass. They have the right of way in these lanes, which are clearly marked on the marine charts. There are two shipping lanes in the Atlantic Ocean. When you pass through them you must be doubly vigilant. Tiny pleasure craft like ours must give way to larger ships.*

### *Fearing the Worst*

Despite the beauty, I was feeling uneasy and slightly seasick that morning. The worst place to be when feeling sick is down in the cabin, but I had work to do. I had to get a grasp on our provisions. I felt driven to count and document every item of food on board since I hadn't done the shopping and had no clue what we had. Being responsible for our meals, I needed to plan them carefully so we wouldn't run out.

"You guys, I'm going to inventory the food. You won't be able to get to the cabin for a couple of hours, so fetch anything you may want—or go to the head!" Patrick raised his eyebrows. When had a cook bossed the skipper around?

"Do you really need to do that?"

"Pat, I'll go mad if I don't do this. How will I know what to cook?"

"I think you're being silly but go ahead."

Confining myself in the belly of the sweltering sloop with the sea rolling mercilessly around me, I removed every item from the lockers under our beds and piled them on the floor, where they immediately scattered as *Alban* rolled from side to side. Sitting on the floor with my legs spread out, I grabbed each item, wrote what it was in my journal, and stuffed it back into one of the lockers under the center berths.

My thoughts swirled as I sorted through the provisions: *Twelve cans of chicken legs, two cans of mackerel. Twenty cans of green beans, two chocolate bars. What if we run out of food? Eleven cans of milk, three bags of rice. What if we wander for weeks lost in the Sargasso Sea? Ten boxes of cornflakes, sixty-two bags of tea. Does Patrick know what he's doing? I feel seasick! These bloody Englishmen drink so much tea! I need some fresh air.*

I gritted my teeth and stood up, my damp hair clinging to my face. I dashed up to the cockpit and sat down next to Patrick.

"My stomach feels funny. This boat is rocking, and I feel sick!"

"The word is roll luv. Boats never *rock*."

"Oh, come on! This boat is *rocking*, and I feel sick! What does it matter if it's *rocking* or *rolling*?"

"The correct word is *roll*."

"Well, phooey!"

We both laughed.

I returned to the hot galley to finish the task I'd set out for myself. The fellows thought I was nuts, but they kept out of my way, staying in the fresh air as I continued to block the path to the head and galley. When I was finished, I stood up, balancing on my bare feet in the rolling boat. I felt tremendous satisfaction.

"Hey guys! All's clear!"

But would the inventory really help? I hadn't a clue what was a reasonable amount to eat each day. I was inclined to starve the lads, as I feared the worst. These poor men didn't know what they had gotten into when they accepted me on board.

I ducked back down into the cabin to make a hasty lunch before my noon to 4:00 p.m. day watch. I spread out a few sardines, some bread, cheese, and sliced oranges. The lads seemed happy about the beers that I had put out for them as well. Bless Mike: he offered to tidy up the galley after lunch.

That day, Patrick changed our watch schedules:

Patrick: 8:00 p.m.–12:00 a.m.

Mike: 12:00 a.m.–4:00 a.m.

Tamar: 4:00 a.m.–8:00 a.m.

This new routine worked to my benefit, as I would get nearly six straight hours of sleep. Patrick would get eight hours and still be able to take sightings with the noon sun, the moon, and the stars. Mike would get the worst schedule, with barely four hours of good sleep, but he didn't complain.

The next dinner was once again horrible: two cans of ravioli and a can of heated up green beans. There was a flicker of a smile across Patrick's face when he saw what was on our plates—he seemed to be continuously amused—but Mike scowled at the scant meal. As a consolation I opened a can of peaches and a tin of biscuits for dessert and made a pot of tea.

Several hours later Patrick announced, "I'm ravenous!"

"Would you like a banana and cornflakes?"

"I'd like a whole roast partridge with gravy and mashed potatoes!"

"Sorry, Patrick. Dream on!" I fetched him a bowl of cornflakes.

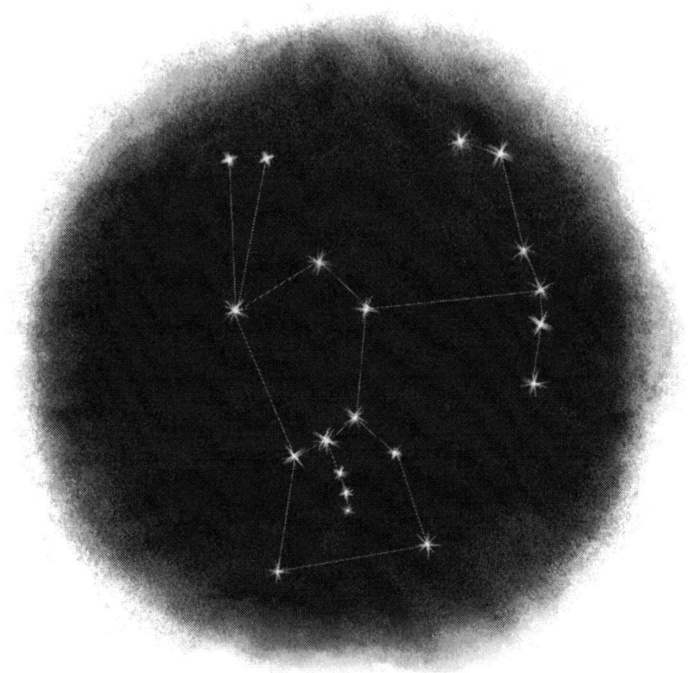

### *Orion*

IT WAS GRIM GETTING UP at four in the morning, but once I was up, it was all right, even pleasant. The sky was cloudy for over an hour, then the slender moon appeared along with the bright constellation of Orion the Hunter, who strides across the celestial realm from east to west. In Greek mythology, he was the handsome son of the sea god Poseidon and Euryale, the daughter of King Minos of Crete. He fell in love with the Pleiades, the seven sisters, daughters of Atlas and Pleione. When Orion started pursuing them, Zeus scooped them up and placed them in the sky. Every night Orion traverses the sky in pursuit of the sisters.

Max's stance onstage was larger than life, much like Orion's in the heavens. Broad-shouldered Orion, with a glittering belt of three stars, commands the night, just as Max did as the Grim Reaper when he pounded the stage of the theater with his feet. Every night as Orion traveled over the twinkly sky, I welcomed Max into my soul. Orion became Max in my imagination.

Gazing up at Orion, I remembered watching rehearsals of the Joffrey Ballet after their summer residency in Tacoma in 1967.

When the ballet company and I had returned to New York, I asked Robert Joffrey if I could sketch his dancers, merging my passion for art and dance. He graciously allowed me to attend as many rehearsals as I wanted.

It was exciting to sit alone in the expansive, empty theater with my sketch pad on my knees, attempting to capture the dancers in motion. When they rehearsed *The Green Table*, dramatic, urgent music filled the theater as I threw lines onto the paper. I was utterly swept away watching Max rehearse for his dream role as Death. I felt I was in a sacred space where no one existed beyond Max, me, and Death.

The enticing scent of coffee hit my nostrils, alerting me that my watch was coming to an end. Patrick emerged from the cabin and handed me a hot mug. "Here, Tam. How was your watch?"

"Thanks, Pat. It was great. Four hours alone at night is a long time, though."

"I can teach you about the stars some night if you wish."

"I'd love that!"

Patrick stayed with me until 8:00 a.m. when my watch was over.

"How about a bit o' breakfast?"

"Sure. What d'you want?"

"Cornflakes, ma'am. I can't survive the day without cornflakes and tea."

I disappeared into the galley and returned with cereal for us both. As we sat in the stern together, quietly enjoying our breakfast, I felt an unspoken attraction between us. He was so real, kind, open, and right in front of me! I craved being loved, but for some reason, I felt afraid and kept my guard up.

"Have a good watch, Pat!"

I gave him a brief hug and escaped to the bow, into my journal, recalling the magic of dawn bursting forth over the ocean. I wanted to remember it forever.

*Gradually, the sky became less tangled, the stars became fewer, and a faint light glowed on the eastern dome. Slowly the light extended itself, and a few strands of clouds were on pink fire. The moon became pale against the vastly changing indigo sky. The sun was coming! Powerfully he climbed up the heavens, announcing his reign over the day. What a welcome sight is day with its warmth and infinitely changing hues!*

## **Zia *out of Luck***

It was 1:00 p.m., Time to connect with our friends. Not only was this an entertaining diversion from the hypnotic ocean waves that rolled ceaselessly, but it provided a tether for all of us who had cut ties to land and loved ones. I felt as if we were held together by an invisible spiderweb dancing on top of the waves.

"*Zia, Zia, Zia,* this is *Alban, Alban, Alban,*" Pat radioed. "Do you receive me? Over."

"*Alban, Alban, Alban,* this is *Zia, Zia, Zia*. Yes, we receive you loud and clear. Over." It was John, the Colonel, replying, as always.

After giving the latitude and longitude of our position, Pat informed our friends that we were 406 miles from the Canary Islands. The Colonel told us that they were 85 miles north of us and a bit ahead. He then informed us they had bad news.

"Our generator broke down and we have no electricity. I repeat, we have no electricity. Our meat is thawing in our deep freeze, and we'll soon have no ice for our gin. We are quite despondent."

"We're sorry to hear that. All's well on *Alban*."

"This is Tom speaking. I'm getting smashed out of me mind. Michiko is in her green crocheted dress, eating cookies and getting sick."

"Tell Michiko we feel sorry for her. Yes, we feel sorry for her."

"Will do. We are signing off now," John said.

"Take care and happy sailing!"

Mike, Pat, and I stood quietly around the navigation table, soaking up the news. Without a generator they wouldn't be able to start their engine. They'd have to sail the entire way unless they could find a way to repair it. They were in a sorry fix, with food thawing in their freezer—and no ice for their gin!

"Daddy's pleasure yacht is a pleasure no more," Patrick said.

Mike wondered how they'd manage. With two thousand square feet of sail on her, she could beat us to Barbados. But if they hit the doldrums, they could drift for days. I thought about how desperate I had been to join *Zia* only a few days before; now I could not be gladder that I was on *Alban*.

We spoke with the *Tamure* fellows as well. Even though they left two days after us, they were catching up, which wasn't surprising, as they were serious and experienced sailors. Everyone wanted to win the "race" to Barbados.

We had been sailing for a few days, and life settled into a comfortable routine. We were adjusting to the rhythm of our watches and to each other. Patrick exuberantly took the sightings and charted our course. He sang often, out of pure joy. He also appeared to enjoy my presence on board.

However, hidden from the men, I felt a growing unease with Mike. Every morning, he wrote in his journal as did I. When he wrote, he seemed to be studying me. He was quiet and observant, and his gaze made me self-conscious. Mike had done nothing to prove my suspicions that he might be writing horrid things about me. That was just how fragile my self-esteem had become, especially having so recently spent all that time subjected to Olaf's criticism.

I concocted yet another miserable meal that night. Mike opened a bottle of red wine, which satisfied the lads a bit. I thought the men might consider firing me for substandard cuisine or attempting to starve them. Putting the plates down in front of each of the lads that night, I sheepishly announced, "I promise that when—*if* we arrive in Barbados, I'll take you out for an extravagant dinner in an elegant restaurant with a steel drum band, and we'll have a heck of a lot of fun."

### *Blessed*

DURING MY NIGHT WATCH ON our fifth day at sea, I did the unthinkable. Having gotten cold and feeling a bit sick, I snuck into my bed, midwatch, for half an hour.

I felt guilty and relieved when I climbed up the companionway to continue my watch. *Alban* was still sailing along with Harry at the wheel. Daylight had begun, and Mike and Pat were snug in their beds. The sea was racing after us in huge, even swells, dark gray with tiny whitecaps. The sky was overcast, but there was a welcome glow of soft pink and yellow on the eastern horizon.

I managed to write the following note in my journal.

*Night watch is bleak: no stars, no moon, only dark-gray and black clouds, a splatter of rain, and the sound of swooshing water on our hull as we sail fast over the sea. There are a few sparkles of phosphorescence in our wake. I'm cold and feel under the weather, so I sneak down into my quarter bed for half an hour, feeling guilty. Harry, our autopilot, is doing the work, but Patrick wants us to be watchful to make sure he keeps us on course. Harry's a contrary fellow and likes to wander. The lads are sound asleep. It can be miserable to be alone for hours in the dark before even a promise of light.*

Suddenly, out of the dimly lit cabin with a laugh and grin, Pat leapt into the cockpit and proclaimed, "Luv, you are *mad* to have come with us! I could be anybody! You have no idea who I am!"

"No kidding!" I said, knowing he was totally right. Carried away with the fun of teasing me, Patrick burst forth in his deep, beautiful voice:

*Mercy on us! We split! We split! Farewell my wife and children!*
*Now would I give a thousand furlongs of sea*
*for an acre of barren ground, long heath, brown furze, anything!*
*The wills above be done! But I would fain die a dry death!*

I clapped my hands. "What's that from?" I knew it was Shakespeare but wasn't sure which play.

"It's Gonzalo in *The Tempest*."

"Ha! You devil!"

Harry squeaked and moaned as we let him steer our fair sloop during the day. He sounded a bit disgruntled at his task. Harry was another companion and a rather unpredictable one, with an ornery nature. He made *Alban* a boat with five personalities on board.

As usual, we gathered around the chart table at 1:00 p.m. to call *Tamure* and *Zia*. We radioed *Tamure* first. Patrick reported that we were 541 miles from Las Palmas. *Tamure* told us they were about 100 miles behind us. We all wanted to hear how *Zia* was doing and if there had been any change in their situation.

"*Zia, Zia, Zia*, this is *Alban, Alban, Alban*. Do you hear me? Over."

"*Alban, Alban, Alban*, this is *Zia, Zia, Zia*. Roger. Over." I recognized the Colonel's voice.

After exchanging coordinates, the Colonel said, "We're rolling like hell, we've still no power for our engine, and there's no wind. You'll probably get to Barbados ahead of us. We're quite discouraged and unhappy. But we caught a fourteen-pound tuna today."

"That's magnificent! We have not caught a fish. I repeat, we have not caught a fish."

"We're sorry to hear that."

I tried to be funny and whispered, "Let me say we're dying of starvation and near mutiny!"

Patrick bristled. "No! We can't say *that* luv!" Later he told me this was because another boat, listening in, could catch the words "starvation" and "mutiny" and possibly send out a Mayday call to rescue us.

"We're signing off now," Patrick radioed. "Enjoy your dinner!"

It was a beautiful day—thick, blue sea, sparkling sunshine, a few clouds on the horizon. After lunch we put up the two headsails and took down the mainsail because the wind was blowing us too far north. The headsails looked so pretty, spreading their wings out on both sides of the sloop.

As we sailed along in the middle of the wide ocean, the immensity of the decision I had made became even more vividly clear to me. Despite my fears, I felt tiny, brave, and blessed, all at once, as if fairy dust had been sprinkled over my life. There was an element of disbelief and astounding magic that I was here on this little sloop, so far out in the Atlantic Ocean.

## *A Just in Case Letter*

When ocean sailing, there's plenty of time to consider your life, and that afternoon, my mind wandered between what was happening in the present moment to *Josefine*, to my parents in the Pacific Northwest, and to the artistic life I had been carving out for myself in New York City. All of this was bundled up into one single moment. Just in case my worst fears came to pass, and we didn't reach Barbados alive, I decided to write a "final" letter to my parents, which I recorded in my journal. Writing the letter somehow helped to ease my fear.

*Dearest Mother and Dad,*

*It is so incredibly beautiful. Blue-gray, pink-gray clouds tumble along the horizon, which defines a complete circle around our sloop. The sky is salmon orange and pale turquoise with a dark gray-blue wash above. The bright planet Venus has appeared, and we are sailing slightly in the wrong direction on calm waters.*

*I'm reading Churchill's "History of the English-Speaking Peoples." These lads have quite a good library on board* Alban. *Dad, I'm also reading Saki!*

*Being at sea is a commitment. There's no exit. For better or worse, we three are together in this adventure, for maybe a month. We are totally alone except for the sky, the sea, us little humans, and God, if you will. Light still lingers in the sky, so I will stay out here for a while, sipping rum!*

*I've been cooking most of the meals, doing the dishes and taking night watches from 4–8 a.m. I am super tired and drugged with the motion of the sea, but it is very beautiful. Tonight, I can SLEEP. No night watches. No shipping lanes. HOORAY! Patrick will set Harry, our automatic pilot, on course and wake up occasionally to make sure all is well. He's a conscientious skipper and sleeps lightly.*

*With oodles of love,*

*Tamar*

## *Prelude to the Storm*

THE MORNING OF OUR SEVENTH day at sea we were moving like lightning through sullen gray waters. There were banks of clouds all around with a few patches of blue, and occasionally the sun shone in silver-white sparkles on the sea. Thanks to Harry, all night we had been moving swiftly in the wrong direction, sometimes as far north as 320 degrees, which would have brought us to Miami and significantly off our desired course of south-southwest at 220 degrees. So, this morning, in wind and rain, with the sun glowing salmon red on the horizon, the lads had to maneuver the sails. I climbed out of the cabin to watch.

It was frightening to be on deck in heavy rain and wind with the boat tossing wildly in huge ocean waves. I struggled to keep my balance so as not to fall into the sea. None of us had paused to put on safety lines. Pat and Mike reefed the mainsail to half its normal height, folding the sail upon the boom and tying it securely so there would be less sail for the precarious wind to play with. Then they raised the headsails. One wrong move could have been disastrous.

Later that morning the weather became tranquil, and once again Pat and Mike raised the mainsail an impressive sixty feet and kept the headsails up. We were flying in the right direction like a bird. The morning clouds had disappeared, and it promised to be a splendid day.

To celebrate our first full week at sea and Mike and Pat's feat with the sails, I put some dark, sweet bread in the oven and served it freshly baked with butter and jam. It was delicious and the lads were happy.

At the appointed hour, the three of us crowded yet again around the chart table, eager to hear news from our friends. "*Zia* Time" was becoming the highlight of our days, a collective joy. Only Patrick spoke in the radio while Mike and I listened intently.

Poor *Zia*. They were now southeast of us. With all two thousand feet of sail up, they had traveled a meager ninety miles in the past twenty-four hours.

"You can have all our fuel if our paths converge or if you care to come by!" said John.

"Thanks, Colonel, that is very kind of you. I repeat, it's very kind of you. But we're bent on beating you to Barbados. Good luck. If we do meet up in this vast ocean, we'll gladly take your fuel."

After that, we radioed *Tamure*. Those lads were going like magic, averaging 140 miles a day. She was not far behind us and could possibly meet up with us somewhere in the next forty hours. That would be a delightful surprise!

Our *Alban* was much lazier than *Tamure*. We let Harry do much of the work, steering according to the wind, yet we had to keep an eye on him. He never seemed to obey his skipper and had a mind of his own as to which direction he wanted to go. At least for now, he continued sailing us west.

That evening, I wanted to treat the lads, as we were still celebrating our seventh day at sea. I spoiled them with a more abundant meal than I'd provided so far. After preparing hors d'oeuvres of liver pâté, sardines in tomato sauce, cheese, and crackers, which the lads ate in the cockpit while drinking beer, I made a baked mackerel casserole with rice. For dessert I opened a can of pudding and poured peaches over the servings. Mike brought out the rum to top it off. All was cozy and nice.

## *Storm*

Our celebration ended too soon. The harsh weather of the morning had been just a preview of a storm to come. After dinner, the winds picked up and raced head on into our bow, rushing at us from the southwest, just the way we wanted to go. *Alban* rolled mercilessly, her decks drenched in rain and seawater, as giant waves crashed over the sloop with a vengeance. We were bucking the sea like a wild horse.

Harry steered, but apparently, he wanted to go to Florida, so the compass had to be monitored every hour. None of us got much sleep that night.

A mountain of seawater broke over our deck as I stood barefoot on my early morning watch in the pounding rain. It was still dark. With my robe's huge hood drawn over my head, I gripped the wheel tightly, terrified.

I wished I were home by the fire with my parents, watching a storm rage outside while snuggling on the sofa. But I was here. I wanted to call Patrick. His steady presence would give me courage. However, I chose to see it through. *You can do this,* I told myself, and repeated it like a mantra.

At some point during the early morning, Patrick discovered that the bilge was full. He ordered Mike to pump, but Mike quickly gave up. I was mad and frightened that the boat would go under. We had a fight. "Mike, we could sink! Keep pumping!" I yelled from the cockpit. "No way. *You* pump!"

"I'm on watch. Patrick told you to pump."

"Fuck Patrick."

I was stunned by his blunt refusal to obey our skipper's orders.

Resuming my watch duty in the cockpit, I didn't pay attention to how the clash resolved between Patrick and Mike. This argument with Mike disturbed me. My discomfort over confrontation had reared its head again.

At the end of my watch, I climbed down the steep companionway, holding tightly to the wooden rails. The sea was crazy wild. Giant waves with curling whitecaps continued to rush straight towards us. *Alban* climbed up the waves and plunged down violently. She was holding her own in mountainous waves, while we humans struggled to keep our balance. I felt sick.

Once inside, I discovered that sometime during my watch, all the sugar had spilled on the floor. I rescued what could be salvaged and swept up the remainder to toss. The boat was rolling wildly from side to side, and the cabin floor was a mess. Before anyone could even make coffee, I would need to clean up the chaos in the galley. It took me two bloody hours to do the dishes from the night before. There were only seconds at a time when I was stable enough to wash or rinse a dish.

Later that morning, the wind howled more fiercely, the rain pounded the deck and porthole windows, and the sky became even darker. There was no way out. I did *not* want to be there, but there was no choice. We had to endure whatever the ocean tossed at us, challenging our wits, stamina, and courage.

Patrick stayed vigilant on deck, in the rain and wind, keeping constant watch over the sails and compass. Mike wrote in his journal at the cabin dining table, peacefully drinking tea. By evening I felt utterly rotten and told the fellows they must manage on their own for supper. I curled up on my wet bed and wanted to die.

As threatening as the storm seemed, I felt aligned with its force because of the storm that inhabited my psyche as well.

We only traveled seventy-eight miles that day.

## *Full Fury Storm*

We had a terrible night leading into our ninth day at sea. The storm continued to build into a fury. The boat rolled like a drunken ass, without navigation lights. All prior glory at sea was forgotten, and I wished I'd never come. *What* shit *this romance with the sea is. I'm just not made for it, and I will never, NEVER again brave the ocean.*

I was miserable from a stomachache, a soaking wet bunk, and sheer fright.

The sea crashed over the bow with greater force than ever, sending waterfalls of ocean down the companionway into the cabin. Patrick was on deck, frantically reefing the sails alone in the deluge. He called for help. "Mike! Get up here!"

"No!"

"Come up here now!"

"No!"

"Damn you!"

There was no time to argue. Patrick remained on deck and continued to fumble with the sails. He had to take them down quickly to reduce the risk that the wind would topple the vessel. He was barely able to see or stand with the heavy rain pounding his face and the waves crashing over the deck.

Patrick didn't ask me to help in this wildly unpredictable situation, and to be honest, I was relieved.

Neither Mike nor I knew how to sail, and if Pat drowned, we'd have been doomed. I wondered if Mike even knew how to make a Mayday call, the universal call for grave and imminent danger at sea. I sure didn't. But that terrible night, wracked with fear, I envisioned a nightmarish call: *"Mayday, Mayday, Mayday, this is* Alban, Alban, Alban. *We are somewhere in the Atlantic Ocean on our way to the West Indies. We lost our skipper overboard and don't know how to sail. We need immediate assistance..."*

It was still dark when Patrick finally came into the cabin, drenched to the bone. The tension could have been cut with a knife. He changed into dry clothes and crept into his sleeping bag, letting Harry handle *Alban* for the rest of the night. Neither Mike nor I said a word. I hugged my knees to my stomach in my wet sleeping bag, too sick to move. I don't think Mike ever emerged from his bed either. None of us were able to sleep with the storm continuing to batter the sloop.

Suddenly, there was a sharp crack, as if timbers had split. We sat up wide-eyed. Patrick leapt up the companionway.

"Our boom broke!"

He stayed on deck awhile, securing the boom until it could be fixed in the light of day. When dawn finally arrived, Patrick cut a strip from old sailcloth, which was stashed in the emergency cupboard, and he and Mike wound four layers tightly around the compromised boom.

The lads did a fine job of wrapping it up, and it was not doing that badly, but when we looked at the boom from the bow of the boat, it was easy to see it was bent. Lovely *Alban* seemed to valiantly accept her wound and bandaging, and on she sailed. At least we had an operating boom that appeared promising enough to get us across the ocean to

Barbados, where it could be repaired.

Patrick looked wretchedly tired that morning. He had certainly demonstrated his sailing experience in his handling of the storm. Knowing we were in Patrick's capable hands gave me a glimmer of confidence in the success of our voyage. But would we really make it? It's amazing how persistent fears can be.

None of us could escape our private dramas, no matter how far away from home we sailed. The storm reflected the turmoil I felt in my inner life—chaotic, unpredictable, wild, with no assurance of survival.

The storm shook me. This time, my vulnerability wasn't triggered by an egomaniacal, stoned captain, but by the force of nature. Before setting out, I knew intellectually that Mother Nature could influence our fates, but it was another thing altogether to experience her full power. My romantic, optimistic soul believed that nature would be kinder now that we had weathered her challenge. But nature isn't kind or unkind. She simply does her thing.

## *Sky Magician*

The next morning, the waves from the storm were still huge...and so on we struggled. There were some stormy nimbus clouds puffing along the horizon, but they were far away. The day looked promising.

This morning's sunrise was the most exquisite sunrise I had ever seen. The clouds raced into a myriad of animal forms: bright pink birds flew wildly above, changing into giraffes and running camels. Small, mauve-colored clouds marched heavily beneath, and lower yet, airy, dark-gray clouds moved swiftly to the north. Far above were brilliant patterns of yellow-gold clouds against a heavenly cerulean blue. And the sun rose red. There must have been a magician up there in the sky painting with pure light. These were the most transparent colors I'd ever seen, from eerie yellow to turquoise, blue, fire pink, and flaming orange. The sky was an ever-changing canvas of windswept, overlapping colors, utterly awe-inspiring.

As I watched the sunrise, I yearned for peace. At sea, set in the grand theater of nature's majesty, my inner turmoil felt like a dreamlike wisp, and I wished it could dissolve into thin air. Instead, tired in the aftermath of the storm, the burden of questions and deep longing returned to haunt me on this beautiful morning.

By late morning the winds had died down. Patrick took sightings of the noon sun with his sextant, calculating our position on the chart. We had traveled 980 miles from Gran Canaria!

## *Wind Gods*

"The wind gods are playing games with us mortals. There's not a blessed breath of the trades", Patrick lamented.

We all gathered around to listen as Patrick radioed *Tamure* and *Zia*. We were curious to hear whether our friends had suffered as brutally at the hands of the storm as we had. *Tamure* was about twenty miles south of us, and it sounded like they were next door. We could hear them clearer than ever before. They'd had a most uncomfortable night, but there was no damage. Everybody was in happy spirits because the sun was out.

Pat relayed that we had a miserable night with a cracked boom, and it was bandaged up in sailcloth. The *Tamure* lads were sorry to hear our story.

"Tim is singing ballads, invoking the trade winds, but so far it has come to naught," one of the *Tamure* fellows said.

"Yes, we hear Tim singing. May he be successful! Have a great sail!" Patrick said.

"Same to you. Good luck with your boom. Goodbye!"

We shook our heads, smiling. Those lads always seemed cheerful.

Next, we called *Zia* and told her our coordinates. The Colonel told us theirs and said she was about three hundred miles southeast of us, lagging even with her many sails. Patrick then spoke of our frantic night and our broken boom.

"We're sorry to hear of your misfortunes," the Colonel said. "We're all listening to the radio with very long faces. We passed a better night. We caught a big dolphin fish yesterday and are going to cook it for lunch."

"Our mouths are watering. I repeat, our mouths are watering. We've only caught one four-inch squid, which we tossed back to sea."

"Our condolences. We hope you have better luck next time." It wasn't likely. Mike just trailed a hook and a line behind the boat, hoping something edible would find its way to us.

We were so exhausted from the past few days, and relieved that we were alive, that we took life easy for the rest of the day. My bed and sleeping bag, given their proximity to the companionway, had gotten doused in seawater when the waves exploded over the deck. Mike helped me carry the mattress on deck and tie it down to dry in the wind and sun. All our sleeping bags needed airing, so *Alban* looked quite homey with our bedding drying on the boom.

## *Ravenous*

During my early morning watch in the dark of night, I once again saw the stars that had been hidden during the storm, and greeted my bewitching ghost lover, Max, who ruled the sky of my dreams. There he was, in the form of Orion, still drawing me towards him.

Finally, we caught the famed trade winds. Patrick had felt just the slightest shift in our sloop and popped up into the cockpit to check. He was right: a northeast wind was blowing us southwest, in the direction we wanted. It wasn't a strong wind, but it was promising. The gods were appeased.

The stars were out, and a sliver of silvery-blue light was on the eastern horizon, foretelling the arrival of the sun. The sea was a beautiful calm, with large, gentle swells. The mainsail was up, taut with the wind, her boom still wrapped in makeshift bandages that were remarkably effective.

Patrick and I stood together, gazing at the gift of another dawn, drinking in the moment. I studied Patrick in the soft light, hiding my attraction to him. He seemed a magical sea-god in my eyes. But I was glad when he broke the spell.

"Have a good morning, Tam. I'm going to catch another wink of sleep before the day begins." I watched him longingly as he descended into the cabin.

At 8:00 a.m. Patrick reappeared from the dim cabin, like a mole emerging from the dark earth, and deeming the coast clear, he leapt into the cockpit.

"Good morning, luv! What a lovely day for taking the sights with my sexy sextant in my hands and my logbook on the table... I am perfectly able!"

Sweet Patrick. His joy was like a kid's, and that is one of the reasons I adored him.

Patrick took over the wheel, and I went down to boil a pot of coffee. I then brought him a steaming hot cup laced with canned milk.

"Would you like fried eggs and bacon this morning, to celebrate making it through that storm? Or pancakes?"

"How about fried eggs *and* pancakes? I'm ravenous!"

After our hearty breakfast, Pat and I tackled the arduous task of cleaning up *Alban*. Our sloop was a huge mess from the night of the storm, and dishes were piled in the sink with open tin cans and bottles. We wiped the floor, washed the dishes, and put everything in its rightful place. Once again, *Alban* was shipshape.

"That's better," Mike said, looking up from his journal at the tidy cabin.

Patrick shrugged. He and I didn't vocalize our irritation that Mike hadn't helped. "Let's get out of here!" I said. I climbed into the open air with Pat following close on my tail. "What *is* it with Mike?"

"He owns the boat."

## *Au Naturel*

THE DAY WAS GLORIOUS AND very hot. After we finished cleaning and had feasted on a simple lunch in the cockpit, I descended into the cabin and stripped. "It's too hot to put on clothes!" I climbed up to the cockpit, and without further ado, I stretched my arms out to feel the sensual wind caress my body and loose hair, the sun's heat bathing my skin.

The men thought this was a hoot. Soon after they, too, appeared stark naked on deck, laughing, singing, and celebrating the freedom of the day. I was glad and lucky that we were all comfortable enough to be naked without the awkwardness of sexual tensions.

A little while later, Patrick exuberantly announced, "Bath time!" He grabbed a bucket, dipped it into the ocean, and poured the salty sea over his body from head to toe, lathering himself with a bar of saltwater soap. He looked hilarious, smothered in white foam. Scrubbing himself thoroughly and dancing in joy, he shouted, "Oh, the degrungeing of Patrick!" Then he dumped another bucket of salt water over his head and stood naked and clean on deck, soaking up the heat of the afternoon sun.

Patrick always seemed to be singing, and that afternoon, as he was drying in the sun, he sang:

*Yummy, yummy, yummy, I've got love in my tummy*
*And I feel like a-lovin' you...*
*Love, you're such a sweet thing, good enough to eat thing*
*And that's just a-what I'm gonna do*
*Ooh, love to hold ya*
*Ooh, love to kiss ya*
*Ooh, love I love it so*

I smiled at what I wanted to believe was his hidden declaration of love through choosing that silly popular song. Mike smiled, too, enjoying the childlike enthusiasm of his skipper.

Capable, romantic, and well-read, Patrick was rather a wizard aboard

*Alban*, calculating mysterious and esoteric knowledge of the heavenly bodies to guide our vessel safely across the sea. Even when he was not on watch duty, he was alert to every nuance of what was going on around us.

I imagined how different things could be between us if I were ready for a love grounded in reality! But my heart was locked tight. The only man I was willing to offer the key to was Max, who was beyond reach.

## *A Luckless Fish*

Later in the afternoon, as we were spurred on by gentle easterly winds at three knots, a flying fish was caught in our mainsail, and it fell to the deck, where it flapped about. The poor fish was in the wrong place at the wrong time, and the glow of its fins and eyes dimmed quickly as it died. Not wanting it to go to waste, I thanked the fish and took it to the galley, where I cleaned it and fried it in butter with lemon juice and dill for Patrick. It was only big enough for just a few bites.

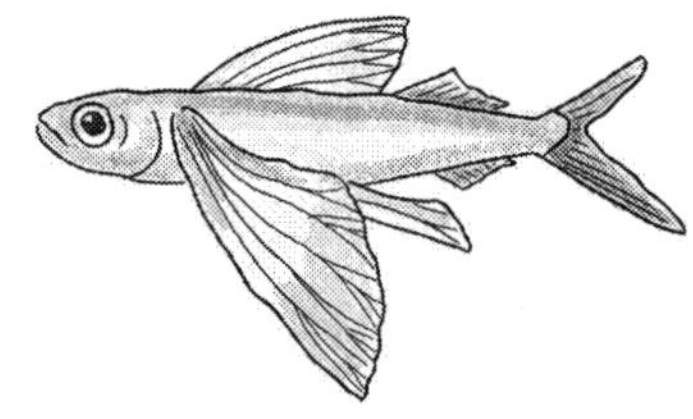

Cleaning this tiny luckless fish reminded me of a day long before, when my dad taught me how to clean a big salmon that I had caught in Gig Harbor as a child. It felt good to relive that experience. So many fond childhood memories had been eclipsed by the torment that my father later caused.

---

One evening, when Daddy came home from the mill, I raced up to him. "Daddy! I caught a big salmon! Come see!"

I dragged him to the deck, where the salmon was in a bucket of cold salt water.

"Tink, how did you manage that?"

"I went rowing and towed a long line behind with a hook and a flasher, and suddenly there was a yank on the line, and I had a fish! I rowed to shore and beached the dinghy. The fish was still on the line! I pulled it in by hand and whacked its head with a club and it died. I caught our dinner!"

Daddy wrapped his arms around me. "Well, Tink, you are a little fisherwoman. I'll fetch a knife and show you how to clean it."

We brought the salmon to the beach. Daddy taught me how to scrape the scales off the fish, so it wasn't slippery. Then he showed me where to plunge the knife in to open its white belly. All the guts oozed in deep purple, red, and pale yellow along the spine.

"Now Tink, scoop out all the innards and dump them into the bucket. We'll feed the fish when you are done." I plunged my hands into the slippery organs and pulled them out. I didn't mind getting my hands deep inside the fish.

"There's one more thing you need to do. You must run your thumbnail up the spine to break the membrane that protects the spinal fluid—like this." I enjoyed the bumpy feel of the vertebrae under my thumbnail and felt proud as punch that Daddy had entrusted me with a sharp knife.

"We can go fishing and catch many more salmon. I'll get you a real rod and line. Now let's cook this fish."

The evening was lovely. The slender moon hung like a jewel in the darkening sky, with the bright planet Venus almost touching her crescent. The air was translucent. Little specks of light pricked through the sky, and bit by bit, the starry universe shone in all its grandeur, as night came upon us.

Patrick decided to scrap night watch, as everything was going well, and we weren't anywhere near a shipping lane. It was a blessing to be able to sleep through the night. Harry was set, and we hung a lantern in our stern in case *Tamure* should approach us.

### *One Thousand Miles*

We had gone one thousand miles by our eleventh day, which called for another celebration. We were over a third of the way to Barbados, in the middle of nowhere. I planned to bake a raspberry cake later that morning out of Mother's Ready Flour, straight from the box.

As I sipped coffee, watching the golden sunrise, Patrick shouted, "Dolphins!" Mike abandoned his tea and journal ritual and rushed out to see the excitement. Dorsal fins sliced through the ocean waves, heading swiftly towards us. I dashed to the bow and lay on my stomach, gazing down at the exquisite creatures who by now were playing in the bow wave of our sloop.

There must have been twenty leaping out of the sea and coming down with exuberant belly flops, sending fountains of spray up from the sea. They swam on their backs, revealing their silvery-white bellies. They swam in pairs, and zigzagged briskly under the hull, their bodies sleek and perfectly adapted to life in the sea. I wondered how they found us, if they had heard our boat from miles away and hurried towards us to play. They swam alongside *Alban* and then, just as quickly as they appeared, they vanished.

What an auspicious way to celebrate our one thousand miles at sea.

Sadly, my attempt to bake a delicious celebration cake was not as successful. I burned it.

"Don't worry, Tamar," Mike said, with a wry smile. "I like charcoal!" I had to laugh.

Patrick took a few crunchy bites to indulge me, followed by a long sip of tea.

"I'm sorry! I really wanted it to be good!"

I spent a lot of time sitting on the edge of *Alban*, dangling my feet into the sea, reading a little of *A History of the English-Speaking Peoples* by Winston Churchill, and *The Short Stories of Saki*. Churchill's history was fascinating but slow reading. Saki's short fiction was pure entertainment, about children who outwitted and got the better of their elders. I knew that Saki was the pen name of H. H. Munro, as he was one of Dad's favorite authors. I had always been curious why Dad enjoyed Saki so much and had great fun reading his stories about the absurd situations stiff aunts and uncles got into when facing intelligent, mischievous, and, often, very naughty children.

One of the things I loved about Dad was that he had an inquiring mind, and he was fascinated by literature, history, art, dance, and music even though his days were spent as a businessman in the lumber industry.

When I wasn't gazing at the printed page, I simply watched the sky and sea as *Alban* climbed up and down the waves. There was no chance of boredom at sea. Every moment of the day and night presented its own magic.

Occasionally Mike joined me, sitting a respectful six feet away on a towel, naked and bent over a book, with his feet dipped into the sea. I would read a bit and gaze at the circle of ocean surrounding our tiny sloop. Nowhere on land could I see so clearly the perfect ball of the earth. We were in the middle of this circle, and the horizon, which was the circle's edge, kept moving with us, so we never reached the horizon while at sea.

Sometimes the clouds looked like a field of daisies, sometimes they became a swooping bird, and other times a carnival of animals chased each other's tails across the horizon, the huge blue dome arching like a cathedral over everything. The sky constantly inspired awe and wonder, putting my individual struggles into perspective. It reminded me that my life is only a tiny part of a much larger story unfolding.

The day was supremely lovely, and there was harmony on board. We each went about our tasks and pleasures and let the day unfold. *Alban* was cruising along with a mountainous sea racing behind, and the wind filled our sails. We were going in the right direction at an exhilarating speed.

## *Constellations*

That night, after Mike had gone to sleep, Patrick and I admired the skies. This was the first night he taught me about the stars and constellations.

"Look, luv. There's Betelgeuse looking orange in Orion's shoulder." Even with my naked eye I could see the star's orange tint. "And see there, Rigel is in Orion's foot, burning blue-white. Rigel is the brightest star in the constellation of Orion. Off to the side you see Sirius, the Dog Star. Look how bright it is! Sirius is the night sky's brightest star." Truly, the Dog Star was huge. "It's much larger than the sun and has a companion star, Sirius B, which is nicknamed the Pup. Can you see it?"

I nodded.

"Orion has a hunting companion up there in the sky," Patrick said, chuckling. "Orion is the dominant constellation in the northern hemisphere in winter. I use Betelgeuse, Rigel, and Sirius to take sightings of our position at night. I also use Cassiopeia's Chair, which looks like an upside-down W in the winter sky, and points to the North Star. Do you see it up there?" Patrick asked, pointing to the big M—the upside-down W—in the sky.

"Yes, I know Cassiopeia's Chair. It's visible in the winter sky over our house out west. I love seeing that big W sailing over our roof."

Patrick smiled and briefly put his arm around me, acknowledging my enthusiasm for the night sky. "Cassiopeia is the queen of the north. When the Big Dipper isn't visible above the horizon, sailors use Cassiopeia to locate the North Star."

Patrick continued his lesson, which I thoroughly enjoyed. "The North Star, or Polaris, is a favorite for navigation because it seems to hold a steady place in the heavens, while all the other stars seem to move across the sky. On occasion, I'll use Jupiter or Venus. Orion's very reliable." He laughed.

Of course, I knew Orion well, but I didn't know the names of the individual stars within it until Patrick instructed me. It's impossible not to see Orion when you live in the northern hemisphere, as the constellation is gigantic and easy to locate in the winter months. It's as easy to locate as the Big Dipper in summertime. I knew Patrick used stars to guide us, but it came as a surprise to learn that he specifically looked to the stars in Orion to find our position at sea. Patrick had no way of knowing how profound our shared fixation on Orion was or what it meant to me. Like so many other secrets I had kept, Max was locked away with them all.

That night, Patrick and I stood next to each other under a heaven of glittering stars, in awe of the mystery and stunning immensity of the universe. There's no better place to be swept off your feet in amazement at how tiny earth is than at sea in a small sailboat.

## *Endless Blue Sea*

Our twelfth day was another peaceful day. Patrick continued to calculate where we were and where we might be tomorrow and the day after tomorrow. The ocean was hypnotic, and I found myself getting sleepy in the day and tired at night. The days flowed into each other; it was hard to distinguish between them. There was always the rhythm of the sun rising and setting; the endless blue sea and more blue sea; gently rolling waves; white, puffy clouds, changing shape and color; and the approach of night. Moments slipped away, becoming the past, bringing in the present, which never stands still.

That night after supper there was occasional rain and splashes of sea at the door. We stayed belowdecks, sitting around the table under the dangling paraffin lamp that spun round and round. The can opener clanked in the sink, and the two-burner gimbaled stove swung back and forth on its two pivot points, always remaining level. We told each other stories over a bottle of wine. The lantern outside swayed in the cockpit. Harry was at the wheel. We were all cozy inside.

## *Halfway to Barbados*

There was not a cloud on the eastern horizon when I awoke at sunrise. In the west was an army of puffy little yellow-pink clouds. It was so warm at 6:30 a.m. that I didn't put on clothes. This was nothing new, as we had been sailing au naturel for the past three days.

Patrick came out on deck, naked as a Greek god, and announced with a grin, "At seven o'clock tonight we'll be halfway to Barbados."

I was impressed that he could predict the exact time.

That morning we caught a second flying fish in our mainsail, and it was Mike's turn to eat it. I wanted to try a different recipe, to see if I could make it tastier than Patrick's had been, so I dunked it in a raw egg;

shook it in a bag with flour; sprinkled on salt, pepper, and marjoram; and lightly fried it in oil. Sweat dripped down my forehead as I stood over the pan. It must have been close to hundred degrees Fahrenheit in the cabin, and we still had to go another six hundred miles farther south.

Over lunch in the cockpit, I presented Mike with the delicacy—a whole flying fish, the head still on. "Here you go, Mike. I hope it's edible."

He took a crunchy bite.

"Not bad."

## Zia *Time*

We all stood around the radio to contact our friends at 1:00 p.m. and discuss our locations and the events of the day. Both *Zia* and *Tamure* sounded very faint. The Colonel explained that *Zia* was having more problems. Their spinnaker was left out overnight and it was torn to shreds. They were all feeling a bit glum.

"We're sorry to hear that. Our boom is holding up. We may get to Barbados before you!"

"Indeed, you may. Our mainsail's up but we're only going three to four knots."

"We'll be halfway to Barbados tonight. We celebrated with banana pancakes this morning." I imagined the folks on *Zia* might celebrate in a grander style, with champagne and caviar and probably roasted pheasant with gravy and mousse au chocolat for dessert.

"That's mighty fine. We're signing off now. Have a great day."

"You, too, Colonel. Good luck!"

*Tamure* was south of us, but it wasn't much better there for the winds.

It was so hot, I wanted desperately to go swimming, but we were moving along at a steady clip and making such good time that it would have been foolish to jump overboard. We had been at sea for almost two weeks, and it was hard for me to imagine that we were 1,500 miles away from anything. As far as the eye could see, it was all ocean, with its unfathomable depth, filled with mysterious deep-sea creatures.

Later in the afternoon, there was a south-southwest wind blowing straight against us. Because of this, Patrick spent more time at the navigation table. At this time of year, Patrick informed me, the trade winds blow stronger and more steadily, so with any luck, a transatlantic journey should be a piece of cake. But one never knows what surprises nature has in store. "This isn't supposed to happen," he said. "The wind gods are expected to blow us straight to the West Indies." We were becalmed for a while, going nowhere in stultifying heat with our sails flapping loosely, and once again, I was tempted to jump in, but Patrick shook his head. "The wind can pick up at any moment, luv. You best stay on board."

It was an extremely peaceful and sleepy-hot day. I finished reading Saki. His short stories had a macabre twist to them and were entertaining, to say the least. They were fun to read, and I could understand why Dad enjoyed them.

Crossing the halfway point made me feel a bit more secure about our prospects of making it to our next port. At this turning point in the journey, I began to wonder how I would navigate my own life once we arrived in Barbados, and I returned to New York.

## *Mike Likes to Cook*

Mike was kind enough to cook dinner that night, and I was greatly relieved to be free of the task. Cooking every day was a drag. He disappeared into the galley, and I occasionally peered down, getting glimpses of him moving about like an animal, sniffing spices, stirring, chopping, and tasting with a spoon to his mouth and a smile of satisfaction.

After what seemed like hours, Mike called, "Dinner's ready!"

"Good! I'm starving," Pat said.

Mike passed up the plates heaped with fried eggs, sausage, curried rice, and peas—a noticeable difference from the scant portions I usually provided. Patrick smacked his thin lips at the bounty and dove into the meal like a hungry wolf. When I exclaimed how good it was, Mike paused his fork and looked at me intently.

"I like to cook. And you, Tamar?" I felt a blush rush to my cheeks.

"I spend hours in the kitchen at home," Mike said.

It was obvious to the guys that I didn't enjoy being stuck in the galley. And it had become blatantly apparent to them that I didn't know much about cooking. In exasperation, I blurted, "What do you want me to do? I'm doing my best!"

Patrick burst into a playful recitation from Samuel Taylor Coleridge's morbid *The Rime of the Ancient Mariner*; I guessed he did this to ease the tension.

*Her lips were red, her looks were free,*
*Her locks were yellow as gold.*
*Her skin was white as leprosy,*
*The Nightmare Life-in-Death was she,*
*Who thicks man's blood with cold.*

*Are those her ribs through which the sun*
*Did peer, as through a grate?*
*And is that woman all her crew?*
*Is that a Death? And are there two?*
*Is Death that woman's mate?*

I gazed at Patrick, giving him a big thank you with my eyes. Avoiding further conflict, I quickly jumped up. "Time to wash the dishes."

Patrick announced that we'd be having night watches as we were passing through the second shipping lane. It was paramount that we kept close watch while sailing through these zones on the marine charts.

## *Navigation*

PATRICK'S EXULTANT MORNING PROCLAMATION FILLED the air. "We've crossed the longitude of forty degrees and are rolling down the bosom of the West!" His exuberance was due to our having traveled eight degrees farther south from our starting point, Las Palmas, and a good many degrees farther west.

Zero degrees is where the equator lies, horizontally dividing the earth into two hemispheres, north and south. It is the widest part of the earth, closest to the sun, and is very hot. Latitude is a measurement of degrees north or south of the equator. Longitude is a vertical line defining any distance east or west of the prime meridian, which runs through Greenwich, England. The prime meridian divides the earth vertically into two hemispheres, east and west.

At the beginning of our voyage, we were about twenty-eight degrees north of the equator (New York is about forty degrees north of the equator) and sixteen degrees west of the prime meridian. To reach Barbados, we had to sail about fifteen degrees farther south, and about forty-four degrees west. This is a huge distance west, and a substantial distance south—almost to the equator.

As Patrick took sightings of Jupiter, he told me that it takes Jupiter twelve years to travel around the sun, whereas we all know that it takes Earth one year to spin around the sun. Jupiter is the largest planet in our solar system and far from the sun.

Life is full of learning, with many layers of meaning. Jupiter is one thing to scientists, another thing to astrologers, something else to sailors, and yet another thing to ordinary people gazing at the sky. In astrology, Jupiter represents luck, inspiration, life purpose, prosperity, the expansion of heart and mind, and joy. I wondered if Jupiter was shining on our tiny boat a ray of hope and good fortune on our passage.

*An unearthly shade of pink streaks the sky like lightning, reaching over the dome, then fades into dusty gray. The sea is an incredible plateau of calm, gently surging, with not even a whitecap. We are moving along at a fine rate with our sick boom and the wind in our headsail.*

*The sun finally comes—a slow fireball of red appearing out of the eastern sea. The cotton wisps overhead are intensely orange, and the sky is deepening into blue and turquoise. After some time, the sun breaks free of the sea, and everything's bathed in light and heat. We are swung into the rhythm of another day.*

We were over halfway to Barbados and were waiting again for the trade winds. There was even a little bird flying around our boat. Patrick thought it came from the West Indies. Perhaps it was a petrel or shearwater, ocean birds that rarely venture to land except to breed. These birds skim over the waves, picking up little fish that are near the surface. It was a welcome sight.

As usual, we radioed *Zia* a short time after noon and spoke to the chatty Colonel. He told us that Alan was cooking Yorkshire pudding that night, and they'd offer us a celebratory dinner when they passed us.

"We'll accept dinner," Patrick said. "Yes, we'll accept your dinner. It will be most welcome."

The Colonel said that Alan had got out his rifle and shot red balloons in the water. "We may see you in a day or so. We'll blow our whistle and pass you the Yorkshire pudding."

"Thank you. That would be lovely. Tell Alan we appreciate his generosity. Best of luck sailing. We're signing off now."

The idea of meeting *Zia* in the middle of the ocean tickled our fancy and we all wondered if it was possible.

It was uncanny how peaceful it was on the water. There was a spooky shadow moving not more than twenty feet from *Alban*, reminding us that nothing is peaceful for long. It was a shark, checking us out.

As we were barely moving this afternoon, Patrick decided to turn on the engine to help us along. This was the second time we had motored in fifteen days, and I was dreading it. *Thump, thump, thump, thump, thump,* the engine made itself known.

After supper, Patrick announced that we did a meager eighty miles that day.

I slept out on deck, as the cabin temperature reached ninety-seven degrees with the engine on. There was a gibbous moon, which would become fuller over the following week. It was so bright it kept me awake.

### *Shooting Cans*

I WONDER IF THE COLONEL'S story about Alan shooting balloons inspired Mike to get his pistol out. Without a single warning, he tossed tin cans overboard one morning, and began to shoot at them as they drifted away from our stern. The piercing crack of the gun was intensely startling and shattered the calm of the day. I freaked. I had no idea Mike had a loaded gun on board.

"Got it!" Mike yelled. All three of us watched the bobbing tin can sink. Then, *BAM!* Another. And yet another. Mike was a good shot.

After I learned about the gun's existence, life on board *Alban* suddenly became more tense and precarious for me. Mike certainly wouldn't shoot Patrick, his lifeline to safely cross the Atlantic, and I seriously doubted he'd shoot me. But accidents happen. The gun's presence added a new fear to my bag. I could tell Patrick was uneasy about the gun, too.

"Patrick? That was scary. What do you think?"

"Tam, don't worry. I'll ask him to take the bullets out and only load the gun when he wants to shoot cans."

Was it common practice for ocean sailing pleasure craft to keep a gun on board? I knew *Zia* had one, and it seemed as if no one was concerned. I tried to convince myself that it was perfectly reasonable, for any number of reasons.

I grew up thinking guns were for one of two things: hunting or killing each other.

Dad had plenty of guns on the wall of the master bedroom, and they never frightened me because I knew what they were for. He loved hunting ducks in eastern Washington, accompanied by his English setters, a few friends, and occasionally, Mother.

One Christmas Mother decorated our elegant eighteen-foot noble fir with hundreds of duck and pheasant feathers she had collected from the birds Dad brought home. No tinsel. No gleaming, colored glass balls or ornaments—just feathers and tiny white lights. I remember standing in the presence of this regal tree, with my arm around my mother.

## *Becalmed*

"*Tamure*, *Tamure*, *Tamure*, THIS IS *Alban*, *Alban*, *Alban*. Do you receive me? Over."

"*Alban*, *Alban*, *Alban*, this is *Tamure*, *Tamure*, *Tamure*. Yes, we receive you loud and clear. Over."

When we contacted our friends this afternoon, there wasn't a breath of wind. We learned that *Tamure* was becalmed, some eighty miles west of us. They had snuck ahead the past few days! Those intrepid New Zealand lads were out of petrol and, without wind, expected to be drifting for the next few days. For amusement, they put their dinghy overboard, tied to their sloop, so they could get off the boat and row a bit. They didn't seem discouraged at all. They seemed to find ways to keep happy in any situation.

Pat said that we had twenty hours of fuel left. We'd try to find them and join them in revelries. He thought we'd meet up in about seventeen hours.

"We're going nowhere, and any diversion would be welcome," one of the New Zealand lads said.

Finding *Tamure* would be like locating a needle in a haystack. On a small sloop, all you can see is a radius of three miles. Higher up on a large ship, there is more visibility. Patrick needed to be accurate to the decimal point in his calculations.

### *Patrick Makes a Move*

ALTHOUGH WE WANTED TO MEET our friends, Pat decided to wait awhile before turning on the engine, as it would add heat to an already unbearably hot afternoon.

"I want to swim. Is it okay?" I said.

His answer was totally different from the last time. "You can do anything you want, luv. I'll fetch the ladder."

So, cautiously, I slipped naked into the sea. Stark naked themselves, the lads looked on.

"You should try it! It's fantastic!" I beamed while treading water.

It was astonishing to swim in the middle of the ocean. It was not like swimming near shore, where I could see or feel the bottom. The depth and darkness of the ocean was palpable. The sea felt thick and dense around me. Down, down, and down the shafts of light penetrated to dark blue and finally vanished in utter darkness and cold, where fantastic and fearsome creatures swam about, luring prey into their gaping jaws with flashing lights on strange antennae. There's life on the ocean floor, where creatures live in perpetual darkness, tremendous pressure, and cold. This was creepy to consider, and awesome, too.

The Birth of Venus—*detail*

I climbed up the ladder, feeling like Venus on her gilded seashell. For an instant, I pictured myself as that mythical being. The moment vanished all too quickly. I shook my hair, as I returned to my ordinary self, and let the sun dry itchy salt on my skin.

I stretched my body and sat on the edge of *Alban,* near the bow, with a towel under my bum. Mike was in the cabin, reading or writing. Patrick was suddenly sitting beside me. He put his arm around me and leaned in to kiss me. He fondled my breasts softly. A shock of excitement went through me. He kissed my neck. I wanted to surrender to this kind, loving, joyful man, but fear took over again. I drew away and gently but firmly took hold of his hand.

"Please, Tamar."

"Not now, Pat. Mike may come up any minute."

"You're beautiful."

"Pat, I'm afraid. I like you very much, but—I don't know. It's too risky. And besides, we may fall into the sea!"

Patrick folded his hands in his lap. "All right, luv."

I looked longingly into his sea-blue eyes. "I'm sorry, Pat. Really, I am."

He sat silently beside me, soaking up the reality of my rejection. I felt desolate and lonely pushing his love away.

Eventually he stood, squeezed my shoulder briefly, and turned to resume his watch duty. I gazed at him fondly and felt very sad.

Late that afternoon the sea was as still as a silk bedspread. Patrick turned on the engine, now on a focused mission to find *Tamure*. He was quiet after our encounter, but he didn't sulk. He was a romantic soul, for sure, but sensible, too.

## *Rendezvous*

THE NEXT MORNING, ON OUR seventeenth day at sea, Patrick kept the engine on even though our cabin would become unbearably hot. We were too excited not to keep motoring. The engine had run all night, so if Patrick's calculations were accurate, we could find *Tamure* at some point that day.

The hours rolled by, and the sun beat mercilessly on the teak deck. The cabin was even more outrageously hot than outside, so I sat with a towel under my bare bum, dangling my feet into the sea and staring ahead at the shimmering water, hoping with my whole being that we'd catch sight of a sail.

Alas, we ran out of fuel, except for a reserve, after motoring for seventeen hours. Patrick calculated we were just fifteen miles north of *Tamure*'s latitude. Our sails flapped listlessly on a satin sea. Pat radioed *Tamure* to let them know we had run out of petrol and gave them our coordinates. There was no chance of meeting this fair sloop now. Just as I'd settled down to write about the awesome sea creatures that we had seen the day before while we were becalmed, Patrick yelled, "Get dressed. We have visitors!" I followed his gaze and caught sight of a sloop heading straight for us, not thirty yards away.

*Holy shit!* I dashed into the dim cabin and rummaged through my clothes, quickly slipping on my dress. Mike and Patrick put on shorts.

I could envision the crew of *Tamure*, for it was indeed our friends, passing the binoculars around, royally amused, as they spied us scrambling for clothing. I couldn't believe my eyes. Four men dressed as pirates, with colorful Tahitian cloth wrapped around their loins and holding cardboard sabers three feet long, whooped a war cry and stomped a wild dance, thrashing their weapons overhead, intent on raid and plunder. Without even rafting up, one pirate, who I knew was Tim, with a black patch over his eye and a red bandana wrapped around his head, jumped on board *Alban* and carried off his booty—me!

I threw my arms around his neck and kicked in mock protest, loving the playful attention and the feel of his strong arms cradling me. He then leapt onto *Tamure* and descended into the galley, triumphant in his conquest.

*A surprise party at sea*

I hugged my pirate prince and didn't want to be released. I fantasized about being held as a happy hostage. We would sail off to the wild blue yonder and live happily ever after, and *Alban* would never catch us, because the pirates of *Tamure* were better sailors. Instead, the men quickly tied the two boats together, and we had a party. Out came the gin and food to celebrate our good fortune.

The seven of us, squished together in the cockpit of *Tamure*, toasted to the fun and improbability of our gathering. We were high as kites and laughed at the creative plunder the New Zealanders had planned with the one charming Irishman.

We learned that *Tamure* had spotted us an hour before, when our mainsail shone in the sunlight. They had just enough petrol in reserve to

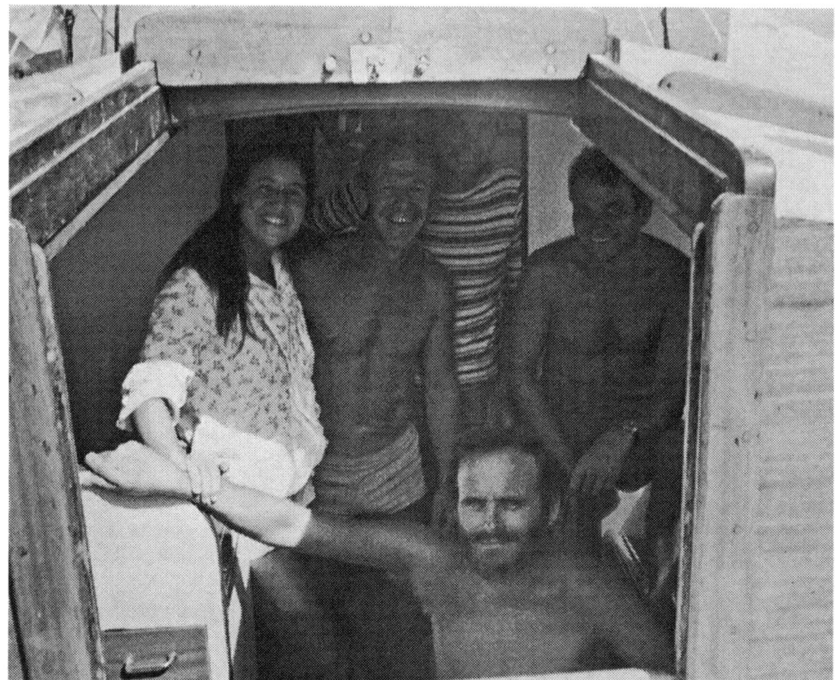

*Tamar with the* Tamure *fellows*

motor up to us. These valiant sailors, who were so intent upon beating us to the West Indies, had reversed their westward course to search for us.

Smack-dab in the middle of the ocean, 1,500 miles away from anything but endless ocean, our two tiny boats had found each other, thanks to the expertise of our skippers, a fair amount of luck, and the playful spirit of these sailors.

By midafternoon the *Tamure* crew had stripped off their loincloths and we all were running around naked and happy. We studied jellyfish, the shimmering blue-and-silver Portuguese men-of-war, which are poisonous and hurt like hell if you get brushed by a few of their endlessly long tentacles. We watched two dolphins play around our boats.

As the afternoon waned and there still was no breath of wind, we leapt into the smooth, bottomless sea, ignoring the threat of sharks. The water was warm, salty, and soft, caressing our bodies.

By evening, we got dressed for dinner. Mike invited the pirates to dine on *Alban,* and he kindly offered to cook the meal: mackerel casserole, peas, and potatoes—the latter gifted to us by the raiders, served with plenty of wine and beer. Mike and Pat were thrilled to receive the potatoes; when they left England, they had decided that neither of them liked potatoes, bread, or sugar. At sea, however, they discovered that these were the delicacies they most ardently craved.

We served dinner by candlelight, crowded around the wooden table in our cabin. Here we were, two little boats tied together in the vast ocean, at latitude 15°15′ north, longitude 42°47′ west. We drank and told stories late into the night. Mike was brilliant. He was our court jester, telling jokes and stories under the influence of abundant booze. To my delight, the party spirit loosened him up. He told one joke that sent us into peals of laughter.

"This fellow was preparing for the ministry. It was his first sermon, and he wanted to do it well. He was afraid, so he decided that instead of the usual water at the pulpit, he'd have a glass of gin. He let the reverend in on the secret because he wanted to do it right. After the sermon, the reverend approached him. 'Very good, son. Very good,' he said. 'But there are two things I want to say: First, you don't say "cheers" to the congregation every time you lift your water glass. Second, David didn't beat *the shit* out of Goliath.'"

Mike continued with a true story about the characters he grew up with on a farm in Ireland. When he was fourteen, there was an old bloke named Jim, who was about eighty-four, who lived on the farm and who hated anything modern. One day someone bought him a bright red tractor, and he spat at it. Mike convinced him to take a drive.

"An old woman stopped the tractor, waving her arms, and asked, 'Would ye help me a little?'

"'Sure, lady,' Jim replied. So old Jim got down and packed the woman next to him. About halfway to her destination, old Jim turned around and whispered loudly to the lady, 'Ye know. There is a little price for this trip.'

"The old woman asked, 'What is it?'

"Jim leaned over and whispered loudly, 'Only a wee bit o' tumblin' in the hay when we get there.'

"'Bless ye, I can't. It wouldn't be much fun for ye.'

"Then she added in a loud whisper, 'I'm seventy-two years old. I'm a little bit like custard pie—with the crust fallen in.'"

I was utterly astonished by the genial side of Mike that emerged that night—he had been so reserved up until this evening. Whether it was the wine, the company, or both, he amused us royally. This was the first time I felt a genuine fondness towards him.

After listening to Mike's entertaining stories and jokes and passing around the wine bottles, we climbed out to the cockpit. Tim played his guitar, and we sang ballads and sea shanties, our voices rising into the sparkling sky.

At 2:30 a.m., with the wind stirring, *Tamure* put up her sails and slipped away on a moonlit sea. We watched her little light slowly disappear. My heart whispered, *God bless you, Tamure.*

Then Pat, Mike, and I fell into our beds, tipsy and thoroughly satisfied with the events of the day.

When we woke the next morning, we were all too pooped to move and quite hungover, so we took our time greeting the day. After several cups of coffee—none of us felt like eating—we hoisted the sails and were moving westward at three knots. Eager to connect with *Tamure* and see how they were, Patrick radioed them midmorning. They were already forty-three miles ahead of us, on a roll to beat us to Barbados.

Mike offered to help clean up from the night before, while Pat manned the boat. From the cockpit, Patrick's lovely voice drifted into the cabin.

*We come on the sloop John B*
*My grandfather and me*
*Around Nassau town we did roam*
*Drinkin' all night*
*Got into a fight*
*Well, I feel so broke up*
*I wanna go home*

*So hoist up the John B's sail*
*See how the mainsail sets*
*Call for the captain ashore*
*Let me go home,*
*let me go home*
*I wanna go home*
*Well, I feel so broke up*
*I wanna go home.*

## *Flocks of Fish*

The sea was exploding with flying fish. We accidentally caught our third one in our sail, and it was my turn to eat it. Those poor fish. All three had leapt out of the sea, spreading their fins like gossamer wings to escape predators from below, only to be caught in our sails. Perhaps we should have tossed them back into the ocean while they had a chance of surviving. They were barely an appetizer and weren't even good to eat.

We had picked up the northeast trade winds, and they moved us along at five to six knots. It was great fun to be sailing again and to hear the rush of water over our hull. When we contacted our friends after lunch, we learned that *Tamure* was 64 miles ahead of us, and *Zia* was lagging far behind, being 210 miles southeast of us.

The Colonel, as usual, was more talkative than the fellows on *Tamure*. "We had quite a day since we last talked. This morning we caught a sturgeon and, when we cut it open, we found quite a variety of little fishes, sea plants, and tiny squid."

"We caught our third flying fish, and it was Tamar's turn to eat it."

"We send our condolences. It looks like we won't catch up with you to pass you our dinner. By the way, do you know that in Grenada there is a lavender hearse named *Bon Voyage*, and the mortuary will give you a free coffin if a relative of yours dies on Christmas Day?"

We all looked at each other, our eyebrows raised in a question, wondering what he was talking about. "You're kidding!" I said. Patrick shushed me with a finger to his mouth.

"Well, no, I don't believe we've heard of that," he said.

## *Cotton Candy World*

That afternoon while *Alban* was flying like a dream, I sat near the bow with a book open on my bare thighs and my feet dangling over the side of the boat. I stared at the printed page, trying to become a bit more worldly by continuing to study Churchill's *A History of the English-Speaking Peoples: The Birth of Britain*, published in 1956.

History had never interested me. It seemed like such a dry, dead subject. I was much too internal and dreamy to concern myself with politics. Yet I knew that I was sorely lacking in the history of Western civilization, and I barely kept up with current events. I felt I needed to prove to the others, and to myself, that I wasn't as dumb as I appeared—that I had an ounce of interest in learning. And in fact, it *was* interesting!

When my mind couldn't absorb another fact about kings or wars, and it became too hot on deck to enjoy the sights of ocean waves and sky, I slipped back down to the interior of *Alban* for a break. Mike was at the table, writing in his journal over a cup of tea. It was here that I took copious notes in my journal about what I'd just read, as if I was in a college course, hoping that some facts would lodge in my brain and give me a better sense of our world.

Mike had observed what I'd been reading. He calmly put down his pen and, for some reason, was compelled to say, "You've been protected in schools all your life. You've never thought, and you know nothing about the world or wars. You, with your boarding school education, think everything's peaches and cream."

I stared back at him, trying to collect myself.

"I know. I'm trying. That's why I'm reading Churchill's book."

"Good for you. It looks like it's shattering your cotton candy world a bit. But reading is not going to make a difference. Life is what it's about. Raw, brutal survival. You live in a world of ease, with your education and money. You've never had to struggle for anything. I've had to work my ass off to buy this boat."

"How do you know I've never struggled? You're not inside my head. You've not the foggiest notion what I suffer."

"Thank God. I only know how you behave, and it's appalling."

"What do you want me to do? Jump off the boat?"

"Listen, my dear. Just get the hell home when we arrive in Barbados."

A dark cloud swept over me. So, Mike *had* been sizing me up. Why must these random people I meet along the way feel entitled to throw harsh criticisms at me and my life?

Mike took a long sip of his tea, staring straight at me without a glimmer of friendliness. Then he picked up his pen and began to write in his journal.

I escaped up the ladder to the cockpit, where Pat was on watch. I stood quietly beside him, with tears welling up in my eyes.

"What's wrong? You look unhappy."

"Mike just tore me to shreds. He hates me!"

"Oh Tam, that's not true."

"Yes, it is. I need to be alone."

I wriggled out of his attempt to console me and went to the bow so I could think.

Lying on my stomach as *Alban* sliced through the cerulean waves, with the sun beating on my bare back, I let the motion of the sea calm my nerves. Staring into the unfathomable blue of the ocean, I reflected that jumping off the boat would be a dramatic way to end my life, but I didn't want to do that. What is life if not a journey—for better, for worse?

Both Olaf and Mike had criticized my spoiled life, harping on the fact that I could do anything I wanted, and all I was doing was drifting aimlessly with no purpose, no goals, no plans for my future. I accepted the notion that I was spoiled and privileged. But how were the lives of Olaf and Mike more meaningful than mine? And how could they so quickly assume that privilege meant no struggle or suffering? My self-worth was like thin glass against the criticisms each of them had hurled at me. Miss Witherspoon, my father, Olaf, and Mike were teamed up like a chorus in a Greek tragedy, chanting relentlessly in the back of mind.

I desperately wanted to be at peace with myself and the world, but at that moment, achieving that goal felt an impossibly long way off. I knew that I had to find my way through the chaos in my soul. I wanted to become a truly loving, confident, and happy person. After all, I was once, before...everything.

For now, I would do what I always did: I would act like everything was normal and fine. I was good at that. It was exactly what Dad and I had done years before when I was home from college, pretending that nothing had happened between us. All was groovy! Even when it wasn't.

I didn't want this *Alban* adventure to turn into a sorrowful journey like I had experienced on *Josefine*, even if I had to lie to myself about it. With a sigh, I let my body soak up the motion of *Alban* carrying us forward. I felt more grounded and ready to greet my companions, appreciating the beauty of the moment and of the afternoon.

"Hey, guys, would you like a cup of tea?"

"That would be lovely, luv. And how about some biscuits?"

"Sure thing!"

I disappeared into the galley, where I put on clothes before indulging the men with English tea. After Mike's caustic remarks, I wanted to restore some normalcy and calm, to make things seem nice. After all, we were living in tight quarters. People are complex beings. Hardly anyone is completely evil or completely good. Mike may have criticized me in an upsetting way, but he was kind to me, too.

That night, Patrick offered to cook. He made mashed potatoes laced with canned milk and butter, then regaled us with amusing stories about his acting career into the evening.

As the sun set, the gibbous moon appeared silken yellow, high in the sky behind us, spreading a golden path across the even, rolling waves of a breathing sea. We were all in the cockpit after dinner, looking up at the sky.

We had a mellow evening. The sun sank, fire red, into the sea, and slowly the stars pricked the fading blue-gray sky. I hoped that the sun's disappearance into his wet bed, heralding another night, would wash away the sting of Mike's cruel remarks. I excused myself and gathered the empty dishes to tidy up the galley before climbing into my sleeping bag and closing my eyes. It had been a challenging day, and I was exhausted.

## *Bioluminescence*

Mike tapped me on my shoulder and said, "Wake up! It's your turn at the wheel." It's hard to be abruptly woken from the land of dreams and be required to immediately operate fully awake. I sat up and rubbed my eyes, struggling to get my bearings.

I could see up the companionway that it was still deepest night, and I could hear the ocean sloshing past *Alban*'s wooden hull. The sky was sprinkled in billions of twinkling stars.

I quietly washed my face, brushed my hair, and put on the Arabian robe I had come to love. I climbed out into the night, scanned the sea for lights, checked the compass, and made sure that Harry was steering on course. All was in order, and it was a glorious night.

The moon was out. The wind was warm. Orion was striding across the sky followed by Sirius, the Dog Star. Cassiopeia's Chair was hidden in thin layers of windswept clouds.

It was in the quietest times when thoughts came out of their hiding places and gathered to swirl in my mind: my sister's death, my parents in their Chambers Creek home, my father's secret letters, silences, words never spoken, questions never asked, Max, Arthur, dance, Olaf, Mike, Patrick, Irene. Here I was, sailing upon the light-splattered waves of the Atlantic, with a soft trail of bioluminescence spreading out behind us—a lost soul trying hard to find my place in the world. In those moments I asked, *What am I doing? Who am I? Why am I here?*

### *Mauve Factor, Dad Again!*

Mike's criticism of me the day before had touched a deep nerve. When criticized, I felt as if I deserved it because I was inherently flawed. Dad's preoccupation with my genetic faults had completely hijacked my confidence. After Naomi died, he became obsessed with the idea that she suffered from schizophrenia and worried that Mark and I also carried the illness. Dad did massive amounts of research and came across the work of Dr. Humphry Osmond at Princeton University, who discovered that something he called the "mauve factor" often appeared in the urine of alcoholic and schizophrenic patients. Dad insisted I get tested for this mauve factor to see if I carried the dreaded disease, and he hounded me about it for years.

For a long time, I refused. What if I had this so-called mauve factor? Even if I had no signs of being schizophrenic, my father would become even more invasive in my life, relentlessly warning me that I'd have a sick child, and insisting I take massive doses of niacin, which Dr. Osmond believed helped schizophrenic patients. I didn't want Dad's notions to have that power over me. His ideas had already affected me enough. However, I finally caved and got tested in 1967, the year before I set sail.

### Tested for Schizophrenia

Fuming with anger and fear, I took the train to Princeton, where Dr. Osmond had his research lab in a beautiful old stone building on campus. After I'd waited a bit, wondering why I had given in to my father, a lab technician gave me a little plastic cup and sent me to the ladies' room to gather my pee.

This was the moment of truth. My body wouldn't lie.

After I handed the cup back to the technician, Dr. Osmond gave me a psychiatric written test while we waited for the results. One question stood out: *Do straight edges of objects ever appear curved or distorted to you?*

"Of course! I'm an artist!" I knew this was not the answer he was looking for, but I couldn't resist having a bit of fun.

Finally, the doctor revealed his findings. "You don't have the mauve factor in your urine."

*Oh my God, thank heavens!* My heart soared with relief.

He said that my written exam showed that I had a flexible mind and that I was fine. But, if ever I had a schizophrenic child, I'd know where to come for help.

Even though I had received good news, I was so furious with Dad for putting this worry in my mind that I refused to tell him the results. This was my one and only tiny bit of rebellion I staged for all the hurt he had showered on my young adult soul. I tenaciously held on to my privacy, knowing he'd be frustrated and even angry. A week after the test, I received a letter, in Dad's signature blue envelope, which I opened with curiosity because I had at last defied him.

*Dearest Tink,*

*I don't think it is quite fair of you to be so guarded to me about the results of your tests you took at Princeton. You remember that I gave you the results of my tests. Why the big secret?*

But this letter had new, devastating warnings, as though he was punishing me for keeping the test results from him.

*All the evidence that I have indicates that you can be normal at 15, 25, 35 and at 45 and finally succumb at 50! There is no conceivable answer to this peculiar prognosis of this disease. On this basis it is quite clear that even though you are completely normal today you might deteriorate next month or next year or in 10 years...*

So, I wasn't clear! At any time, I could succumb to the disease that dad believed haunted our family genetics for generations. As I held this letter in my hand, I sank into a deep funk. Dad still had the upper hand. I was furious. Why couldn't he leave me alone?

Who would want to marry a woman whose family tree was riddled with "sick" people, and who could become ill at any moment? If I ever found the courage to let someone into my heart, I was afraid they'd run away after learning the "truth."

## *Circling the Moon*

Patrick popped out of the cabin and burst into a sea shanty. His deep, jolly voice infused me with much needed joy, and I joined in on the chorus. We sang at the top of our lungs, which brought Mike bleary-eyed out on deck.

*Oh, the times were hard and the wages low.*
*Leave her, Johnny, leave her.*
*And the grub was bad, and the gales did blow,*
*And it's time for us to leave her.*

*Leave her, Johnny, leave her.*
*Oh, leave her, Johnny, leave her.*
*For the voyage is done and the winds don't blow,*
*And it's time for us to leave her.*

The days quickly became so hot that it was difficult to get through them. It was too unbearable and bright to be outside, where the tropical sun beat mercilessly down on the teak deck, so I confined myself to the sweltering cabin, lying on my bunk. Day after day, Mike sat at the table, watching me off and on while he wrote in his journal. It was very uncomfortable.

Lazily daydreaming, I realized that in December 1968, precisely when I was hunting for a boat to take me across the ocean, three astronauts were circling the moon in the *Apollo 8* spacecraft. They beamed images of our planet back to earth. It was humanity's first glimpse of earth from outer space, inspiring awe at the stunning blue ball that is our home.

The perspective the astronauts gave to us through those photographs, and that the wide ocean had been giving to me, caused me to wonder about our purpose on earth. Is it simply to recognize the miracle that we are here, that we can move, breathe, and talk? Is our purpose to take care of our precious home? Humans are on a fascinating journey on this jewel of a planet, and there is no telling how our collective story will evolve. But, on that hot day, surrounded by water, I had no answers.

## *A Spectacular Sight*

The day was listless and scalding. I prepared a lunch of tuna fish, hard-boiled eggs, slices of cheese with crackers, and a bean salad. The fellows drank cold beer; all I craved was water. After lunch I served tea, and we spoke to our friends on the other boats over the radio. *Tamure* was racing ahead of us. *Zia* was well behind. She'd never catch up unless some unforeseen event occurred.

At 3:46 p.m. Patrick called us on deck in great elation. "Look! On the horizon! There are four symmetrical poles on our port side. I declare it's a ship."

Mike perked up. "Give me the glasses... What the...?" He handed the binoculars back to Patrick.

"By Christ, that is a sail!"

Patrick calculated that we were on converging courses, both of us under full sail.

Hours later, as the blazing tropical sun sank low over the horizon, Patrick shouted, "Get dressed!" Both Mike and I knew that Patrick meant the ship was approaching. It was stifling hot, and we'd all gotten used to going about our days naked. We threw clothes on and scampered up the companionway into the cockpit. The huge vessel that we'd spotted earlier was only about twenty-five yards away from us now. She dwarfed our little sloop. She was a four-masted tall ship, in full glory with all nineteen sails taut in the wind.

We studied her through our binoculars, giving each other turns. There were many fellows on board dressed in white shorts and shirts, standing at attention. Others, in long white pants, wearing navy jackets and white flat caps were lined up along the bulwark. Two guys were lying in the bow net, which is attached to the bowsprit in larger boats.

The ship then turned so she was parallel to us. I was so ecstatic I couldn't believe my eyes. Through binoculars, Patrick could see her name, *Juan Sebastián de Elcano*. Too awestruck to even fetch my camera, I tried furiously to sketch her in my journal.

*Tall ship* Juan Sebastián de Elcano

Pat narrated what he saw: her crew, like ants, scurried to take down their topsails, adjusting her direction to the southwest after sailing past us not twenty-five yards away. We waved wildly at the ship as it sailed away. Slowly she disappeared into the setting sun, dusty orange sails rising out of a Prussian-blue sea against a brilliant red-orange sky.

Encountering *Juan Sebastián de Elcano* was truly astonishing luck. We had to be exactly at the right place at the right time on the vast ocean to have crossed paths. We guessed the captain went out of his way to peek at us. She had come straight towards us, then turned around and traced her journey back west.

Over dinner—a pot of potatoes smothered in butter, a can of chicken legs served with canned beans, and a little swig of aquavit to celebrate the occasion—we mulled over the fantastical visitation.

The gibbous waxing moon, rising behind us, was almost full. A long, hot, and satisfying day was over.

## *Closer and Closer*

Near the end of my watch the next morning, soft, gentle clouds were again a parade of fanciful animals. A fragment of the sky turned from a platinum yellow into an eerie green. Slowly the clouds caught fire. On the far side of the dome above the western horizon rested downy cloud pillows veiled in a soft bed of lavender, still in the netherworld of dream. Jupiter was the only planet left in the sky.

As the sun rose, the clouds spun into a most stupendous white, and the sky was a deepening blue. The cloud animals broke into a gallop and became white and light gray. Gold was brimming around the sun and an otherworldly fluorescent green was on the horizon.

We were nearing the end of our voyage, and so, too, the rhythm of life we'd settled into together aboard *Alban*. I felt like we'd been naked children in the Garden of Eden. People going about their lives, singing, dancing, working, crying—all of life outside this moment seemed just a dream.

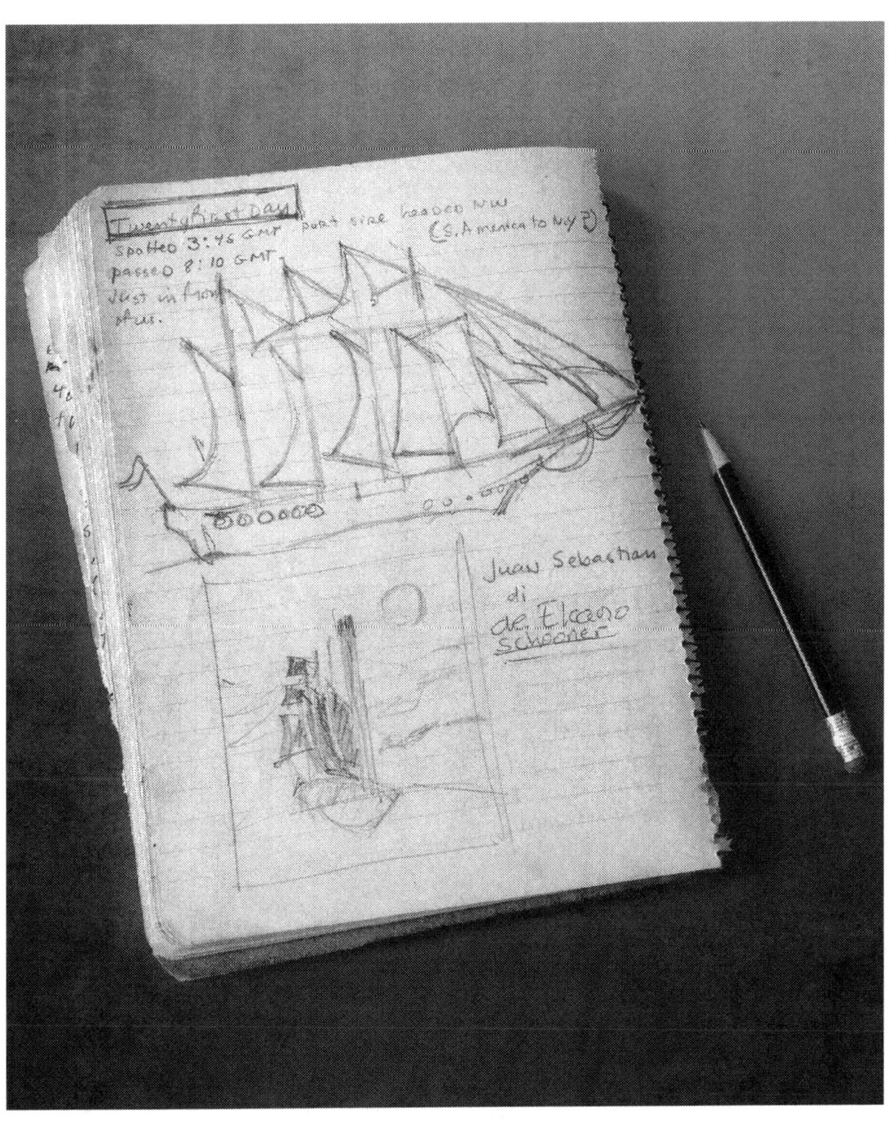
Twenty First Day
Spotted 3:45 GMT
passed 8:10 GMT
Just in front
port side headed NW
(S. America to NY?)
Juan Sebastian
di
de Elcano
schooner

"Coffee, luv?"

"Yes, please!"

Pat went into the cabin and joined me in the cockpit after handing me a mug of coffee with canned milk. Standing side by side, sipping our coffee, he burst into a folk song. "The Sloop John B" had become a favorite of ours on the boat. At top of our lungs, we sang:

*First mate, he got drunk*
*And broke in the captain's trunk*
*Constable had to come and take him away*
*Sheriff John Stone*
*Why don't you leave me alone?*
*Well, I feel so broke up*
*I wanna go home*

*So hoist up the John B's sail*
*See how the mainsail sets*
*Call for the captain ashore*
*Let me go home, let me go home*
*I feel so broke up*
*I wanna go home*

I didn't want to go home, not really. Not if home meant to Tacoma and my parents. If home meant New York City, then yes. I wanted to continue to dance, explore art, and connect with a few friends—most of all, Max. I was sure that a healing journey lay ahead.

I was between two worlds—the open sea and life on land. Yet it wasn't possible to stay in this in-between place. I understood that, in life, one chapter ends, and another begins. It had been a glorious, fun adventure despite some drama—an experience to treasure forever. Our life on the boat was a minuscule world within the wider world. It would take some adjusting to step out of this reality and expand my life again.

As we approached the West Indies—a series of exotic islands strung out like jewels in the tropical ocean—I could imagine the steel drum music and the dancing feet of the islanders. A whole new world was opening, like a curtain rising on the stage of a theater, yet I was already feeling sad at the thought of leaving the sea behind.

### *Splish Splash*

As a cloud darkened the sky that afternoon, we watched it drop heavy rain a mile or so from us. Pat could tell it was coming towards us and saw one thing: shower time. We rushed to place several buckets on deck to catch the rain. All three of us fetched our bars of soap and towels from the cabin, and then stood naked on deck, eagerly waiting for the rain.

"Here it comes!"

I lifted my face and closed my eyes to feel the downpour pummel my skin, and I opened my mouth wide to taste it. I lathered my hair with soap and scrubbed furiously to try and beat the end of the squall. We had time to wash ourselves completely. Afterwards we were squeaky clean and shouting for joy. I wrapped my towel around me, and suddenly an old song from the 1950s popped into my head and I sang it with gusto, dancing as Pat laughed and joined in on the fun. Mike thoroughly enjoyed our silliness as we pranced about.

*Splish splash, I was taking a bath*
*Long about a Saturday night, yeah*
*Rub dub, just relaxing in the tub*
*Thinkin' everything was alright*
*Well, I stepped out the tub, put my feet on the floor*
*I wrapped the towel around me, and I opened the door,*
*and then a splish, splash, I jumped back in the bath*
*Well, how was I to know there was a party going on?*

The rainstorm had left the seas in turmoil, and it was impossible to work in the galley that night. Water poured down the companionway, and the boat rolled madly. I was attempting to prepare dinner using knives, a can opener, the pot, and a frying pan—all the while trying to drink a glass of wine, which was pure madness.

Later that night, I sat naked on deck, with a full belly and silken clean hair, and enjoyed the confused, stormy sky. I peeked down into the cabin, and saw Patrick reclining naked in his berth, grinning like a Cheshire cat, tapping his fingers on his chest. He was one happy sailor.

Our sails luffed. It looked as if we'd be becalmed, but the sea was surging black and pushing us along. There was a contented hush on board.

## *Overwhelming Splendor*

THE FEBRUARY FULL MOON WAS setting on the western horizon when it was still dark outside, just as the sun was preparing to roll out of bed in the east. Patrick called to me to come up and see the bright moon and morning sunrise. All my life I'd thrilled to the magic of the full moon. In my mind's eye, I could easily call up the image of the huge, orange moon rising over Gig Harbor, rolling out a glittering path on the rumpled, dark sea.

In coastal waters one becomes acutely aware of the moon's influence on the tides. In the Pacific Northwest, the sea can rise ten to twelve vertical feet in one day. In the open ocean, water bulges out towards the moon, but it is impossible to see this effect because there is no land visible to delineate the movement from high to low water.

"Not another sunrise!" I buried my face in my sleeping bag. "My brain can't contain another image. I'm full up. This is overdose!" Even splendor is overwhelming when there's just too much of it.

"Well, luv, it's a new day. Come up and sing with me." He was in high spirits.

"What the hell... All right."

I rubbed my eyes, brushed my clean hair, put a pot of coffee on, and climbed out into the dawn. Patrick welcomed the day with a bawdy song. To the tune of "The Twelve Days of Christmas," he sang:

*On the first day of Christmas, I took to bed with me*
*My Lord Montague of Bulee.*
*On the second day of Christmas, I took to bed with me*
*Two virgin maids and my Lord Montague of Bulee.*
*On the third day of Christmas, I took to bed with me*
*Three Boy Scouts, two virgin maids,*
*and my Lord Montague of Bulee...*

I didn't like this song one bit. The words were too indecent even for my free-spirited brain, especially at the crack of dawn. "Why did you get me up for this?" Pat seemed chagrined that I was such a prude.

"Okay, luv, here's another one you might like," and, in his deep baritone, he began to sing a lovely West Indian song. I knew this sweet love song and joined in, thoroughly enjoying the shift in mood.

*Yellow bird, up high in banana tree*
*Yellow bird, you sit all alone like me*
*Did your lady friend leave her nest again?*
*That is very sad, makes me feel so bad*
*You can fly away, in the sky away*
*You're more lucky than me.*

By noon we were ripping along at six to seven knots. It was exhilarating. *Alban* was galloping like a mare. The famed trade winds were blowing from the north-northeast. We traveled 146 miles and only had 464 more to Barbados. We were in high spirits when we called *Zia,* but the Colonel said they weren't doing so well. They were over two hundred miles behind us, and it would be nearly impossible to catch up. *Tamure,* on the other hand, was about two days ahead of us, consistently logging more mileage than *Alban*, at an average of 168 miles a day. To top it off, these fearless sailors caught an eighteen-pound dolphin fish! Nothing had found its way to our hook trailing behind *Alban*.

### *A Green Streak*

After supper we gathered around the marine radio and to while away the time, we listened to doleful hymns and Swedish sermons in the bright moonlight. Suddenly, there was a flash of light in the sky and a big crashing sound. The whole cabin was lit up for an instant.

Pat quickly leapt into action and switched off the radio. Then all three of us scrambled up to the cockpit just in time to see the tail end of a brilliant arc of green fire swoop across the sky.

"Christ! What was that? A comet? A shooting star?" I said.

Comets and shooting stars don't make noise. Patrick thought there was some electrical link between whatever it was that raced across the night sky and our radio, and that the radio had caused the noise. We waited to see if there was any more activity that would reveal something about what we had seen, but all was silent, except for the swoosh of water passing over our swiftly moving hull. Later I enjoyed imagining that, perhaps, the little prince from Saint-Exupéry's children's story had come to greet us.

### *Too Many Voices*

All day the sky looked stormy and foreboding, with a green haze on the horizon. Despite this, it was a sleepy, dreamy, and peaceful day on *Alban*. I had learned how to stay out of the line of fire with Mike. This way, I could focus on enjoying our journey.

As our lovely queen, *Alban*, graciously carried us over the sea, and the three of us went about our lives in the tiny space, my companions still had no idea what churned around in my head and heart as they carried me across the ocean.

We were approaching the end of our ocean voyage, and I was struggling with what was next for me. What was I going to do? And what would it be like to return to the noise and chaos of a teeming asphalt jungle? I had left that world an eternity ago. I felt a sense of belonging at sea, just as I always had felt at home in the Pacific Northwest.

While I had carved out an exhilarating life in NYC, I never intended for it to become my permanent home. For the time being though, I knew the city offered the creative resources I needed to heal and grow.

## *Almost There*

Exploring the west indies before returning would be a welcome distraction. The closer we got to Barbados, the more I wanted to hang out in those idyllic islands before returning to my life in New York City.

Patrick could hardly believe our speed. "Whooooo-Hoooo-Hooo! We're barreling down on Barbados with only two hundred eighty-five miles to go!" Mike looked up and laughed. We were ripping along in mountains of blue sea that curled white behind us as the waves broke and rushed towards us. I felt great joy and admired our good skipper immensely.

Over the radio, *Zia* came in very faintly. She was 390 miles behind us, and everyone on board was in low spirits. *Tamure* was 150 miles ahead, also going six knots. With luck, she'd be in Barbados the following night. Patrick thought that we'd be slipping around the southeast corner of Barbados just as the moon was rising on the day after tomorrow.

We also picked up *Josefine*. I was surprised she was close by, and only now nearing Barbados, because she had left two weeks ahead of us. I didn't want to engage with her.

We began to see ocean birds soaring over the waves—a sure sign we were near land and approaching the end of our voyage. To our delight, more dolphins appeared, swimming in perfect harmony, crisscrossing each other at our bow.

Flying fish showed up in flocks, spreading out their fins like wings to soar over the waves. The air felt denser due to the tropical heat and moisture.

## *Only a Dream*

ON OUR TWENTY-SIXTH DAY AT sea Mike woke me at midnight. I was in the middle of an intense dream.

"Time to get up!" he said, shaking me gently. "It's clear as a bell."

I yawned and stretched, grappling with memories of my dream, and slipped into my hooded robe, as it was still cool during the night despite the intense heat of the days. When I stepped into the cockpit, a sudden deluge of water poured out of the sky.

"Ack! It's raining! Didn't you say that the sky was clear, Mike?" There was no response—Mike was already in la-la land.

Just as quickly as it had arrived, the rain stopped, and all was clear again as though it had come from a single cloud. The waning moon rose like an orange pumpkin climbing out of her dark, wet bed. Thousands of stars twinkled, slowly giving way to the majesty of the moon, with powerful Orion striding ahead of her.

As I stood at the wheel, I tried my best to pull from my mind the strange dream I was having when Mike woke me for my watch. I was perplexed by the dream because in it, my subconscious had turned Patrick into a villain. It made no sense.

We were sailing along on a bright moonlit night, the mainsail out to port, the headsail out to starboard, very much looking like a bird. *Alban* was surfing up and down huge waves. Mike and I were in the cockpit, reading by moonlight. Patrick wanted to sleep on deck, but the moon was too bright. Without saying anything, he rigged up a dark canvas sheet and spread it around the cockpit.

Mike shouted angrily, "Can you please not put that here? We're reading." Patrick looked at him and said simply, "I want to go to sleep."

Mike threatened to jump overboard and then did. I said, "No! No! No! This can't happen. It's only a dream."

### *Land Ahead*

Later that morning, Mike and I were sitting in the cabin at the rectangular table, drinking tea and writing in our journals, when we heard Patrick shout, "Land ahead!"

We jumped up and scrambled to the cockpit. Staring at the horizon, we saw a shimmering mirage of pale brown and green. Land! It was far away but unmistakable. We hadn't run out of food or water, and no one had been murdered. Three strangers, captive on a small boat for nearly a month, with some tensions, for sure, but overall, it had been easy sailing.

I gave Pat a gigantic hug of appreciation. It wasn't until this moment that I released all my fears of being lost at sea.

Patrick radioed the customs and immigration office to notify them of our expected arrival in port. While Mike and I cheerfully tidied up the boat for customs, Patrick stood at the helm, steering us towards land.

# chapter eight
# WEST INDIES

### *Barbados*

We anchored in Bridgetown, Barbados late in the evening. We weren't allowed to go ashore until we cleared customs, so we spent the time drinking a bottle of wine over supper. Our long journey had come to its end. We feasted on the sights of harbor lights and the sounds of people on land shouting, singing, and laughing. It was crazymaking to be in port and need to stay on board.

Patrick burst into a Caribbean song to while away the time. The song, "Angelina", was familiar to me, and the lyrics brought fond memories of Dad playing our concertina beside summer campfires. Music lightened the mood on board, and we sang to the stars late into the night.

*Angelina, Angelina,*
*please bring down your concertina*
*And play a welcome for me*
*cause I'll be coming home from sea*

## *Spiffed Up*

We woke early the next morning. Pat put on a pair of khaki Bermuda shorts and a long-sleeved blue cotton shirt. Mike wore white shorts and a short-sleeved white polo shirt with a collar and an open neck. They both were clean-shaven and looking smart. I wore my yellow dress with sandals and braided my hair. When we were all as spiffy as we could get, we sat in the cockpit drinking coffee, anxiously waiting for the customs official.

This was no small affair. The fellows had been through it before, and so had I. We knew to be on our best behavior and to reply to questions seriously and respectfully. There was no joking or teasing allowed. Mike would be required to provide proof of his ownership of *Alban* as well as a passenger and crew list, and we would have to present our declarations of health and clearance from our last port of call. All spirits, wine, tobacco, and plant and animal products had to be listed. We had to be prepared to have our luggage and personal belongings rummaged through by the officer, who would ask about our last port of entry and how long we would be in Barbados.

The customs officer finally motored up to us, and Mike invited him on board. He wanted to see the boat, so we climbed into the cabin and sat around the table as the officer inspected our documents. Mike had to hand over his gun and ammunition to the officer, to be retained until his departure from port. All went smoothly, much to our relief.

The tricky part for me was the final question. "Where are you going after you leave Barbados?" Mike said that he planned to sail to Grenada, where he'd charter *Alban* for a few months before returning to England. Patrick would stay with Mike as skipper and then also return to England. I hadn't discussed my hopes of continuing to Grenada with *Alban* and needed a serious talk with the lads. Fudging a bit, I told the officer that I'd fly back to my home in New York City after the fellows left for Grenada.

The officer had completed his check. We shook hands with him and waved as he departed. We climbed into *Alban*'s inflatable dinghy and headed for the Bridgetown wharf, where we tied up and were instantly surrounded by the commotion of graceful dark-brown people going hither and yon, vibrant colors, laughter, and the sounds of steel drums playing on the street corners. It was as though we had entered a carnival.

## *Mother's Letter*

Walking on land for the first time in weeks was a strange sensation, as we still felt the rolling boat under our feet. We walked like we had been drinking for hours. This made us all laugh.

We were eager to meet our friends from *Tamure* and envisioned a night of revelry with them, hanging out in a nice restaurant and kicking up our heels to a steel band playing dancing music. We couldn't wait to swap stories and celebrate our safe voyages across the ocean.

First on our schedule was the post office, to check our mail. I was overjoyed that a letter from Mother was waiting for me. It thrilled me to see her neat printing on the envelope and hold something that she had touched, as I had missed her dearly throughout our journey. I excused myself from my companions, wanting to go to a café where I could treasure the quiet moment and savor her letter.

It was not a long letter.

*Dearest Darling,*

*We have sad news. Max is dead. He was found in his car on the side of a freeway going into New York City. We are so sorry to greet you with this sorrow. David went to his funeral. Please cable us about your safe arrival in Barbados.*

*I love you,*

*Mother*

For a moment I did not hear the bustle around me.

Max dead?

Too stunned to even cry, I stared at the words printed on the page. I felt as if I had been hit hard in my stomach from out of nowhere.

*Max dead. Gone. Forever.*

A cloud of bleak despair settled over me.

I folded Mother's letter, returned it to the envelope, and stuffed it into my bag. In a trance, I stood up and left the café, stumbling into the hot, bustling city. The world outside felt surreal and coldly indifferent to my sorrow.

I wandered to the dinghy and waited for the lads. I tried to hide my grief from strangers hanging out on the wharf but couldn't hold back tears that streamed down my cheeks. When Patrick and Mike approached, I flung my arms around Pat and wept.

"Max is dead! Mother just wrote that Max is dead."

Patrick held me close until I calmed down.

"Max was a friend I knew in New York. I'm so sorry. I can't go out with you tonight. You'll have to join the *Tamure* fellows on your own. Please tell them how sorry I am. I was looking forward to our night out. Can you take me back to *Alban*?"

"Sure, Tam," Patrick said. "We were going to the boat to catch a wee nap before the night's revelry. I'm sorry to hear of your loss." Mike looked at me and nodded his condolences.

When the time came to meet up with the *Tamure* folks, Pat and Mike climbed into the inflatable dinghy. "You'll be okay, Tam?" Patrick said.

"I think so."

I watched the lads head for the wharf, leaving behind a V-shaped trail of white froth. I longed to be with them, but I was in no condition to be social. Since Mother hadn't told me the circumstances of Max's death, my imagination grappled with possible scenarios, including the worst of all—murder or suicide.

I climbed down the steps into *Alban*'s cabin, lit two candles, sat at the table, and composed a letter to Mother in my journal.

*Dearest Mother,*

*I am numb with grief. When I try to think what could have happened, I am struck only with grim tales. Then a sudden wave of sadness. Then numb all over again.*

*You might have surmised that I loved Max. We even had something happening between us. Perhaps it was not much on his account, but on mine it was. I want to say that there are two people on this earth that I love: one is you, and the other is Max. I love my brother, but it's not the same thing: we scarcely know each other anymore.*

*By the way, it was very nice of David to go to the funeral.*

*Right now, I'm sitting alone in the boat. There are two candles burning. It's way past midnight, and the night is clear. It comforts me a little to be writing to you. The others are on shore celebrating our arrival with the Tamure folks. They all know what's happened, and they are very kind.*

*Well, my dearest Mother,*

*In utmost sorrow,*

*Tamar*

The next day I went on my own to nearby Carlisle Bay. I needed to be alone and chase out the heavy grief in my heart. There was no one else in sight. I swam naked in the clear water and lay in the sun. I ran as fast and far as I could, barefoot on the hot sand, feeling my strength and the joy of movement. For a few moments, I forgot Max.

## *Chance Encounter*

Two days after we arrived, we watched *Josefine* enter the bay under sail and anchor not far from us. Soon after, I ran into Jay at the laundromat in town. Tossing my laundry bag on the floor, I raced up to him and gave him a hug.

"Jay, how was your trip?"

"Horrible, actually. Let's get a drink while we wait for the laundry."

He looked quite handsome with his new mustache, and after hunting around unsuccessfully for a cocktail lounge, we bought two oranges, sat beside a fountain, and had an entertaining chat. *Josefine*'s voyage had taken forty-one days—ours, twenty-six. He said it had been a miserable, tense journey, and the Danes continued to ration the water. The two English boys, whom Olaf took on to replace Andy and Steve, proved to be problematic. Jay admitted that he added quite a bit of antagonism, too.

He mentioned that the Danes were no longer keen on chartering the boat as they had originally planned. She had proven too much to handle, so they wanted to sell her in St. Thomas.

That surprised me, although I understood that picking up random people in different ports had brought on tensions and conflicts that they had not been able to foresee. Every one of us had been lured to *Josefine* by the romance of the sea. And every one of us had contributed to the stress on board.

After picking up our laundry, we walked together to the port. When I gazed at that sixty-six-foot black gaff-rigged ketch that had so captured my heart in Ibiza, I felt indifferent to her. The formerly glorious *Josefine* simply looked grungy from this distance despite all the work scraping, painting, and varnishing Jay told me they had done. I couldn't separate the physical boat from my unpleasant memories and the stories I heard from Jay. I was disenchanted, to say the least.

Jay zipped me back to *Alban* in *Josefine*'s lovely clinker lifeboat.

"Thanks, Jay. It was great to see you. Do say hi to Anja and Bine."

"Bine wants to see you. She keeps begging Anja to ask you aboard."

"That's kind, but I'm not sure if I'm up to it." I couldn't imagine facing Olaf. "Let me think about it."

Jay started the motor and backed away from *Alban*. He certainly was a decent fellow. I had felt a calmness settle over me in his presence and was sad we'd be parting ways for good, soon. I knew that once we left Bridgetown, I'd probably never see him again.

That night I confined myself once again to *Alban*, where I could be alone as my companions let loose in town. I was hungry but had no appetite. I sipped hot milk with honey for some comfort, then lay on my bed, utterly exhausted but wide awake into the night.

### *The Potters and the Moores*

During the week, the crews of *Alban* and *Tamure* became acquainted with various expats who had made Barbados their home. Seen as adventurers from all over the globe, who could entertain with our seafaring stories, we were invited to some of their parties.

One day, the Potters and the Moores, folks some of us had met in town, invited us to a family party at their estate, several miles outside of Bridgetown. The *Tamure* fellows, Jerry, David, Mac, and Tim, rented a car and drove all seven of us to the estate, crammed like sardines into the front and back seats. I welcomed the distraction of going off with the guys, after the heaviness of the prior days.

I squished into the back seat between Pat and Mike. My pirate, Tim, was next to Pat. If I had been in a better mood, I may have enjoyed flirting with both lads. They seemed to be rivals, competing for my attention. Instead, I relaxed into the familiar proximity of my *Alban* companions and enjoyed the sultry air streaming into the car through the rolled-down windows. All the boys were in great spirits, excited by the intriguing invitation and the chance to get free drinks.

When we arrived at our destination, we scrambled out of the car, laughing and relieved to be released from the furnace inside. Someone opened the door to the grand house and led us through the cool entry to a covered veranda in the back, looking over the sea. The Potters and the Moores were gathered there, and after introductions, we were quickly offered rum and Sprite.

Old Mr. Potter, whom everyone called Potsie, sat in a wicker rocking chair, giant hands folded over his big belly, wearing round violet sunglasses with gold rims. Mrs. Potter sat next to him in a sturdy wicker chair, frail, with thin lips, white hair, and a faltering voice. She told us about her work taking care of the elderly in a special home and arranging meals for them. I wondered how old the old people she took care of were, as she looked old as the hills herself.

Mr. Moore, the Potters' son-in-law, was tall and lean, sporting a small, red mustache and short golden hair. He was perhaps in his late forties and wore white shorts and a loose flowered shirt. His wife, the Potters' daughter, was wearing a sleeveless blue linen dress; she was wide-eyed, short, and plump.

The Moores were chatting about finances, the value of land, and possibly building a house for their newly married daughter, Patty, who was about twenty-three. She and her husband, Harold, were both rather heavy and nicely in love. Another daughter, Lynne, was about seventeen, wide-eyed, gracious, and warm, with a turned-up nose and flashing braces, only revealed by a quick smile. She was very thin, like her father, but wore blue like her mother—turquoise slacks and a flowered shirt. Lynne bustled about, serving drinks to her family and their international guests.

"Lynne, I wish you wouldn't sit on the rail," Mrs. Moore said. "It makes me nervous. You might fall over."

"All right, Mummy," she said, and slid gracefully off the rail.

"Why don't you fall over?" Harold, her new brother-in-law asked. "Then she wouldn't be nervous!" It was a jovial atmosphere, and I loved their sense of humor. In my family, we never bantered with each other.

Tim was sprawled in a comfortable chair, looking dashing and relaxed with his dark beard, dark glasses, white cutoffs, and a Tahitian straw hat. He was pleasantly joking with the family. "Let's see... There are about three generations here..."

"Yes, and I'm beginning to feel it!" Potsie's big belly heaved in a sigh.

Beer, rum, and Sprite flowed, loosening everyone up. David, from *Tamure,* sat on the far side of the veranda. "I could live here forever. I can imagine ending up in a house like this." It sounded like he'd had enough of the roving life and was looking forward to a settled life in a real house. Maybe he'd tell his kids and grandkids tales of his ocean sailing adventures, when he had been young and carefree, with Jerry, Mac, and Tim, including our party in the mid-Atlantic.

I could relate to his comment. I had no desire to embark on another ocean voyage once this adventure was over. I, too, looked forward to settling in a house with a bunch of kids running about.

The late afternoon sun spread a soft light through the tropical trees and onto the grounds of white sand. The waves swished gently over the reef. It was a languid afternoon, hot and mellow. A golden retriever lay in the shade of a palm tree, nursing her litter of puppies, bringing me back to my parents' home, with their English setters, and the night that my sister died when I was playing with Lola's puppies.

Mrs. Moore and Lynne gave us a tour of their palatial residence. I, too, had grown up in a large house, but it was more like a cathedral than a home despite Mother's attempts to make it cozy. The Moores' place seemed more human, and I could imagine the fun the kids had growing up in it.

A large watercolor in the spacious living room caught my eye: a river lined with trees and Mediterranean houses, a steepled church in the distance. Below the painting stood a dark wooden shelf with a wedding portrait on it and two other family photos. Glancing at the loving images, I felt admiration for what they displayed and a sting of sadness at the void in my life. Up a set of creaking stairs were four huge bedrooms filled with mirrors and dressers. The home was clearly large enough to house three generations of Potters and Moores under one roof.

We returned to the veranda after the tour, where we all visited merrily throughout the afternoon. It was an idyllic scene. The day certainly had made a great impression on me. I saw firsthand how it was possible to have a more relaxed, fun family life than I had known.

As everybody was saying goodbye our hosts said, "I'm so glad you could come" and "You must come again!" We knew it was highly unlikely that we would ever meet again, but it was a fun interlude to tuck away in our hearts.

## *Reunion with* Josefine

*JOSEFINE* WAS STILL IN PORT, and one afternoon I bumped into Jay again. "Let me take you to the ketch. Anja and Bine really want to see you."

I hesitated, considering whether spending time with Bine might buoy my spirits.

"Okay. Sure."

I was filled with dread and anticipation as we sped over the harbor. When we approached the old ketch, Jay hollered, but nobody was on deck. We climbed up the steep rope ladder and clambered over the bulwark to the wooden deck, where Fang nearly knocked me over.

"Fang! I've missed you!" My heart ached as I rubbed her ears and head.

"You've got a visitor!" Jay yelled down into the interior.

While the Danes climbed up the companionway, I glanced at the beauty of *Josefine* and all the hard work Jay said they had done while crossing the Atlantic—scraping, painting, polishing, and varnishing. She looked great—not at all grungy, as she had appeared the other day from a distance.

Up popped Olaf, followed by Bine and Anja, cradling their baby. Olaf grinned and shook my hand. "Welcome aboard. It's been a long time." I was stunned. It appeared that he had forgotten the hard times. Bine gave me a hug, and Anja appeared glad to see me.

We descended into the interior of the cabin, where Anja made coffee and brought out a plate of cookies. Olaf joined us; Stefan was nowhere in sight. We chitchatted about my sailing adventures on *Alban* and my plans to either return to New York or explore the West Indies for a bit.

Olaf confirmed what Jay had said—that *Josefine* proved to be too much for them, and they planned to sell her in St. Thomas after enjoying the West Indies a while. Olaf said it had been a hard decision, but they had to be realistic, and that perhaps they'd return to Denmark.

Although I felt no animosity from Olaf during our conversation, I still didn't trust him fully. He made no reference to the money he owed

Arthur. I was hoping he would bring it up on his own, and because he hadn't, I worried that he wasn't planning to repay the money. I felt responsible because I had orchestrated the loan, but I was scared to open the topic with Olaf.

Farewells were spoken, and Jay took me back to *Alban*.

As I watched Jay leave, I puzzled over my visit on *Josefine*. What did I know about people? Olaf seemed to have morphed back to the charming fellow whom Arthur and I met in Ibiza. He had been under a tremendous amount of stress during the shipwreck, negotiating to get *Josefine* off the beach and repaired in dry dock. That, it seems, had brought out the worst in him.

## *Dinner with the Colonel*

*Zia* finally appeared in the harbor on February 11, and was safe and sound in Bridgetown. Mike, Patrick, and I had dinner on board with the Colonel that night; all the other passengers and crew, including the cook, had disembarked to kick up their heels in town and celebrate their arrival after all their tribulations at sea.

We savored the fine meal Alan had prepared of fresh dolphin fish smothered in lemon and dill, white rice in onions and garlic, glazed carrots, and, for dessert, canned pears in crystal glass bowls drizzled with melted chocolate and rum. The relaxed evening was a welcome and much needed respite for me. We thoroughly enjoyed ourselves, sitting around the wooden table in *Zia*'s large lounge, regaling the Colonel with the story of the whacky pirate raid in the middle of the Atlantic by the *Tamure* lads, and being entertained by the chatty Colonel—the lovely, warm man who had spoken to us most of the way across the wide sea.

## *Too Many Goodbyes*

*Tamure* had been in Bridgetown for just over a week, but the crew wanted to catch the carnival in Trinidad, the southernmost island in the West Indies, on their way to the Panama Canal. From there, they would head across the Pacific Ocean, back to their homes in New Zealand. Tim intended to fly back to Ireland from Trinidad, to tie the knot with his fiancée.

I was sad saying goodbye to my fun pirate from our brief, high seas encounter. We hugged, long and sweet.

"Take care, Tamar."

"You, too, Tim. I'll miss you. Best wishes for your marriage."

Walking away, I felt wistful. There was no one on the horizon who wished to tie the knot with me.

I also was sad about losing my connection with the intrepid New Zealand lads, Jerry, David, and Mac, who would have roamed the high seas for nearly three years by the time they reached home. Yet they all seemed to get along splendidly. I felt like it was another forever goodbye, although we promised to write and stay connected.

### *French West Indies*

Mike and Patrick were now busy planning the next leg of their trip. Mike wanted to take a little tour of the French West Indies before sailing south to Grenada. I wondered if they'd let me stay on to Grenada. I wanted to remain on *Alban* because I could not wrap my head around finding another boat or returning to New York without exploring the West Indies.

Barbados had been my agreed upon destination aboard *Alban*. When we arrived, no one mentioned my leaving, so I saw that as my window of opportunity to ask about staying aboard. I avoided speaking to Mike about it until the last minute. My moodiness over Max's death had reconfigured our rapport, and I had no idea how Mike would respond.

A few days before *Alban*'s departure, I got up the nerve to ask Mike if I could accompany them to Grenada. "I'll get off just as soon as we arrive there, I promise." I was fully aware that I had promised to leave *Alban* once we arrived in Barbados, so what good were my promises? Much to my surprise and relief, he agreed.

63°
62°
61°
60°
14°
13°
12°
11°
10°
N
W
E
S
Castries
Saint Lucia
Laborie
Barbados
Chateubelair
Saint Vincent
Bridgetown
The Grenadines
Carribean
North
Atlantic
St. George's
Grenada
Trinidad
and
Tobago
Venezuela

*West Indies*

## *St. Lucia*

WE SET SAIL FOR CASTRIES, the largest port on the northwest side of St. Lucia, after twelve days in Barbados. *Tamure* was long gone, and *Zia* was staying in port, so we wouldn't be keeping radio contact with her, either. Everything felt precarious and I already missed the camaraderie of the other ships.

It was glorious being under sail again, however, this time in a turquoise sea. Our white sails billowed tight in the warm wind. I thought about the fun we could have at our next destination, taking part in a carnival jump-up.

When I mentioned this, Mike snapped, "If you want to buy the boat you can dance, otherwise she's sailing on. We've got no time to fuck around like you. This is business, chick."

I thought that was damn mean.

"You're like a bit of flotsam floating about in the sea with no purpose," he said.

Flotsam is the worthless junk that drifts about the ocean, and it moves only at the whims of the ocean currents. I understood too well what he meant.

My fragile self-esteem plummeted once again. And, once again, I had no words.

I thought about Andy, how feisty and confident he was at only eighteen, and how he was able to respond to situations on the fly. He had the guts to fight back. I clearly saw how he benefited from his inner strength. Would I ever learn? Would I ever be strong enough to stand up to harsh criticisms?

Later that evening I was on night watch for the first time in two weeks. The air was soft and warm, the sky brilliant with a multitude of stars. Mike and Pat were asleep. I looked for Orion and thought of Max. I felt as if the sky were falling.

The next morning, we slipped by the Pitons of St. Lucia, rising from the blue sea like two immense pyramids covered in lush green and speckled in the sunlight.

By the time we arrived in Castries on Thursday morning, Mike seemed to have forgotten "his very important business," and was ready to attend a jump-up. We were told that it started at 2:00 p.m. The next person we encountered said it started at 3:00 p.m., and our cab driver said between 3:00 and 4:00 p.m. We eventually learned that the jump-up was not carnival, but occurred once a week and was a fun time for the locals to dance to steel drum music, drink plenty of rum, and have a grand time—like a giant street party.

We never found it. Instead of partying, we had a late lunch at the Reef Bar restaurant, nestled on the bay, surrounded by palm hills and yachts. It was a tropical luxury sort of place, where yachting folk liked to hang out when on land and be served a nice meal.

At the entrance to the restaurant was a large cage with a giant, wrinkled turtle, dozing in the heat. It looked ancient.

"Poor turtle," I whispered under my breath.

A waiter met us at the door and guided us through a dark, cool room full of empty tables, where imitation paintings of a cardinal by El Greco, one of Cezanne's paintings of his uncle Dominique, and a Renoir hung on the walls. Outside on the covered veranda we were guided to a table and studied the menu. All we wanted was junk food—greasy cheeseburgers with french fries—and plenty of it.

It was a listless, hot afternoon. An hour passed and there was no sign of our food. A donkey brayed loudly. Dogs barked. Flies buzzed around the tables. The three of us sat quietly, enjoying the atmosphere. I felt a dreamy peacefulness settle over us, as if all our tensions had been washed away.

As my companions were nodding off to dreamland, our lunch finally arrived.

"Sorry for the wee nap!" Patrick said. "Let's dig in!"

That evening Mike went out on the town alone, and Patrick and I stayed on the boat, safely tied to the wharf. We had a peaceful evening under the stars.

Sometime during the night or wee morning hours, Mike must have returned, because when I climbed out of bed, there he was, quietly drinking coffee at the table.

"Morning, Mike! Did you have a good time last night?"

"Yes, quite. But it's none of your business, dear."

He seemed to be clearly miffed at me and felt entitled to snap harsh words, which didn't help my mood or the *Alban* vibe.

We left Castries around 11:00 a.m. to begin our journey south to Grenada. Our destination that night was Laborie, a quaint fishing village on the south end of St. Lucia. It was fine sailing that day, in a sparkling-blue, gentle sea.

Despite my appreciation for the splendor that surrounded us, the weight that pressed down on my heart and mind grew heavier as I sensed the journey coming to an end. I was in tears most of the morning and afternoon. Patrick tried to console me.

"You shouldn't be unhappy. We're sailing in the West Indies under perfect conditions. You can do anything you want; you are free. What more can you want?"

"Peace! I feel absolutely hopeless."

"Oh, Tam! You're not hopeless. You can cook. You can row a dinghy..."

"Who gives a *fuck* if I can row a dinghy?"

Patrick's attempt to cheer me only frustrated me more, and neither he nor Mike knew what to make of me. They knew I was suffering from the death of a friend, but they had no idea how deep my pain ran. I was incapable of confessing to them the history I had brought with me. They couldn't know how, as fragile as I was, a few sharp words could affect my soul like a match on dry tinder. At the same time, as a hostage to my own suffering, I was blind to the impact I had on those around me.

I became irrational. I was so insecure and depressed that the most insignificant conversations were absurd.

"Would you like some peaches, Mike?"

"Why yes, that would be nice."

"Do you want them now or later?"

"Whenever you like."

"Are you *sure* you want some peaches?"

"Listen, babe, you do whatever you like."

### *Despicable Me*

ONE DAY AS WE WERE sailing down the west coast of St. Lucia, Patrick proclaimed out of the blue, "No man would want to marry you. You are attractive at first, but you are shattering after people get to know you."

I just stared at him while his insult landed. The shock of his words was twofold: that they came out of the mouth of Patrick, who had been a steady friend on the trip, and that without knowing about my father, the letters, or Max, he had managed to strike, with precision, my deepest fear. I was confounded as to how I seemed to attract blunt, diminishing verbal attacks from men. The last remnant of my self-esteem was extinguished then and there.

I wrote in my journal,

*What a useless and despicable person I am. My inner dialogue wails:*

*If people abhor me, mock me, make fun of me, there's no use being here. What am I giving to people? Nothing! I'm stupid, rude, and selfish. I live in a fantasy of self-interest. I'm quite a joke on this planet. I'm appallingly blatant, misguided, and screwed up. I give nothing but annoyance to people.*

We sailed into Laborie, on the south end of St. Lucia, before nightfall. A slender moon hung over the bay. We anchored and, with little conversation, sipped wine while watching a boat load bananas. Buxom women in long cotton skirts with yellow, blue, red, and white checks moved quickly, helping the men load the boat.

Patrick once again burst into song, this time, "Day-O." His voice startled and annoyed me, as it broke my quiet stupor. However, by the time he got to the third line of the tune, I woke as if from the saddest dream I'd ever had and found myself singing along.

*Day-o, day-ay-ay-o*
*Daylight come and me wan' go home*
*Work all night on a drink a rum*
*Daylight come and me wan' go home*

## Hopeful

I woke at dawn. The sky was beautiful: silken pink and blue, with a rainbow. Rainbows had always made me feel hopeful, as though they were a fortuitous gift from the gods. We got underway by eight, heading for Chateaubelair on St. Vincent, but there was no wind. The sails flapped uselessly. Patrick didn't want to turn on the engine because the temperature in the cabin would rise to one hundred degrees. So, there we sat, yet hoping to arrive by nightfall.

I was still feeling down, but being once again without wind brought back fond memories of our pirate party in the middle of the Atlantic Ocean; our revelry now seemed like a century ago, and so much had changed since we reached the West Indies.

Gazing at sparkles dancing on the surface of the water, I drew a deep breath and let it out slowly. Soothed by the beauty in front of me, I felt a tiny flicker deep inside me and remembered I wanted to be happy.

By one o'clock we were sailing between two beautiful islands, La Belle Helene and St. Vincent, at three knots. La Belle Helene was smoke blue, and St. Vincent appeared a deep, sunlit green. Four sailboats crept up on us in the silken blue distance. Schools of fish jumped out of the sea, bodies glistening in the sun, and dove back in, leaving little pools of expanding waves like raindrops on the sea. Ocean birds dove after the little fish.

## *St. Vincent*

WE ARRIVED IN CHATEAUBELAIR, THE largest fishing village on the west side of St. Vincent, about five o'clock that evening, and the lads lowered the anchor and furled the sail. With our binoculars on the village, we noticed a maze of plantations; greenheart and banana trees; a black-sand beach with pigs, dogs, chickens, and half-naked children running about; smoke rising from shanties partially hidden in rows of coconut trees; and donkeys braying. Boats with gunnysack sails were returning from fishing along the coast. This scene was far from the fancy world of yachts we had been visiting.

Without a thought, I donned my orange crocheted bikini, plunged headfirst into the murky green water, and swam to shore. A cluster of kids ran to meet me, but I caught sight of Patrick waving frantically from *Alban*; I had forgotten we had to clear customs and swam back to the boat as fast as possible.

Clearing customs proved to be a delightful, relaxed affair here, unlike any we had yet encountered. As night settled over the village, we motored *Alban* to a dilapidated wooden dock, where we were met by a broad-shouldered policeman who took us to the Sea View Bar.

A Mrs. Frances and her young daughter welcomed us. When I stood in the entry to the bar, gazing at the room, I felt curiosity and amusement. A policeman, who was also the customs official, taking us to a bar? "This is the customs office?"

Patrick only shrugged, going with the flow of island life.

The room was shabby, with high ceilings, several chairs without seats, and TV trays. In the center of the room was an oblong table covered in a plastic cloth sprinkled with images of yellow bananas and bright oranges. A vase full of plastic flowers adorned the table, and some real, wilted flowers decorated another table in the corner. Girlie pictures of women in skimpy bikinis covered the pea-green walls, along with entertaining signs that read, "H. B. Dublin is licensed to sell intoxicating liquor," and "Absolutely no spitting. If you must spit, spit here. We want you to feel at home."

Three men with lined faces, slanting black eyes, and broad noses entered the shack. We assumed they were customs officials. Our policeman waved them over. After introductions, he invited them to join us. We ordered a pitcher of Guinness, "The Drink That's Good For You," along with a can of orange juice for me, and a bowl of ice. Rich, coffee-colored ale with a frothy white foam spilled from the jug as Patrick poured it into the glasses.

"Is there any place we can get a bite to eat?" asked Pat, who was always hungry.

"You mean for dinner?" our guide asked.

"No, just anything."

"Yes, up the road a bit, you can get some fried fish or canned stew."

"Fine. Perhaps we can have it brought here?" Pat asked.

"Oh, no," was the unanimous reply from the locals.

"That's all right. We can walk," Pat said.

Mike chimed in, saying, "When I'm ninety-seven, if I keep drinking rum, perhaps I won't be able to walk. But I can walk now!"

"Can you get drinks there?" Pat asked.

"No."

"Oh. Should we bring the food to the drinks or the drinks to the food?"

The resounding reply was "Food to the drinks!" So quicker than scat, Mike whirled off with a slender policeman.

He returned sometime later with a plate of fried fish heads, highly seasoned, and a paper bag of bread. He held an uncooked leg of mutton.

"Mrs. Frances, the angels told me you were a beautiful cook.

They told me so." Mrs. Frances smiled and graciously took the mutton from Mike.

An hour and a half later, after much dancing and drinking, Mrs. Frances's daughter brought out a huge bowl of meat and white yams. Then another, and yet another until there were seven heaping bowls of steaming food in front of us.

It was a most enjoyable customs interrogation. Not one question asked. The last word I wrote in my journal that night was "*Fantastic.*"

## *The Grenadines*

We left St. Vincent early the next morning and arrived in Bequia, the most northern island in the Grenadines. I would be parting ways with the lads once we reached Grenada. I still hadn't a plan for my return to New York, but I knew that I wanted to poke around the island for a bit because it was unlikely that I'd ever get the opportunity again.

Over the next couple of days, we continued to island-hop until we finally reached Grenada. The atmosphere on board was relatively calm and peaceful, as we all kept pretty much to ourselves.

## *Grenada*

We arrived in St. George's Town, Grenada, on February 26. I remained on *Alban* for a few more days to adjust to leaving the sloop that had been my home for the past six weeks. I needed to find a place to stay. Mike wanted to charter her, but she was a mess and needed quite a bit of work that the lads estimated would take three or four weeks. There would be no place for me once they began the repairs to make *Alban* shipshape for chartering.

I sent my parents and Arthur a cable to alert them of my safe arrival in Grenada.

To Arthur I wrote: "In Grenada. Come meet *Alban* lads. Please. Love, T." I wanted to show him off and thought his common sense might even lend me some credibility. Also, I had to discuss with Arthur how to get his money back from Olaf.

## *Farewell,* Alban

I FOUND A CHEAP BOARDINGHOUSE outside of St. George's Town, where I could walk the several miles along the water to town each day. It was time to say farewell to my companions in the wildest adventure I'd ever had.

I thanked Mike for taking me on board and mentioned how sorry I was for starving them. I confessed how afraid I was that we'd run out of food and water.

"No problem, Tamar. You did add some color and helped to stave off the boredom of the crossing. Find something to do in New York that gives you focus."

Ah, that advice seemed to be offered with genuine kindness.

"Patrick, thanks a million for taking us safely across the ocean. Remember the dark joke you spun when we were beginning our voyage—how crazy I was to sign up with you when I had no idea who you were? Well, you didn't know who I was, either. We all survived!"

He hugged me close. There was an undeniable bond between us and an ache of longing in my heart.

"If Arthur comes, let's get together in town. I'd love for you to meet him."

"Sure, Tam. That would be great."

"Please come visit me in Tacoma. I'd like my parents to meet you both." All three of us exchanged addresses. Despite the recent tensions between us, we had all shared a remarkable experience and recognized that we were forever bonded by our common adventure.

It seemed surreal to be leaving *Alban* and striking out on my own. Yet, it was exhilarating to be alone, on my own two feet, for the first time in months.

## *Murder in the Guesthouse*

It was a dangerous time to be on the island. The upheavals were intense. Murders, torture, and brutality were all too common. Eric Gairy was the premier of Grenada when we arrived. Ruthless yet charming and charismatic, he had formed his own secret police force, the Mongoose Gang, which consisted of criminals who had been convicted of robbery, assault, and physical aggression. These tough fellows defended Gairy's government.

Although I wasn't fully aware of the politics, I did understand that the scene was alarming, and it wasn't safe to be out late at night alone—especially as a woman. I had enough sense to return to my boardinghouse before dark.

Not everyone was so lucky. In the house where I stayed, there was one other boarder—a reclusive, pudgy man with thin hair and watery eyes; he may have been German. One late night I heard moaning coming from his room. Scared out of my wits, I rushed downstairs to find the owner of the house.

"Come quick! I think the fellow in the next room is hurt!"

We raced upstairs and heard the man's desperate moaning. We could not reach him, as his door was bolted from the inside. The owner called the police, but by the time they arrived and bashed in the door, he was dead—with a bloody wound on his skull.

I stood aghast at the horrible sight. I'd never laid eyes on a dead man before, especially one whose skull had been bashed in and who was lying in a pool of blood. This fellow seemed innocent and incapable of starting a fight. I felt dizzy, sick to my stomach, and scared. The scene haunted me.

Yet, as vulnerable as that gruesome event had left me feeling, the lure of this West Indian island inspired me to stay on.

## *Arthur Visits*

The evening after Arthur's arrival, the *Alban* lads joined us in a bar. After ordering drinks, we found a round table in a corner, where we could have a decent chat. Arthur had all sorts of questions to ask the English fellows, sorting out in his own mind the adventures we had crossing the Atlantic.

The next day, Arthur and I enjoyed getting caught up on the events of our separate lives over the past months. It was fabulous to be with my good friend again. I felt at home with him, here in this exotic place. He was the one guiding light that shone a steady beam of love and acceptance my way. Eventually, we discussed what could be done about the money I'd asked him to loan Olaf. I explained that the *Josefine* folks had decided the old ketch was too much to handle, and they were headed to St. Thomas, where they intended to sell her.

After we'd mulled it over together, Arthur suggested, "Perhaps you could impound the boat."

The idea shocked me. "How would I ever do that?"

Arthur remembered a student we both had met at Barnard, who now lived in St. Thomas. "Maybe Adele can help." We agreed that I should contact her to see if she would help me locate *Josefine* or give me some suggestions on how to proceed. It was a far-fetched idea, especially since we weren't close friends. Still, I managed to get her phone number from a mutual friend.

Arthur stayed only a few days. I was on a mission to collect the two thousand dollars and deliver it into his hands when I returned to New York. I felt a tremendous cloud of dread at the thought of impounding *Josefine*. Could I do this? Would I do this?

### *Sketching in the Market*

Since I knew the Danes intended to spend some time exploring the West Indies before heading to St. Thomas, I took a few weeks to gather my wits and take advantage of my time in Grenada. The place I loved most was the local market. It was full of noise, wandering tourists, hustling locals, colorful fruit and vegetables, and aromatic spices. West Indian men and women carried baskets on their heads loaded with coconuts,

sweet potatoes, mangoes, papayas, okra, tomatoes, bananas, sweet corn, tamarind, plantain, and passion fruit. Some men carried live chickens on their heads in boxes!

Over the next several days, I noticed three women who came to sell produce in the same spot each market day. Wanting to practice my art skills, I asked if I could draw them. In their melodic West Indian accents, they gladly agreed. They seemed amused by my request. That afternoon I bought a sketchbook and a ballpoint pen and eagerly returned to the market the next morning.

After greeting the women, I sat on a bench, with my sketch pad on my lap, far enough away from their booth so that I didn't interfere with their work. The women were obviously good friends or relatives. They chatted away as they sold their goods and occasionally glanced at me, bursting into laughter.

Focusing my attention on something that was rooted in everyday life gave me satisfaction and joy. As my pen sketched the women and I began filling in the shadows and their expressions, I entered moments of deep creative flow, where time vanished, and I was at one with my work. I was happy with my sketches and felt they resonated with all the love and passion I was feeling as I drew. It was good to be making art again.

## *Gorgeous* Ticonderoga

WANDERING AROUND THE DOCKS ONE day, I stopped to gaze at the most gorgeous sailboat I had ever seen. She was huge, graceful, and in perfect condition—a ketch like *Zia* but bigger and incredibly elegant.

As I stood there gawking, a handsome young fellow emerged from the boat. After only a few minutes chitchatting, he asked if I'd like to work for him as sous-chef for their charters. That took me by complete surprise, as I hadn't been looking for work or to board a new boat. But I didn't have to think twice; that ketch was glorious.

I was thrilled to become part of the crew of this ketch, once again sailing among the pristine islands of the West Indies. It turned out to be much easier and more fun to be the assistant cook than to be responsible for planning and creating meals as I had done on *Alban*, even if all I did

*The ketch* Ticonderoga

was open cans and mix the contents up into a big pot. The attractive young chef, Gabriel, was capable, preparing delicious and exotic dishes I'd never heard of before. All I had to do was to follow his instructions and be helpful.

In my tiny West Indian exercise book, I jotted down some of the elaborate meals we prepared: Buckingham eggs, harlequin salad, Spanish omelets, chicken Divan, macaroni salad, poached eggs, pineapple salad with chestnuts and raisins, lobster Americaine; the list goes on.

*Gabriel*

I was halfway infatuated with the chef. He was an energetic, clean-shaven young fellow about five feet ten inches, slim and strong, with thick, short, sandy-colored hair; blue eyes and strong eyebrows; and a square jaw. He excelled at managing the decadent meals and fancy happy-hour treats. I sketched a portrait of him in ballpoint pen, so I would remember his beautiful and somewhat sad face.

The chef and I spent hours in the galley together, but it was just as well that he concentrated on doing his job and not flirting with me. I felt useful. For the first time, I had a paid job, and I appreciated that the rapport between us was so easy.

# chapter nine
# LAST MISSION

### *A Hard Decision*

Summer was approaching and it was time to head back to the city. I loved the color, warmth, and pace of life on a tropical island, but I knew I had to face reality.

Before I could take off, I had to get Arthur's money back from Olaf. I thought long and hard about it and concluded that Arthur's suggestion to impound the boat was the only way to go. I didn't feel confident that I had the strength to stand my ground were I to confront Olaf directly about the money.

Impounding *Josefine* felt like a bold measure and scared me to death. Yet, I also was very angry with Olaf, as he had made no moves to repay what he owed. Had I been more mature at the time, I could have asked him how he intended to repay the loan. But I was not mature and didn't dare risk another one of his attacks. I was fragile, frightened, and insecure.

I was also fueled by a fierce protectiveness of Arthur and of our friendship, which was a critical lifeline for me. Arthur had given me unconditional and steadfast support, and I didn't want him to think I took his generosity for granted. Impounding *Josefine* was the hardest decision I had ever had to make.

With trepidation I phoned Adele from the boardinghouse in Grenada. "Adele? This is Tamar, from Barnard. Do you remember me?"

"Sure! You were good friends with Irene."

"Yes. I'm in a pickle and am wondering if you can help me..."

"What is it?"

I explained the situation and my fear that the Danes had no intention of paying back the loan. I described the ketch and wondered if she would check to see if *Josefine* was in St. Thomas.

"Yes, I can do that for you."

I relaxed a notch. Then I mustered the courage to ask what I really wanted from her—how to impound the boat. She seemed to grasp the seriousness of my request. After pausing, she suggested that perhaps her brother, Morgan, could help. She kindly gave me his contact information and said she'd let him know to expect a call. I was bowled over by her helpfulness and very grateful.

I waited a few days to give Adele time to relay the message to her brother. When he and I finally spoke on the phone, he confirmed that *Josefine* was anchored in Charlotte Amalie, the main harbor in St. Thomas. He would arrange the impound.

### *St. Thomas*

I flew to St. Thomas the next day and checked into a pensione that Morgan had recommended.

We met in a small café, where he laid out the plans to impound *Josefine*, anchored serenely in the bay. He had already contacted the authorities, who were waiting for my arrival to act. He would take me out to *Josefine* early the next morning; I would climb aboard, then the authorities would step in. I was not instructed to say anything about impounding their boat. I was simply told to visit with them.

An act of such aggression towards the unsuspecting Danes seemed positively despicable. I truly cared for Anja and Bine. I knew Anja would be mortified by what I was about to do. I felt ill at the thought.

### *A Heart-Wrenching Deed*

THE FATEFUL MORNING DAWNED. THE harbor was calm with barely a breeze. The sun had risen, promising a hot day, but the morning air was still cool. I met Morgan at the main wharf in the harbor and climbed into his open skiff, feeling tremendous guilt, shame, and fear at the prospect ahead.

Olaf was on deck as we approached the big black ketch. I waved.

"Hi, Olaf! May I come on board?"

I could tell he was surprised to see me. I had not seen them since we left Barbados in February, and this was July.

"Sure!" He let down the rope ladder.

"I'll be back in an hour," Morgan promised, and the skiff sped away, leaving me alone to face the consequences of my action.

Anja, holding their baby, climbed up from the galley and welcomed me aboard. Bine ran to give me a hug, which made me feel worse. Fang raced over and sniffed me up and down, wagging her tail. I rubbed her soft black ears, overcome with emotion and near to tears.

It was too late to reconsider.

Olaf left Anja, Bine, and me at the communal table to chat about our recent adventures. She offered me tea, but I declined. I'm sure I was visibly shaking. This was one of the longest hours I've ever endured.

While we were sharing stories, we heard a motorboat approach, and a man call out, "Ship ahoy! Anybody aboard?" My heart sank, knowing full well what was happening. We climbed out on deck, and I watched the drama unfold.

The policeman announced from his boat that unless their outstanding debt of two thousand dollars was paid immediately, *Josefine* would be impounded.

"Well, fuck!" Olaf muttered. He glared at me, clenching his hands.

Anja said, "I can't believe this!"

"Anja, I'm so sorry."

There was stunned silence on *Josefine*. I was shaking uncontrollably. Without saying a word, and without glancing back at Anja and Bine, I climbed down the ladder and jumped into the skiff. The police took the ketch into custody and gave them twenty-four hours to come up with the cash.

I felt deeply saddened. I knew I had severed our relationship beyond repair.

Back at the wharf, with a heavy heart, I thanked Adele's brother.

"Let's see what happens tomorrow morning," he said. "I'll be in touch."

The next morning, Olaf handed the authorities two thousand dollars cash. The *Josefine* saga was closed. Despite the outcome, I already regretted it.

## *Return to New York*

I DEPARTED FROM ST. THOMAS for New York on July 5. The weight I'd felt as I left began to mingle with nervous excitement as the plane landed at JFK airport.

Arthur met me at the airport. He spotted me first. With a crowd of people swirling around, going in every which direction, there he stood waving, his distinctive figure dressed in white pants and a long-sleeved blue cotton shirt.

We raced to each other and hugged. Fumbling in my bag, I brought out a large envelope. "It worked! I was terrified, but it worked!"

"Tamar, I never thought I'd see that money again. It couldn't have been easy. I'm impressed, thank you."

After collecting my backpack from the carousel, Arthur flagged a taxi. Reentering my life, as the taxi navigated the crowded city streets of New York, I took a deep breath. I had been gone for an entire year. Arthur left me at the entrance to my building on West Fourteenth Street. After climbing up the three flights of stairs, I unlocked the door to my loft and paused to gaze at the serenity of the space I had created before embarking on my sailing adventures.

### *Home*

MY LOFT WAS COZY AND familiar. I had always felt grounded and blessed in this space. My cousin Rich had taken good care of it, and everything was as I'd left it. My huge easel was still set up near the north-facing windows looking onto bustling Fourteenth Street, oil paints neatly laid out on a table. My ficus plant was thriving in the corner. The long door-table with cushions on the floor held out the promise of many more nights enjoying the company of friends.

My bed, with the sun dancing on the India print curtains around it, looked even more huge and inviting than ever. My mind flashed back to that night with Max. The entire year at sea seemed to collapse, as if it had never happened. It was as though the sheets were still warm from that stormy night we shared not long before I left.

### *A Serious Conversation*

UPMOST ON MY MIND WAS connecting with my friend David, who had been to Max's funeral. I hoped he could tell me what happened.

After I'd spent a few days settling in, David and I met in a small café on Madison Avenue. It was nestled down a few steps, partly underground, so it had an intimate, private atmosphere, perfect for a serious conversation. I arrived early and found a table for two with a white tablecloth and an apricot rose in a vase. I sat watching the door, expectant and eager to hear the news but dreading it, too.

As soon as I saw his tall, thin, blond figure in the door of the café, I rushed up to him. "It's so good to see you, David. Follow me.

I've got a table."

We ordered coffee and a poppy-seed cake to split between us. I reached across the table and held his hands. "Tell me about Max, please. What happened?"

David hesitated. Then in his quiet voice, looking at me with his kind, blue eyes, he told me that the memorial service had been a small gathering held in a chapel on Lexington Avenue and Fifty-Second Street. Clive Barnes, the dance critic for the *New York Times*, gave a moving eulogy. Max's Chilean wife spoke about how she was the only true love of his life.

David paused as I took this in.

"Max was found in his car parked on the side of the freeway going into New York City. He stabbed himself in his stomach."

I stared at David, horrified. That wild night spent in my loft with Max rushed back to my mind like a tsunami. Was he considering suicide when he paced my floor that night?

"Oh my God. Mother didn't tell me how he died."

After a long silence, I said quietly, "Thank you for telling me."

As we got up to leave, I said, "Let's get together at a happier time and catch up more. I'd love to tell you all about my sailing adventures." I had to leave quickly before my feelings showed. David had no idea about Max and me, and I wasn't prepared to have that conversation.

## *Safe Harbor*

AS I EMERGED FROM THE subway at Fourteenth Street and Sixth Avenue, the stultifying heat, traffic, bright sun, and noise overwhelmed me. When I reached the sanctuary of my loft, I made a cup of peppermint tea with honey and sat quietly at my small table. Holding the warm cup in both hands, I took a deep breath.

Max! God, Max!

He was gone.

Still, he filled the loft.

Contemplating the last time I saw him, I ached. The power and agony of his soul had drawn me to him and mirrored my own torment. We had shared a mere moment in each other's lives, a complicated, beautiful moment. I could see now that he had always been on his own journey in his brief and astonishing life, and it had nothing to do with me. The life I dreamt of for myself could never have happened with Max. I had to let him go.

The time had come to find my own strength and my place in the world. The weight of my fantasies, fears, and grief had oppressed me for too long. I had just returned from a year at sea, yet a whole new adventure had already begun—a quest to heal.

Since I was fifteen, I had been navigating profound confusion and trauma without a language or a map to guide me. My father's words were etched deeply into my soul but could not have the last say over my life. My dear sister's absence had come to hold its own sacred place in my heart.

As I held the warm teacup, a wave of comfort and possibility came over me. I glimpsed Hope peeking out of Pandora's box. I felt alive in the solitude and safety of that moment.

Here in my loft, bathed by the afternoon sun streaming in, I held with compassion the wounded young woman I had been and was. I felt ready to reclaim the life I was born to live—of joy, satisfaction, curiosity, and love.

*Dad, Naomi, Tamar, Mother, Mark, 1948*

# Reflections

***The heart of man is very much like the sea.***
***It has its storms, it has its tides,***
***and in its depths, it has its pearls too.***
—Vincent van Gogh

Looking back on this journey, I am amazed by the random characters I encountered along the way. As I've been writing this saga, they've come to life in full Technicolor, and I embrace them all with love in my heart. We were very young when this story unfolded, and I view us through the lens of kindness that has come with the perspective of time. I'm sure that we could chuckle over some of the absurdities that happened and appreciate each other for who we've become.

My life has encompassed the dark and the light, betrayals and regrets, losses and loves, joys and sorrows, continually learning what it is to be human and how to connect with the wider view of life on our precious planet. The journey will advance until the curtain closes on the final act of the spark of life that was me.

Flung out into the grand experiment of life, I alighted in a particular time, in a particular family, in a particular culture, to make the best of my journey.

# Epilogue

Goodbyes for me are always wistful. As my life unfolds, I have no idea which characters I encounter along the way will continue to be woven though the rich pattern of my life's tapestry. Reviewing my sailing adventures, I see how deeply each person has remained a part of my psyche. Even now, over fifty years later, they come with me, a white-haired old lady, still enjoying the ocean, still growing.

How I'd like to meet the characters in these pages today—to embrace them in warmth for our shared experiences, in wonder of who we once were.

***Patrick Blackwell*** and I corresponded throughout the 1970s; he even visited my parents in Tacoma. I was thrilled that he traveled so far to connect with them, though I was still living in New York and was unable to join him.

After sailing with *Alban*, he returned to England and lived a few years at Chiswick, London. He continued to visit his elderly mum in Devon and to make summer deliveries of yachts. In one letter, he mentioned the journal I kept during our *Alban* adventure. I must have confessed to him how insecure I had felt recording bits about our relationships, for fear that Mike might snoop into my private writing, so my journal lacked a lot of juicy bits.

> *My Dear Tam,*
> *If you do type up the "Saga of the Alban," it would be interesting to see how it was through your eyes. I don't think you have anything to worry about over that trip and I'm sure your "undress" has colored the story of our mid-Atlantic rendezvous as much for the crews of the Tamure as for me. I feel badly now at the thought of suppressing a journal which might have made fascinating reading now...*
> *Love, Patrick*

In 1989, a few years after I married, I received a surprising and beautiful handwritten letter from ***Mike Lynch.*** We had not been in touch since we parted in Grenada twenty years before, and he had no idea what I had been doing after leaving *Alban*. Fortunately, he tracked me down through my parents.

He informed me that Patrick had died—so young! He couldn't have been over fifty or fifty-five. He also told me that *Alban* had caught fire and sunk in the Caribbean; no one was hurt, but she couldn't be salvaged, so that was an unfortunate finale to the lovely antique sloop in which we had our grand adventure.

Mike married a West Indian woman and brought her to England, where he left advertising for good and set up a butterfly farm outside of London. I was astounded. Mike? Butterflies? Was he kidding? He mentioned that his wife had recently died of breast cancer, leaving their two teenage sons.

He confessed in this letter that he really did like me, and that he thought it would be fun to swap our journals of the Atlantic crossing. I was fascinated; was he willing to let me read everything he had written about me? I had believed all his musings were disparaging or harshly critical.

I'll never know. I let Mike's letter sit in a drawer at home, thrilled to have received it, but too busy to reply. I was so caught up with my new marriage, as well as raising two young stepdaughters and my own child, that I let go of a beautiful link to my past. We lost touch, and no amount of googling can bring him back to the surface. In one of my moves, I lost Mike's letter and, with it, my last connection to *Alban* and my voyage across the ocean.

I am still in touch with ***Arthur.*** He lives in the Rocky Mountains with his wife. Thanks to her generosity, acceptance of me, and wisdom, we have remained good friends throughout all these decades.

When he was ninety-two, I phoned him to find out what his

recollections were of how we got tangled up with *Josefine*. He didn't remember getting "tangled" with the ketch! He recalled that the generator failed as we were coming into port, and he had to keep the engine running because, without a generator, he wouldn't be able to start the motor. He thought we may have met the *Josefine* folks in a bar, and they invited us on board. I am flabbergasted by the difference in our memory when we experienced the same situation. My memory of the event is crystal clear in my mind. Our engine quit. We had to dock under sail. We got tangled up with *Josefine*. Yet, with the drifting mists of time, who knows?

***Maximiliano Zomosa*** was on his own trajectory, playing out the drama of his life, having no clue about the impact he had on me. There is a *Tacoma News Tribune* article from November 6, 1968, two months before he committed suicide, revealing that Max was going to make his home in Tacoma, where he would settle with his (other) wife, a former Joffrey Ballet dancer, who was pregnant with their first child. He planned to retire from dance and resume his interest in the medical profession.

Max continues to live in my heart, all these years later. In my mind's eye, whenever I see the constellation of Orion in the winter sky, striding over the brilliant heavens—the mighty Hunter who guided our little sloop over the vast ocean—I greet Max, and I send him love.

Regretfully, I never kept in touch with ***Andy and Steve Malasky.*** I hope their lives have been satisfying and fun. I hope Andy married Dusty!

I lost all contact with the ***Danish family***. I tried hard to find them online but was unsuccessful. Despite everything, I truly would have loved to keep in touch. When I think back on the events surrounding the impound, I feel deep regret and wish I'd known a better way to resolve the issue at the time. The hurt we caused each other saddens me but does not eclipse the gratitude I feel for having known *Josefine* and the people aboard with whom I shared an astonishing and unique experience.

I was excited to discover current news of ***Josefine*** while I was in the early stages of writing this saga. I'm not sure how many owners she's had, but when I discovered her on the internet, she was moored in Devon, England, where she was a tall ship training vessel. She was also used for day and overnight charters that accommodated up to twelve people. She looked gorgeous, with a nifty white hull; it was clear that she was cared for and maintained in top condition. Recently, she was for sale again, listed in the August 2021 issue of *Classic Boat* magazine, with a yellow hull. I'm pleased to say that she still looks great.

Built in 1931 as a fishing boat, by Anderson and Ferdinandsen, in Gilleleje, Denmark, she is a forty-ton vessel—extremely beautiful and seaworthy. Sixty-six feet long, fifteen feet wide, with a Douglas fir and Oregon pine deck and Douglas fir masts. Refits: 1975 to 1976 and 2000 to 2002.

***The Swede*:** To this day I wonder what we would have done if that generous stranger had not come forward. I hope his random act of kindness has been rewarded many times throughout his life.

***I wasn't wrong! The sea IS dangerous!***

Ybo, an old friend, recently told me a harrowing story about a tall ship that went missing along the coast of Africa. His niece, a young woman from Holland, taught celestial navigation on this boat. They had stopped at Ibiza, where Ybo's niece broke her leg riding a horse. The tall ship continued without her, sailing along the African coast towards the Canary Islands. No one ever heard from any of them again. The sea claimed them all.

I beat myself up for being such a scaredy-cat about ocean journeying. This story, as sad as it is, confirms that the sea *is* unpredictable. That said, while it's important to respect our instincts, it's important to take risks, too. If I had listened to all my fears and acted upon them, I'd never have sailed the high seas. I'd never have done anything.

Seeing ***Juan Sebastián de Elcano*** in the vast ocean was the most spectacular sight of our ocean crossing. When we saw her, she was on her way through the Panama Canal to San Francisco. I still wonder if she'd gone out of her way to check us out, because she turned around and retraced her voyage.

This magnificent ship is a four-masted barkentine, and when fully rigged, she has 30,892 square feet of sail. She's the third largest tall ship in the world, 371 feet long. Launched in 1927, she is one of the oldest tall ships still in operation, used as a training vessel for the Royal Spanish Navy and as an ambassador of peace, as she continues to sail around the world. *Juan Sebastián de Elcano* has been at sea for ninety-six years recording almost two million nautical miles in all the seas of the world.

***David Grant Noble*** has remained a cherished friend. He is a photographer, teacher, and author living in New Mexico with his lifelong partner, Ruth, whom he met at my loft party! He has published many books on the American Southwest, and recently a book about his experiences during the Vietnam War, *Saigon to Pleiku: A Counterintelligence Agent in Vietnam's Central Highlands, 1962–1963.*

***Ticonderoga*: *Ti*,** a clipper-bowed ketch, is one of the most beloved yachts in the world. *Ti* was launched in 1936 as a day-sailing family boat, but she surprised the world by her speed, and soon became a famous racing yacht. She has won more races than any ocean racer in history. *Ti* is seventy-two feet long, with her mainmast rising a stunning eighty-six feet high. This mast had been hewn from a 120-year-old Sitka spruce in British Columbia. She was designed by the legendary naval architect L. Francis Herreshoff.

***7 East Tenth Street:*** This five-story building was bought by NYU in 1996 and is now a center for Jewish student life. Formerly a Lockwood de Forest house, it is one of the most beautiful buildings in New York City.

***Naomi:*** Many years after Naomi's death, I learned that she had attempted suicide earlier, as a teenager. It was Mother who shared this heartbreaking information with me. That this huge event had been kept a secret for so many years astounds me.

Looking back, however, I understand why my parents would have chosen to protect Mark and me from this knowledge. I also understand how worried my parents must have been over the health and safety of Naomi.

Seventeen years after her death, Dad confessed that she had died by suicide; she took an overdose of sleeping pills.

She remains with me every day of my life. I hold her in my heart with tenderness, love, and a wistful sadness. I wish so much that we had the chance to grow old together.

***My brother, Mark,*** is an artist, creating stunning stained-glass lamps and whimsical tiny paintings. He married Phyllis Weyerhaeuser, and they had two children, Karl and Naomi. Karl was a gentle and brilliant young man, studying for his PhD in Greek and Roman classics, when he died by suicide, a result of anxiety and depression. Naomi is a strong, courageous young woman with a heart of gold. She is married and recently had a baby girl, Karla-Jean.

I found the following letter stashed in my journal, which I wrote to Mark on the day we left the Canary Islands to cross the Atlantic, and never sent to him:

*January 11, 1969*
*Las Palmas, Gran Canaria*

*Dearest Mark,*

*I have a SUPER IDEA—Why don't we live in Canada one winter or spring? I know someone marvelous (Andy) he has a beautiful girlfriend (Dusty)—you could find somebody, I could find somebody—and we could let our hair grow to our feet if we want.*

*Thinking of you on your birthday, and practically every other day for that matter. I love you. Take care.*

*Write me in care of British Yacht Alban*
*Royal Barbadian Yacht Club*
*Bridgetown, Barbados, West Indies*
*Should be there in 3 weeks.*
*Sail today—What a trip it will be! Can hardly imagine.*

*LOVE YOU,*
*Tamar*

***Mother*:** Mother lived to be eighty years old. We were blessed with a serene relationship throughout our lives. She was the sunshine of my childhood and the guiding light of my life. Only recently, I received an email from my best friend, Irene, in which she perfectly described my mother: "There was an aura of peace around her. She was a spirit—more like a bird than a human being."

In contrast to the darkness of the letters I received from my father, my mother's letters were a source of fresh air and were a lifeline. These lines are from some of my favorites.

*Darling, dearest Tamar, if I could send you the Sun who is shining on me right now, in the bed, after a stormy night, I would. If I could give you the avocado I just ate, I would. If I could give you my peace and warmth, you know I would.*

*...I hope to grow, to evolve into a grand old crone! Wisdom, Humour, where are you—maybe just around the corner.*

*I am GLAD, so much, that you were born. I wish you love above all—in your own heart and in others for you. You know you have all mine and Dad's and Uncle's and even Mark's, yes—*

***Dad*:** My father also lived to be eighty years old. After my return to New York in 1969, he never sent me another frightening letter. I spent years intentionally healing from the trauma caused by his letters and secrecy. The best of us both was able to outlast the problems between us. He was delighted with my sailing adventures and proud of my success with the whale project, which I created shortly after returning from my year at sea. By the time that I had my baby, Dad welcomed his grandchild into our lives, never uttering a word of criticism or dark forebodings. My daughter adored her opa.

I say hello to my father every day when I pass by his photo in my stairwell and feel only love in my heart.

*Mother on her 50th birthday*

*Dad, right after my daughter was born*

*Tamar and Maya, 1981*

***Me:*** Soon after I returned to New York, I found a great sense of purpose through the creation of Whale Workshops for schoolchildren, combining science with the language arts. The large whales had become an endangered species, and I hoped that the children I taught would grow into caring stewards of our planet.

During that time, I collected children's whale art and poetry, a selection of which was published by Scrimshaw Press in 1975 with the title *There's a Sound in the Sea... A Child's-Eye View of the Whale.* The Smithsonian Institution made the original paintings and poems into a two-year traveling exhibition in the United States and Canada, and it even went to Norway for the United Nations Marine Mammal Conference in 1976!

It would take me ten more years to finally find a way to recover from the emotional trauma that my father had unwittingly subjected me to. Through dance, art, and voice, I was able to emerge healed. In 1981 I welcomed a beautiful baby girl into the world. From the day she was born, she has brought me pure joy.

Today, my life overflows with blessings, including my daughter, two granddaughters, a wonderful son-in-law, creative projects, and many dear friends.

## Food Chart for *Alban*

When I examine the chart today, I feel sorry for the lads. Patrick told me later that he and Mike lived for two months on the food left over from the Atlantic crossing.

| Item | Quantity at start | Amount we ate |
|---|---|---|
| Canned chicken legs | 12 | 4 |
| Minced beef | 4 | 2 |
| Meatballs & curried rice | 4 | 2 |
| Ravioli | 4 | 2 |
| Risotto | 5 | 4 |
| Baked beans | 9 | 2 |
| Curried beans | 3 | 1 |
| Irish stew | 7 | 1 |
| Mackerel | 2 | 2 |
| Mixed vegetables | 9 | 3 |
| Canned carrots | 4 | 2 |
| Peas | 22 | 9 |
| Spinach | 3 | 1 |
| Green beans | 20 | 6 |
| Pimentos | 4 | 2 |
| Tomato paste | 10 | 3 |
| Canned pears | 2 | 1 |
| Canned peaches | 6 | 2 |
| Cartons of milk | 26 | 15 |
| Boxes cornflakes | 10 | 5 |
| Boxes rice cereal | 4 | 2 |
| Tins coffee | 3 | 3 |
| Tea bags | 62 | 62 |

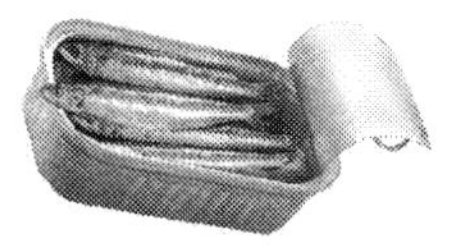

| Item | Quantity at start | Amount we ate |
|---|---|---|
| Chocolate bars | 2 | 2 |
| Sugar | 10 lbs | 8 lbs |
| Bags flour | 2 | 2 |
| Dozen eggs | 6 | 4 |
| Cheddar cheese | 2 | 1 |
| Dry bread | 4 | 2 |
| Biscuit tins | 4 | 4 |
| Large olive oil | 1 | 1 |
| Corned beef | 11 | 3 |
| Luncheon meat | 5 | 4 |
| Ham | 2 | 1 |
| Danish pork & ham | 3 | 1 |
| Cans liver pâté | 6 | 4 |
| Cans Danish bacon | 4 | 4 |
| Can ox tongues | 1 | 1 |
| Tongue & turkey rolls | 6 | 4 |
| Canned tuna | 9 | 7 |
| Sardines in oil | 6 | 2 |
| Sardines in tomato sauce | 15 | 9 |
| Pudding | 4 | 3 |
| Bags rice | 3 | 1 |
| Boxes macaroni | 5 | 2 |
| Bags spaghetti pasta | 6 | 2 |

**Betelgeuse:** *one of two very bright stars in the constellation of Orion. It is in Orion's shoulder and burns orange.*
**Bilge pump:** *an important pump, either manual or electric, to discharge water overboard*
**Bioluminescence:** *the production of light by a living organism. Many are found in the marine habitats, from the ocean surface to the deep seafloor. Fish or plankton that glow in the dark when the sea is disturbed*
**Boom:** *a movable horizontal pole attached to the mast and the foot of a sail to allow the boat to catch the wind*
**Bow:** *the front of a boat*
**Bowsprit:** *a spar extending from the bow of a craft to increase the amount of sail the boat carries*
**Captain's quarters:** *where the captain (and family) sleep, usually located in the aft (stern) of a boat*
**Caulking:** *sealing the spaces between hull planks to make watertight*
**Chronometer:** *an extremely accurate clock to determine one's longitude at sea*
**Cleat:** *a fixture of wood or metal attached to a dock, mast, or deck, with two prongs around which a rope may be fastened*
**Cockpit:** *a depressed area on the deck in the aft end of a boat where the controls are*
**Companionway:** *stairs going from deck to cabin*
**Compass:** *a device that always points to the magnetic north. Used to determine direction through 360 degrees*
**Deck:** *a platform capping the hull of a boat at the base of the rail*
**Equator:** *lies at zero degrees*
**Fender:** *a cushion between a boat and a dock or two boats to prevent them from rubbing against each other*
**Flotsam:** *floating debris resulting from a shipwreck*
**Gaff:** *the spar (pole) upon which the top of a four-sided sail is extended*

**Gaff-rigged:** *describing a sailing vessel with four-sided sails*

**Galley:** *the kitchen area of a boat*

**Gimbal:** *keeps a stove or compass in a horizontal plane, despite the boat's rolling in waves*

**Gunwale/Gunnel:** *the raised edge where the deck meets the boat's sides*

**Head:** *toilet*

**Headsail:** *a triangular sail forward of the mainmast on a one- or two-masted boat*

**Horizon:** *the apparent line between the ocean and the sky that an observer sees when voyaging across the seas. Since the world is round, this line continually moves as you sail the high seas.*

**Inflatable boats:** *for emergencies at sea. Oars, water, food, flares, and a mirror are stashed with these lifesaving dinghies.*

**Jib:** *headsail*

**Jupiter:** *the largest planet in our solar system and the fifth from the sun. It takes ten hours for Jupiter to rotate on its axis, and twelve years to travel around the sun. It's used in celestial navigation.*

**Keel:** *the main timber of most hulls; the backbone of the hull, on the bottom of the boat*

**Ketch:** *a two-masted sailboat with the taller mast in front of the shorter mizzenmast*

**Knot:** *unit of speed; one nautical mile per hour*

**Latitude:** *how many degrees north or south of the equator you are*

**Locker:** *an enclosed space to store sails, anchors, tools, and supplies*

**Longitude:** *an imaginary line defining any distance from the prime meridian, which runs through Greenwich, England. It divides the world into two hemispheres—east and west.*

**Mainsail:** *the principal sail on the mainmast*

**Marine radio:** *onboard VHF transceiver used for two-way communication*

**Mast:** *a vertical spar on a sailing vessel to which a sail is attached. The sail can slide up and down the mast.*

**Meridian:** *an imaginary circle on the earth's surface passing through both poles, defining longitude. It divides the earth into east and west hemispheres. All meridians are at right angles to the equator.*

**Mizzenmast:** *the mast behind the mainmast of a ketch*

***Nautical Almanac:*** *a yearly publication showing the tide tables, the rising and setting of the sun and moon, weather forecasts, and positions of celestial bodies to help navigators determine where they are at sea*

**Nautical mile:** *a land mile is 5,280 feet. A nautical mile is 6,076 feet. So, 2,700 nautical miles across the Atlantic Ocean equals 3,107 land miles.*

**Navigation table:** *the table in a boat where the navigational instruments and charts are kept*

**Orion:** *the Hunter; a brilliant constellation in the winter sky in the northern hemisphere*

**Port:** *the left side of a vessel when facing forward*

**Quarter berth:** *my bed on* Alban, *partially tucked under the cockpit*

**Rigel:** *one of two very bright stars in the constellation of Orion. It burns blue in Orion's foot.*

**Rudder:** *a flat piece of wood mounted to the sternpost of a boat that can be rotated by a tiller or wheel to control the direction of a boat*

**Schooner:** *a sailing vessel with two masts, the taller one being behind the shorter mast*

**Sextant:** *a navigational instrument used to measure the angular distance of the sun, moon, stars, and planets to determine one's position at sea*

**Sirius, the Dog Star:** *the brightest star in the night sky in the northern hemisphere. It is at Orion's feet.*

**Sloop:** *a sailboat with one mast*

**Stern:** *the rear end of a vessel*

**Starboard:** *the right side of a vessel when facing forward*

**Wheelhouse:** *the pilot house on deck where a captain or crew member steers*

## Cast of Characters

**Adele:** an acquaintance from Barnard College

***Alban*:** forty-two-foot sloop built in England (1929)

**Andy Malasky:** teenage boy sailing from Ibiza on *Josefine*

**Anja:** Married to Olaf, mother of Bine

**Arthur:** a good friend, scientist, and inventor

**Bine:** Anja and Olaf's daughter

**Chauncey L. Griggs:** father (Tacoma, WA, 1909–1989)

**David G. Noble:** a good family friend, photographer, writer, teacher

**Eric Britton:** staged the party where I met Arthur, which changed the course of my life. Sustainability and climate activist

**Fang:** black Lab on *Josefine*

**Irene Vandermolen:** my best friend and college roommate

**Jay:** passenger on *Josefine*

**Johanna Frieda Clement:** mother (Black Forest, Germany 1916–Tacoma, WA, 1997)

**Mark L. Griggs:** brother (San Francisco, CA, 1946)

**Martha Graham:** founder of modern dance in the twentieth century (1894–1991)

**Maximiliano Zomosa:** lead male dancer in the Joffrey Ballet, known for his riveting portrayal of Death in *The Green Table* (1938–1969)

**Merce Cunningham:** choreographer and dancer (1919–2009)

**Mike Lynch:** owner of *Alban*

**Moores:** ex-pats in Barbados

**Morgan:** Adele's brother from St. Thomas, USVI

**Nancy Jane Bare:** creative and inspiring dance teacher at Annie Wright Seminary, who studied with Martha Graham in New York City

**Naomi Griggs:** sister (Tacoma, WA, 1940–1962)

**Olaf:** captain of *Josefine*

**Patrick Blackwell:** skipper of *Alban*

**Potters:** expats in Barbados

**Robin McAllister:** a friend at boarding school

**Stefan:** Olaf's brother and first mate

**Steve Malasky:** teenage boy sailing from Ibiza on *Josefine*

**Suzy Creamcheese:** mysterious passenger on *Josefine* with a name coined by Frank Zappa

**Wilhelm Karl Clement:** mother's brother, Uncle Bill (Black Forest, Germany, 1919–San Francisco, CA, 2022)

**Miss Witherspoon:** instructor of religious education and in charge of the boarders at Miss Hall's School, Pittsfield, Massachusetts

# Places

Alicante, Spain
Barbados: Bridgetown, West Indies
Canary Islands: Gran Canaria, Las Palmas
French West Indies
Gibraltar, Spain
Gig Harbor, WA
Grenada, St. George's Town
Grenadines
Ibiza: Balearic Islands, Mediterranean Sea
Ireland: Cliffs of Moher
Madrid, Spain
New York City
Salt Spring Island, BC, Canada
Santa Pola, Spain
St. Lucia: Castries
St. Thomas, US Virgin Islands: Charlotte Amalie
St. Vincent, West Indies
Strait of Gibraltar
Tacoma, WA
Tangiers, Morocco
Torrevieja, Spain
West Indies
Westport, WA

All photos are by Tamar Griggs and the Griggs family, unless otherwise indicated. All illustrations are by Anna Melious, unless otherwise indicated.

**Page 3 — Baby Tamar**
Photo by Virna Haffer, Tacoma 1942
Permission granted by her granddaughter through David F. Martin, curator of Cascadia Art Museum, Edmonds, WA

**Page 8 — Gig Harbor**
The photo of the handmade sail and dinghy was digitally altered. The sail, held together by safety pins, and the boat were not retouched. To best illustrate the story as I've told it in my book, I chose to edit out a second person.

**Page 16 — Irene**
Photo by Leonard Lee Rue III
Permission granted by Irene Vandermolen

**Page 23 — Naomi**
Photo by Virna Haffer, Tacoma 1960
Permission granted by her granddaughter through David F. Martin, curator of Cascadia Art Museum, Edmonds, WA

**Page 30 — 7 East Tenth Street, NYC**
© Karen Tweedy-Holmes 2020
Permission granted by Karen Tweedy-Holmes

**Page 34 — Clowns**
Etching by Tamar Griggs

**Page 37 — *Abduction of the Sabine Women***

Nicolas Poussin, 17th century, Met Museum, NYC. Public domain.

**Page 163 — Sailing naked**

Photo by Patrick Blackwell, Tamar Griggs collection

**Page 175 — *Birth of Venus*, detail**

Sandro Botticelli, Italian Renaissance artist, 15th century. Public domain.

**Page 178 — Tamar with the *Tamure* fellows**

Photo by Patrick Blackwell, Tamar Griggs collection

**Page 191 — *Juan Sebastián de Elcano***

Unknown source: Every effort was made to find the photographer (photo is probably in the public domain). This is a digitally embellished variation of the original photo sourced online.

**Page 193 — *Juan Sebastián de Elcano***

Sketch by Tamar Griggs

**Pages 228 & 229 — Grenada Market Women**

Sketches by Tamar Griggs

**Page 231 — *Ticonderoga***

Image created by Amy Melious after an original photograph by Lucy Tulloch. Permission granted by Lucy Tulloch.

**Page 231 — Gabriel**

Sketch by Tamar Griggs

**Page 240 — Griggs family**
Photo by Richards Studio Photographs, 1948
Northwest Room at the Tacoma Public Library
Citation Number: D37188-2
Permission granted by the Tacoma Public Library Archives

**Page 248: Merry Christmas**
Painting by Mark L. Griggs

**Page 251 — Dad**
Photo by Irene Vandermolen

**Page 252 — Tamar and Maya**
Tamar Griggs collection

**Chapter heading images**
Stock images purchased from istock.com with alterations by Amy Melious, except for Gig Harbor and Tacoma, which were created by Amy Melious.

**Title page image**
istock.com/Ani_Ka

**Page 239, 254, 255, 261, 268**
Images by Amy Melious

**Page 268**
Stock image purchased from istock.com/7romawka7 with coloring by Amy Melious

**Page 159 — "Yummy, Yummy, Yummy"**
Words and Music by Arthur Resnick and Joe Levine


**Page 195 — "Splish Splash"**
Words and Music by Bobby Darin and Murray Kaufman


Words and Music by BOBBY DARIN and JEAN MURRAY

**Page 197 — "Yellow bird"**

Words by Alan Bergman and Marilyn Bergman

Music by Norman Luboff



Walton Music

A division of GIA Publications, Inc.

Licensor: Walton Music Corp.

Writers: Alan and Marilyn Bergman (lyrics), Norman Luboff (music)

Licensor Control: 50.00%

Permission granted

**Page 203 — "Angelina"**

Fair use

Songwriters: Doris Fisher / Allan Roberts / Jacques Larue

Adaptation: Jacques Larue

**Page 221 — "Day-o" (The Banana Boat Song)**

# Acknowledgments

Although writing is a solitary occupation, there are many people who have encouraged me and helped me shape my saga into this book.

Thanks to my friends who read the manuscript in its early stages and gave me encouragement: Brenda deRoos, Pam Jewson, Joan Cobham, and my neighbor, Bob deRoos, who helped me with sailing terms.

I'm indebted to my editor extraordinaire, Joelle Yudin, who believed in me and my story. She was savvy and tenacious as she encouraged me to dive ever deeper than I was inclined to go into my story. Beneath the sea was a complex inner world that Joelle helped me to access. Working with her was a delight. She wholly engaged with my story, and the characters in it, while helping me navigate the tangle of my memory.

Heartfelt thanks to poet Jeannette Encinias, author of *Queen Owl Wings*, who read my manuscript and encouraged me to finish it.

Wendy Dale, who taught an internet course on the structure of memoir, was awesome! I learned a heck of a lot from her lively and fun classes. A tough yet compassionate teacher, she was expert at pointing out writing that did not meet the standards of memoir. With her guidance, another dimension to my saga opened. Thanks, Wendy, for your wisdom and instruction.

Robert Kenney, my copy editor, went beyond the call of duty not only finding punctuation and grammar errors, but also finding inconsistencies in geography and dates, and pointing out where the story was confusing.

Susan Rolph, who took care of my toy poodle with love and devotion whenever I needed to concentrate on writing, and have a day or evening without distraction, was a blessing.

Working with Anna Melious, who designed my cover and did the illustrations in the book, was pure joy.

She added whimsy to my story, giving it a light touch, when much of the story is dark. When she presented me with her cover design, I knew that I had to finish the book. It was too beautiful and mysterious to abandon my writing, and I had been ready to quit.

The guiding light of my journey was Amy Melious, who has worked with me for over five years. I wanted her to teach me Photoshop, but she quickly discovered how disorganized I was, so she dove into the daunting task of cataloging my five hundred thousand digital photos. Deviating from my photography came as a surprise to both of us. She jumped into the ocean with me and spread fairy dust on my spirit when I was down in the dumps and ready to bail. Her wisdom and insight tempered my story, and we had a heck of a lot of fun going over bits, laughing and debating about what to include, and what to delete. Amy put her heart and soul into my memoir, and I am astounded how deeply she understood what I was trying to say and how she brought it into the light. Thank you, dear friend, for being with me on this wild journey into my past.

*Happy at Sea*

TAMAR GRIGGS is a photographer, writer, and naturalist.

Raised on the shores of Washington State, she developed a life-long fascination with the sea.

Tamar earned a Bachelor of Education degree, with a double minor in biology and English, from Simon Fraser University.

For many years, Tamar contributed to her local newspaper. *Tales from Bold Bluff* was a series of articles chronicling life in a remote seaside cabin in British Columbia, and the sometimes zany experiences with weather, wildlife, and humans she encountered.

She takes great delight in her family and island life with her adorable toy poodle.

Tamar began writing her memoir, *Tamar at Sea*, as she entered her 80th year.

Manufactured by Amazon.ca
Bolton, ON